This is a powerful story and a must-read cautionary tale for anyone who wonders why fraud is rampant in corporate America, and for all those who naïvely believe it is not.

Patrick Burns
Co-Director of Taxpayers Against Fraud (TAF)
Washington, DC

Jim Holzrichter is a remarkable man and courageous citizen who had the integrity to take action and the sometimes unbelievable fortitude to see it through. Without Jim and others like him, billions of American tax dollars wrongly lost to negligence and unscrupulous fraud would go undetected.

Michael Behn
Lead attorney for the joined private & DoJ qui tam cases
Principal of Behn & Wyetzner, Chartered

Jim Holzrichter and his entire family are American heroes. In the end, it was not just about winning a case against a rogue contractor for those of us representing the US government and taxpayer, but about not failing Jim and his deserving family.

Richard Zott
DOD — DCIS Special Agent (retired)
(US Department of Defense — Defense Criminal Investigative Service of the Inspector General Office)
Lead criminal investigator and Holzrichter handler for secret informant status

In a very protracted battle that went on for years, Jim Holzrichter stood tall when most people would have given up. He carried the personal brunt of the load for an extremely long time and in the big picture made a very big difference. It is an incredible story. The book is a great read.

Major General Charles (Chuck) R. Henry
DOD (retired)
Former Deputy Director and Senior Acquisitions Executive for Department of Defense — Defense Logistics Agency *and* Commander, Defense Contract Management Command

Thank you:

A JUST
CAUSE

James H. Holzrichter, Sr.
with Patrick A. Horton, Ph.D.

Thank you!

At a time in American history in which personal responsibility, integrity, and the very ideals upon which this country was founded appear all-too-easily sold, abandoned, or neglected into oblivion, this is the inspiring story of one man who could not turn his back on doing what was right, the family who stood by and with him, and the heroes both in government and out who stood up and *showed* up to see him through.

It is a chillingly personal story of the insidious dangers and devastating reach of unbridled and un-American corporate power, corruption, and greed. It is a heroic reflection of attainable possibility and a cautionary tale of potential decline for a nation teetering on the brink between unfinished greatness and its own demise. It is both inspiration and practical guide into finding our way as individuals, families, and a nation.

It is, above all else, a celebration of heroes.

Patrick A. Horton, PhD

For information about books/CDs/DVDs or
to invite James H. Holzrichter to speak, please visit
www.jameshholzrichterconsultancy.com

OR contact

A Just Cause Publications
PO Box 596
McHenry, Illinois
60050

First published and printed in the United States of America

Author services (copyediting, digital and print formatting, distribution, and consulting) provided by B10 Mediaworx (b10mediaworx.com).

Library of Congress Cataloging-in-Publication Data:

Holzrichter, James H. 1954
A Just Cause
    Hardback ISBN: 978-0-9891676-0-4
    Paperback ISBN: 978-0-9891676-1-1
    eBook ISBN: 978-0-9891676-2-8

Holzrichter, James H. 1954 –

        1. Whistleblower   2. Whistleblowing
        3. Qui Tam   4. Corporate Fraud

A JUST CAUSE

Dedicated to my beloved wife, Mary, and to my precious children, who did not choose to be part of this journey, but who stood together to endure what no family should ever be challenged to endure.

TABLE OF CONTENTS

FOREWORD

The general public is largely unaware of the treacherous and uneven path journeyed by whistleblowers. Marked to an exceptional degree by silence, mystery, and misunderstanding, whistleblowers, time and time again, stand up, show up, and suit up for the American people, oftentimes to the detriment of their own personal security, serenity, and even safety. Indeed, the "typical" whistleblower remains an elusive figure, even though they are widely credited with being the driving force behind the federal government's anti-fraud efforts. The reality is that whistleblowers oftentimes toil on behalf of the public interest well outside of the limelight, buried beneath layers of misdirected clichés, and concealed behind the protections of statutory-seal provisions and attorney-client privileges. Thus, the story of a typical whistleblower appears as a series of disconnected images ranging from the courageous champion of morality, fearless and unbending, to the uncertain insider, reluctantly challenging corporate giants. It is often difficult to reconcile the varied images into a single picture.

Others have certainly tried. In fact, in recent years, there has been a growing fascination about whistleblowers, inspiring prose and film, and begetting "whistleblower experts" of every stripe. The mass media has further fed the popular interest by cloaking or burdening various individuals with the "whistleblower" label. Yet even in this heyday of increased interest, the tale of true whistleblowers seems distorted and diluted, with narratives cobbled together by those who are unburdened by experience.

Unfortunately, the person behind the whistleblower mask often seems to be missing from the story, briefly floating in and out of the timeline. In turn, for the apologists for corporate fraudsters, "whistleblower" has become an easy shorthand for the faceless disgruntled employee who exacts his revenge by sinking the corporate ship.

On the other side of the ledger, advocates are quick to bestow the "whistleblower" crown on countless champions of justice, oftentimes whitewashing the individual's inner struggles of doubt and misfortune. So steadfastly have people clung to these extreme views that we still lack an account that fully reveals the inner and outer struggles of the whistleblower and distills them into a fully developed portrait.

By sharing his firsthand, unvarnished experience of struggle and survival, Jim Holzrichter finally provides us with a more complete picture of what it actually means to blow the whistle on dishonest corporations. As his all-too-real story ably shows, whistleblowing is not an event, but a process fraught with obstacles large and small. This reality should be fully understood and appreciated, especially by those who are contemplating blowing the whistle on corporate fraud.

Admittedly, not all whistleblowers travel the same path; however, Holzrichter's long, hard-fought odyssey exposes the full gamut of the whistleblowing experience. Indeed, the proverbial silver lining is that his personal story maps out the landscape, exposes the potential pitfalls, and reveals the terrain, permitting others to fully understand the treacherous personal and professional journey that awaits would-be whistleblowers even as it illustrates the self-survival importance of our supporting and protecting them as a nation.

Joseph E. B. "Jeb" White, Esq.
Former President & C.E.O.
Taxpayers Against Fraud

PREFACE

There are some very common and often emotionally charged misconceptions about whistleblowers and whistleblowing that we should clarify at the outset, not the least of which is the idea that anyone ever sets out to *be* a whistleblower with even a little knowledge of what that entails.[1] Based on my own beliefs and now seriously extensive experience working with others, it is important to note that those who come to be designated as whistleblowers are not particularly different from most of those around them in any consistent way. They are very often simply ordinary people in extraordinary situations.

This stands in contrast, of course, to the more popular tabloid versions or Hollywood movies that posit extreme and opposing notions that whistleblowers are particularly heroic (at least before they begin the path to that which imposes the label on them) or that they are otherwise simply malfeasant troublemakers, with an inflated-to-delusional self-importance moving them to challenge the status quo no matter what that is. Similarly, it is fewer still of those who come to be labeled "whistleblower" that fit the stereotype of disrupter intent on upsetting the lives and livelihoods of others out of some self-absorbed left-leaning ideology. And, contrary to popular belief (by the public at large or the coworkers who may spurn them), it is naïve or even foolish to believe most whistleblowers were in situations that would have taken care of themselves if left alone.

---

1 The term "whistleblower" is actually a fairly formal designation and legally only applied in certain kinds of situations. It is derived from British constables who blow a whistle when they see a possible problem as a warning or alert to interrupt its progress or as precursor to more formal intervention.

What is perhaps most important to understand about most who come to be labeled as "whistleblowers" (those who come to stand in federally protected conflict with their respective employer or setting) is that what turns into a battle of wills and resources generally began as nothing more than low-level attempts at problem-solving and conflict resolution. In many cases (and very much the case in my situation), we only receive the designation and become inescapably embroiled in what follows after having crossed some invisible line—or series of invisible lines—in which events and actions we did not anticipate or expect take on a life of their own, impossibly irreversible and seemingly unstoppable by the time they are known. This, again, is often without the whistleblower-to-be having known anything occurred or had been put into motion at all at the time.

In my own case, however naïve and, in certain respects seriously misguided, my own larger intentions were in bringing a number of procedural and tracking problems related to materials management to my supervisor for consideration and correction. I actually believed I was protecting the giant defense contractor I worked for from harm: first in facilitating the identification and correction of some procedural problem areas that could make them look bad if seen by the outside world out of context; and second, identifying actions of a few seemingly isolated rogue employees.

The most important distinction here that set my own job and circumstances apart from most others who also come to be designated as whistleblowers or troublemakers for wanting to help or protect those they work for, was that I was working for one of the largest and, by necessity, most secretive defense contractors in all these United States of America. What set my specific personal circumstances apart from most others who also worked there at the moment this story formally begins was the fact that my still-expanding job responsibilities had already grown in truly significant ways, which gave me a substantially more intimate and global view of things than was normally allowed.

This was, after all, home of the still-beyond-top-secret Stealth Bomber.

As an ordinary citizen and regular working stiff whose life, like so many others, is shaped on a daily basis indirectly (and thus largely goes unperceived) by the US military industrial complex, my job and renewed hopes for the so-called American Dream put me squarely in the belly of the beast, and my family and me in what would soon be the eye of a very long storm.

It was an adventure that began with my simply trying to identify and correct some problems on behalf of the giant that put unseen events in motion. It challenged me to try to help that very same giant correct itself and its alleged transgressions, even when they were under intensive secret federal investigation. My role as an active undercover informant, that with its ever-present risks of exposure, became an ongoing nightmare. What began with the discovery of a few inexplicably mishandled electronic cables would begin to pull at the threads of a fabric ranging from alleged incompetence to negligent practices that could have cost all government contracts on their own. It was a fabric that, as alleged,[2] was to prove willfully deceptive and decidedly fraudulent in its systematic acceptance of deceptive practices and intentional attempts to cover them up.

By the time the case was finally ready to come to trial over a decade and a half later, it had grown in scope to include charges of negligence and malfeasance as massive as defrauding the US government and American taxpayer with claims that the device that would give stealth to the Stealth Bomber was ready for production—allowing the contractor to continue billing for its falsely claimed completed development and move on to billing for its next (but nonexistent) steps to production. And in the prolonged progression of things, as a collection of heroes gathered over time to help make things at least somewhat right, my family and I suffered horribly just trying to survive—including a humiliating stay at a homeless shelter that stank of human feces and urine, the entry hallway greeting us with, "Six arrived, five will die."

While my own personal story and that of my family may be more than a little on the extreme side of things in terms of top-secret circumstances and the epic scale of events that would ultimately involve almost every level of federal government, there remains a great deal it shares with virtually all potential change agents or whistleblowers. Perhaps more to the point for the widest possible audiences here and recognition of its full

---

[2] It must be noted here and kept in mind throughout this text that all charges raised against Northrop Grumman, however much they were publicly documented, remain alleged under the filing and settlement of the case as conditions of settling prior to going to court.

implications for us as a people and a nation, it applies in varying degrees to every working person or community member who has ever been placed in a position of having to take risks to correct problems of even the most mundane kind, choose what is right, or simply being endangered for knowing or speaking up about too much. We cannot survive, let alone thrive, at this crucial time in history feeling helpless, defining ourselves not by what we are for and strive to be, so much as by what we fear and what we are against. What emerges, quite unintentionally on my part, are the reminders of just how much it is our shared responsibility to choose and create who and what we want to be.

In many ways this book will illustrate or at least touch on all the above and in fact lay out a story that, while profoundly personal, is at the same time undeniably epic and decidedly dramatic. But for the moment, I would like to be clear about my own much more circumscribed intentions in writing the book and its most personal invitations to the reader. The grander implications and influences are a byproduct of this journey that was made with the help of so many.

For me, the writing of this book (nothing short of a grateful celebration of life) is also an inadequate acknowledgment of those heroes who played a part. It is an attempt to provide a little inspiration and direction for those finding themselves in remotely similar circumstances, as well as for all those who aim to protect, support, or guide them. It is an opportunity to once again fully regain my own long-silenced voice and offer the same opportunity for my family. It is a bit of a meditation on the very question passed on to me by my father and provided such a touchstone throughout it all:

When is it ever wrong to do the right thing?

In retrospect, the writing of this book was a dauntingly enormous, emotionally challenging, and oftentimes mentally elusive endeavor. First of all, the complexities and nearly two-decade-long duration of the *initial* case made for vastly more detail and sprawling history than could easily be fit in a single volume. Secondly, revisiting the whole journey required reliving the trauma involved, many of which were still as emotionally charged as when we went through them. Thirdly, because as often as I had shared the details of the story, I did not yet see it as a whole; I had to let go of much of what I thought I knew to be able to see it all very differently and understand many dynamics, dimensions, and interconnections I had never seen before. Then, of course, there was the mechanically challenging issue of the contrasting periods of time to be covered—from mere hours and days (however intense) to sprawling years that ultimately spanned decades.

Mostly, it was a challenge to make sense of the order and connective threads that enabled me to tell the very personal aspects of the story without getting lost in mind-numbing facts. In the end, it was the challenge to be able to step more fully into the present and genuinely shed much of the past that took the greatest courage and yielded the greatest healing and release.

This latter effort, which would have been challenging enough on its own, was further complicated as a second round of lawsuits was still unfolding when work on the book began. At times, it seemed as though the whole nightmare would never end. Fortunately, I had the remarkable support of my beloved family, who already ranked highly among the heroes throughout the story, most especially my wife, Mary. And as additional good fortune would have it, I also had the perfect writing guide and eclectically adept collaborator to help me find my way through all of this, who, in the process, became a valued friend.

Welcome to my story, my family, and a celebration of heroes.

1
A FAMILY ON THE BRINK

I cannot say I slept well the night before my scheduled meeting with my supervisor, Tom Clyder, which was to change everything in my life and my family's for decades to come. On one hand, it was important stuff I was going to bring to his attention, which had significant ramifications for both the company as a whole and for some handful of still-unknown employees whose lives and livelihoods could be affected by the possible implications of the data I was going to show him. On the other hand, I was firmly convinced I was looking out for the company's best interests and those of my colleagues who worked for it with dedication, honesty, and integrity.

I comforted myself only to the extent I needed comforting, which was the belief that if someone or any number of someones were, in fact, violating policies and protocols for how we handled and tracked materials for the development and production of tools of war, their being held accountable was clearly appropriate. The only slight leap of faith I thought I was making at the time (and the basis for a slight gnawing concern) was that everyone would be handled fairly after the evaluation of what I was about to share. If there were any greater concern at the moment, it was that I admittedly did not yet know who *these* individuals were or how they might retaliate. It never occurred to me that my concerns would need to be with the company itself.

I did not expect this impending meeting to be an earthshaking event or a hugely transformative encounter, however urgent the preliminary information and possible issues seemed to be. If anything, I thought this meeting would simply bring home that:

a) there were some problems in materials acquisition and manage-ment that, if left unaddressed, would be of potentially significant consequence for the company; and

b) I was doing a very good thing bringing the problems I seemed to have found into the open and proper channels to be addressed and corrected.

If anything, I thought it would also bring to light the need for more systematic companywide monitoring processes in general (to assure detec-tion and correction of such problems on an ongoing basis); the fact that it was my own native skills and naturally systematic approach to things that had brought the issues to light; and highlight the need for and initial ap-proaches to better detection.

While possible recognition and more opportunities to stretch my mental and professional wings definitely had appeal, the greater satisfac-tion came from the perceived fact that it would help and actually protect my employer from unneeded and accidental harm. Enhancing my own value at a time when many others were losing their jobs due to massive layoffs was also desirable, but not the main point, and in fact, recognition posed some risk. To the extent that this meeting was to draw attention to my job's expanding scope and perspective that cut across normally strict partitions in organization and information, it would open my efforts to some scrutiny in this highly security-minded environment. Hopefully, it would be recognized as a decidedly win-win situation that would make my job more secure and in very many ways more effective. This would allow me to take care of my family in the lifestyle and security we had come to enjoy, all the more precious after just a year and a half of sobriety, and still in early recovery from alcoholism and drug addiction that had taken their own toll on my family and me. Besides, the general focus of the meeting and the domains up for discussion were already known, even if the specific problems or concerns were not.

Given my take on things at the time, it would have seemed odd and even a little ironic to have any major concerns or trepidations about the meeting or the information and issues to be revealed. After all, if the problems I believed I had uncovered were anything like they appeared to be, I was looking out for the well-being of the company and identifying problems they surely would want to know about and correct. Not only did the data suggest waste to the tens of thousands to even millions of dollars related to the acquisition and handling of parts and materials for research and development, it suggested they needed a much better means of tracking it all in such a highly compartmentalized setting. I felt that discovery of their existence by the government or other customers would simply look bad for the company. At the time, I had nothing but the best of intentions and no idea what the impact of explicitly raising these issues was to have on my life and the life of my family for the next two decades.

On the face of it, my situation and the story of my life (about to spin invisibly on a dime) were not all that different from anyone who has ever held any job or has been part of a family, group, or community in which they discovered problem areas that call for attention to avoid bigger problems down the road or just to make things run better—at least, not at this point.

Truthfully, I was happy to have any job at all, and now most especially the one I had. I was happy to be able to go to work every day to provide for my family in ways I had not always been able to given my lack of an advanced formal education or degrees. This job gave me the opportunity to use my mind and inborn skills; it offered me the possibility of expanding my ability to show what I could do; it provided an increasingly better life for my family—and I was grateful for it. The irony is that the very corporate source of our newfound middle-class comfort and stability would soon become the very thing that assaulted it and coldly tore down any semblance of comfort or stability with the vast resources and forces at its disposal with increasingly calculated malice.

This is where my story may diverge somewhat at ground level from that of most other people confronted with issues or problems in the workplace. Other than the fact that I worked for Northrop Defense Systems Division,[3] one of the largest and, by necessity, most secretive defense contractors in the country, my family and I were still

---

3 It would later become Northrop-Grumman.

finding our way through the first couple of years of my newfound sobriety from alcoholism and drug addiction. Ours was a family already on the brink from the damage I had caused myself and them, from undergoing the healing after all those shocks to our systems, with an intensified need for stability and security. Thus, I was very grateful and, in fact, particularly loyal to this company which had paid for and supported my treatment and recovery, and subsequently had given me the opportunity to set up programming to help other employees find their way out of addiction.

If there was anyone who did not want to find trouble or rock the proverbial boat, it was me. I did not want to draw attention to myself. After all, the squeaky wheel gets replaced and this was a place in which people were suddenly terminated and removed without warning. It was a place that kept everything compartmentalized and secretively distinct. However, if what I had discovered in my newly expanded job duties and their related hours of investigations revealed what I thought they did, it was important to bring the information forward to correct the problems for several reasons:

First, because if they were discovered, the continued existence of contracts and contracting could be at stake.

Second, at least in my mind at the time, if the problems and patterns I had uncovered were true, the waste would have added up to hundreds of thousands, if not millions, of misspent taxpayer dollars.

Adjust that to mean *hundreds* of millions in waste and errors in material tracking and billing being passed on to the government, and you have the beginnings of the degree to which I had underestimated my situation and misunderstood what I had begun getting myself into. Notwithstanding, and more to the point of what was to follow, it was quite possible I had discovered outright fraud on the part of what I then believed were a few rogue individuals. If not corrected and handled internally, it could threaten the continued existence of the company as a whole. The only real and immediate concern I had was that it was not totally clear who might be involved or what the resulting consequences of exposing them would be. There was also the very real concern of not wanting to erroneously do any harm to anyone who was innocent, but tools in the hands of others who were corrupt It was the beginning of not knowing whom to trust.

Because I was very much looking out for the well-being of the company, what is most striking to me in retrospect is that I assumed the company itself was naïvely ignorant of practices and events that could conceivably threaten its very funding and existence. In my misplaced trust in the integrity and intentions of the puppeteers who ran Northrop D.S.D., my biggest concern was *for* them. I was concerned that what I had already discovered would be *misconstrued* by outsiders if revealed out of context. In retrospect, what was most naïve on my part was the extent to which I thought I was taking some small and calculated risk in relation to coworkers who could threaten my job, balanced against the intrinsically ethical goal of protecting my employer who should then appreciate and protect me in return.

I was a fool.

After arriving at work and parking my car the morning of my meeting, I went to pick up the copies of the paperwork I was going to give to my immediate supervisor, Tom Clyder. The corridor outside the window to the central photocopying center provided a reminder of just what kind of security and ongoing monitoring was characteristic of the facility: It was one of the more public areas in which cameras hidden behind all-seeing mirror-like globes were positioned at all ends and corners of more public hallways, with several more along the way. Normally, you did not consciously think about them as they were just part of the ever-present security you also took for granted. However, it made its ongoing imprint and reminded you that you were, in fact, ever exposed and under scrutiny of some sort no matter what or where.

There were the ever-present security officers dispersed throughout the building. And every so often, there was the indelible sight of seeing security arrive at someone's work station without warning, boxes in hand, to have them pack up and immediately escorted out of the building. Presumably, this was because of layoffs rather than some breach of security or protocol, but who could know? If one had any warning, it was perhaps suddenly discovering the lack of computer access moments before security arrived.

At the moment, the two primary reminders of the security here were the mirrored bubbles watching me pick up the papers I had copied, and the fact that the only place you could make copies was in this central location, generally requiring a specific tracking or project number to log.

The copy clerk serving the window looked at the order sheet and repeated out loud for confirmation that I had only wanted one set of copies. I would have liked an additional set to have taken home with me the night before in order to look them over. Or maybe I would have wanted to have them in hand as I gave thought to what my next steps should be in gathering more information about the problematic data I had found, as well as how to correct and to track them better. However, the problem with having an extra copy made to take out of the building was, of course, that you were not to take anything out of the building.

There were reasons for all this secrecy and high-level security, after all. It was so secret that in your daily routine, you did not discuss even with coworkers what you were working on or privy to, just as you did not want to know what they were working on or privy to unless you had a need to know. My problem (which I did not yet fully recognize or appreciate at the time) was that my expanded job duties in Product Assurance included tracking how and when parts and materials failed in the development process, and in what numbers they did so. My view cut across the divisions and secretive compartmentalization that normally kept others from knowing what went on in the next project, cubicle, or facility.

As I took my completed copy job from the clerk through the window, I found myself wondering if my subtle pensiveness or distraction in pondering where and how protocols that were crucial to the functioning of the facility might be impaired or violated was detectable. Glancing at the mirrored bubbles, aware I was trying not to seem like I was glancing at the mirrored bubbles, I only partially realized the weight of that notion. It was a weight soon to increase many thousandfold.

I would have hated the idea of not getting to follow through with the problem-solving I had started. In part, because the issues I had started to uncover needed attention and correction, and I felt I could fix them. I also would have hated the idea that I would lose my only foreseeable shot at seeing and showing what I could do. As I made my way to my supervisor's office, reports in hand, I rehearsed the best way to put them in context and then present them in the most useful and constructive way. My thoughts also drifted back to my days in the Coast Guard. It was there where, with only a GED and a very fragmented life to date, my test scores from the Naval Battery Tests placed me so high in the placement process that I was given the choice of going into whatever training and area I wanted. Having decided at a very early age that I wanted to be an electronics engineer, I chose Aviation Electronics and was one of the first to be admitted without some kind of advanced degree, prior college, or demonstrated prior training and ability.

With a failure rate of over 50% (the repercussions of flunking out being a one-year isolated duty tour to a Loran C station somewhere in the darkest corners of the earth), I was one of the eleven out of twenty-eight who even completed the program. I subsequently worked with considerable success and advancement, including becoming a second class petty officer (E-5) at a young age and on the first go-'round from testing, which was a marked feat in itself. My current job was only the second time in my life I had been given a real opportunity to challenge myself to test my abilities and educational skills. I admit that in that moment, I relished the chance to do still more, stretch my wings, and show my stuff.

Little did I know that it was already quite possible I was under surveillance by outside government agents and agencies. I would find out a remarkably short time later that there were already very high-level governmental agents and large-scale agencies on the alert for problems at Northrop.

As I turned the last corner in this labyrinth of a building to arrive at my life-changing meeting, I had no idea I was soon to become the central focus and player in their investigations. Still less did I know as I arrived at my supervisor's office that very soon two of the government's federal agents would be parking in front of my home, knocking on my door, and changing the course of my life forever.

In retrospect, I had already crossed a number of invisible lines of no return simply by virtue of where my ever-expanding job duties had taken me, and what I had started to uncover along those paths. But in the last dwindling minutes before the life-changing meeting with my supervisor, I really had no inkling of what I was about to put into irreversible motion.

As I knocked on the door to Clyder's office, my thoughts and, admittedly, my prayers of gratitude were focused on where my life had gone and that I could now provide for my family and give them what I did not have as a child. For reasons both equally selfish and altruistic, I wanted to make sure they had all the things in life I myself had not known in my early years (and then almost destroyed by my increasingly out-of-control drinking and drug use).

I wanted my children to know their father as I had not known my own, an emotionally war-damaged man and alcoholic, in and out of mental institutions. More than anything else in life, I wanted them to have unquestioned stability, security, and love. I wanted to make up for and help correct any harm I had done prior to my recent recovery. I wanted them all, and most especially my wife, Mary, to have the best of everything life had to offer, the best of the so-called American Dream. My current job was both the means and the key to providing it all for them. As far as I could tell, life was very good and only getting better.

I could not have been more wrong.

2
A MIRAGE OF HOPE

In all likelihood, my job at Northrop was always a bit of a distorted fantasy or, more accurately, a mirage of hope. In retrospect, my job was probably always destined to pit the unsavory practices of the corporation against my own desire for stability, a life of honesty, integrity, and hard work.

Invisible lines had been crossed.

I did not know it yet, but I had seen more than I should have seen and knew more than I should know.

More invisible lines crossed.

Moreover, it was known at least to my immediate supervisor that I had come across some problems otherwise "overlooked."

As I accepted Clyder's greeting and followed his instruction to sit in the chair facing his desk, I was about to cross another one of those invisible lines of no return. I had no inkling that this company and this job—that had given me so much, that I thought was going to allow me to create so much more—would soon turn on me. I had no inkling that it would go well beyond taking it all away, then move on to trying to dismiss, isolate, discredit, and destroy me, and that in so doing, it would put my family though many years of living hell. This was to be an unfortunate and, for some time unrecognized, tipping point in life for myself, my family, and an army of colleagues not yet met.

Sitting there in Clyder's office waiting for him to finish what he was doing on his computer, I took the time to remember the encounter I had with the person who was to facilitate my getting a job at Northrop in the first place.

His name was Jack Martin and we only met a couple of times at a bar. I did not share any details of the instabilities in my life leading to that point. What I did share was a desire for a job that would be stable and make use of the skills I had developed when in the electronics and engineering program in the Coast Guard. He seemed to appreciate that I actually got into that program based entirely on aptitude tests and gained entry without the kinds of advanced degrees most of my competition brought with them. He did not ask why I did not have such degrees or why I had a GED rather than a high school diploma and I did not offer. What he did appreciate was the quality of my training and experience and the fact that the majority of those who were admitted to the program were drummed out before completing their training. All he cared about was that I had some useful skills and need for a job to match. I cared about the same things and I knew that, without ever being able to acquire degrees to prove I could do what I could already do, this kind of opportunity would not likely come along again.

He arranged an interview with human resources and in 1984 I began work building testing equipment from the schematics from engineers. I was soon helping to improve and refine their schematics. It was not a glamorous job by any means, but for someone who knew as a kid he wanted to be an electrical engineer, at least I was in the right playground. And, after rehab, I was promoted to Senior Technician and helped create a company program to help others with alcohol and drug problems.

The equipment I helped manufacture to test other equipment was highly sophisticated and essential to the successful development of some of the most sophisticated and sensitive warfare technology in the world. Straight out of the gate, my ability to enhance the work and the testing equipment was quickly recognized as worthy of some attention and respect. This resulted in some early and rapid increases in responsibilities and pay. It very much contributed to stability of income and ended the need to keep moving. The problem, as I have said, was that my alcoholism was worsening, along with my more rapidly destructive addiction to cocaine that worsened my behavior many fold. This combined with or simply magnified the dysfunctions of my youth, with its serious lack of example or comprehension of adulthood and will have some continuing threads as this story unfolds.

Having found employment stability and having already gone through a number of small but important promotions and raises, it was terrifying to call into human resources at Northrop from the rehabilitation hospital I had entered to tell them I needed a leave of absence and to arrange for reimbursement to the hospital. The message from the other end was neither supportive nor threatening. It was calm and matter-of-fact. It was both better and worse that they were now on alert regarding my problem, which had escaped their notice to that point. All of which is to say, the corporation was there for me when I needed it. It had helped provide stability so I could hit the realities of my addictions head-on. I had one shot at this. Now it was on me to make it work or screw it up. I felt I owed them and I committed myself all the more to my job performance. I committed myself to the well-being of the company in the same way I felt they had supported mine. I trusted that the goodness I saw in them (or at least wanted to see in them at the moment) was all-pervasive and real, and that it would be enduring as well. I admit once again, I was fooled.

It was against this backdrop that I returned to my regular job with renewed focus and commitment. It was against this backdrop that I excelled in what I was doing and kept getting to do more. It was against this backdrop and being able to shore up the foundations of my life and that of my family that, in fairly short order, I was transitioned from working as a tech into a larger, more administrative playground of Quality Assurance. In a scant year and a half of work and still fresh with newfound sobriety, it put me in a position to observe the very issues related to materials management—the issues that would provoke the meeting I was now having.

In many ways, the expanded monitoring and tracking duties I found myself doing did not start out to be particularly different from my day-to-day functions in Product Assurance. A research-and-development entity like Northrop goes through many millions of dollars' worth of parts. The expectation is that in any given engineering or development job, a reasonable quantity of such materials and parts will be estimated and built into the project bid, along with subsequent funding and/or ongoing payments to keep the flow of parts and work going on that project. It is expected that a good number of these parts and materials will be used up in the trial and error of development and thus removed from inventory. Others will prove to be defective and returned to the source vendor for replacement or re-imbursement while ones kept as replacement parts will simply be scrapped if not usable elsewhere. When materials and parts are not used and/or are not returnable, they are sometimes still usable in other projects, so they can be rolled forward in inventory and assigned to secondary pro-jects.

Theoretically, in terms of government contracts, this balances out. Thus, the charges for the subsequent projects to the government can be reduced by that amount, as the materials and parts are already in stock. The obstacle to doing this efficiently is the secrecy with which all projects are conducted and the separation of projects by limiting everyone to a need-to-know status. One project literally has no idea what other projects are doing, using, or taking out of inventory.

Much of my previous job as a senior tech involved 1) handling parts and materials directly related to creating testing equipment (always built into projected costs of doing business and subsequent bids and contracts); 2) contact with more parts and materials in helping to do the actual testing of equipment being developed as a whole; and 3) evaluating the perfor-mance or failure of specific parts and materials for various projects.

In my newer capacity in Product Assurance, some of my most fun-damental responsibilities were simply monitoring aspects of materials acquisition, tracking, and management related to documenting failure rates for them. It occurred to me that it was also useful to know when and how such failures occurred in their progressive handling by engineering, production, etc., so I instigated more systematic approaches to tracking the concrete flow of parts and materials through the system. This involved operating with a perspective that, by necessity, cut across specific project boundaries and across projects when unused parts and materials were transferred. On the face of it, this was very important, as it was a unique perspective, especially when I decided it would be good to go through old reports.

In my earliest steps in getting more systematic about looking at the whole, which was, remember, not visible to any but a very few who had access, the two concerns I was about to share with Clyder came to my attention and raised several more as-yet-not-fully-formed but emerging concerns.

The first specific problem was in regard to a specific type of electronic cable used which had been ordered in the quantity expected to be needed for research and development of one particular project. That is to say, the parts were meant to be consumed, destroyed in development, or would fail on their own. To that end, an acceptable proportion of excess was built in to the bid. The cables had been scrapped and wiped from inventory in both real and tracking terms (i.e., they were destroyed and disposed of and recorded thusly) with tracking records reflecting they were excess and no longer needed.

The smaller part of the problem, if I understood the records correctly, was that someone had accidentally determined that a substantial quantity of the cables were no longer needed for the given project and that they were not forwardable for any other projects, so they were scrapped and wiped from inventory. However, they were, in fact, still needed and would have to be reordered from the vendor, who would have to be paid a second time for the same part.

The bigger part of this problem was that a new and different order had been created that marked the prior cables as obsolete. Further, the new order hid the fact that the exact same cable was being ordered a second time by changing three numbers at the end of the parts designation. This was an act that would have required someone to intentionally hide the redundant billing to the government under the guise of new parts rather than acknowledge the error, with the project and corporation absorbing the cost of accidental loss. What concerned me was not that human error had occurred, but that it had been covered up in a way that the parts were charged to the government a second time.

The second problem was that it appeared there had been, on more than one occasion, other parts ordered that were wiped from the system and disposed of *on delivery*. If they had been determined to be faulty on delivery, they should have been returned to the vendor for replacement or credit. As it was, they were never passed along to their parent project for use and thus were neither consumed nor failed. And in being wiped from inventory records and physically disposed of, clearly they were not transferable to unrelated projects. That would have required approval for the initial order to be placed.

All in all, both seemed very odd occurrences and either indicators of problematic procedural issues or questionable maneuvers by as-yet-unknown individual employees. Either way, if discovered by any outside auditing entity or monitoring body, it could look like sloppy management on Northrop's part, either for not having prevented such errors or abuses from occurring at all or, even more so, for not having caught and corrected them with systems that, by government regulations, were supposed to be put in place to assure accurate handling and reporting.

Sitting now in Clyder's office, and having his attention, I reminded him that I had shared these issues along the way when I thought I had run into a couple of aberrations or abnormalities. I reminded him that he had encouraged me to look into it for clarity and usefulness in problem-solving.

As I began going over the details of the reports I had brought, then moved on to what appeared to be the problems I saw between the lines, I could not read his reaction at all. I shared my own concerns over the possible implications for the company if not effectively cleared up, corrected, and prevented from occurring again. I additionally clarified my comments and concerns to specific problems in lost revenues from unduly wasted parts, distortions in the historical data needed for effective contract bids, and how it could look if an audit were conducted by the customer.

At the risk of some redundancy here, my concern at that moment was not even remotely over possible wrongdoing on the part of Northrop as a corporation or government contractor. It was to assure its well-being and protect it from possible interpretations from the outside, or abuses by a select few from within. I probably redefined trusting and loyal as an employee, as blind and naïve as I turned out to be. I was, after all, not just a loyal, but a *grateful* employee.

Clyder listened with interest but no readable response or reaction. He asked what I made of it all and what I thought would be needed to develop a clearer picture of what we were looking at. I had no truly good answer for the first part, as, given my trust in the company and its intended procedures and values, these occurrences just seemed odd. To determine what had occurred would require further research with details of what had happened at each step, from ground level up. I needed to research how any of it had occurred with the kinds of approval it would have been required. Lastly, I needed to determine what was wrong or missing in the system for this kind of thing to occur without being caught and corrected by someone.

In spite of my motives, I had some discomfort over coming up on the company radar as being someone who had the range of perspective I did. But even if I had any concerns at that time, it was that I did not know who was involved in authorizing the purchases or turning a blind eye to any of the problems I thought I was detecting. In the case of parts being swept from inventory on arrival, I could not even begin to imagine what kinds of glitches in procedure existed or what benefits to those involved could be or what they might look like. I also had no idea how isolated or common any of it might be. In retrospect, I suppose what is most interesting is that neither of us brought up or discussed any of this. We simply agreed it needed more investigation and that I was in the position for and in possession of the skillsets needed to do it.

We ended the meeting with an agreement to revisit the issues when I had more information. There were three closely interconnected things I did not know when I returned to my cubicle down the hall, which was half the distance toward *his* supervisor's office in the other direction.

The first was that I had no idea what he might share with his supervisor (who was thus also my boss) and when. They did not get along and she was as often as not publicly abusive toward Tom and, to my own discomfort, crude and rude in general. She swore like a sailor and always impressed me as trying a little too hard to appear tough and in charge in a man's world.

What I additionally did not know then and still do not know now is if Clyder knew that she and Northrop were already under federal investigation for abuses by some of the employees tied to the second set of problems I had started to uncover. It would not be until some years later that I would discover that several parts vendors had reported to the federal government that one particular Northrop buyer had been shaking them down for personal gain in exchange for priority in trade. This was a clear violation of stated company policy, all legal considerations, and the strict governing regulations of the United States government in contracting with Northrop at all.

What I most especially did not know at the time and would not even begin to grasp until some time later (and only when it was too late) was that I had just crossed what was probably the single most significant invisible and irreversible line in this entire journey. At that moment, the nightmare that was to become my life and that of my longsuffering family had been set in stone. It was not that I had just officially announced finding problems with procedures and possibly a few rogue employees: I had discovered the first visible signs to institutionally intentional and pervasive practices that if fully known and verifiable by the right parties, could threaten the very existence of the company itself.

As anyone who has ever held a job anywhere or worked with others in a group or community of any kind or any setting can tell you, sooner or later you are going to run into problems of one kind or another that call for a resolution in order to keep things running smoothly, make them run better, and prevent problems of all sizes and scope.

Once again, such problems can be a matter of safety, efficiency, and productivity. They can be a matter of fairness or compliance with some accepted personal or collective values or norm. They can be a matter of moral and perhaps even legal consequence. On a larger scale, they can actually affect the well-being and nature of our communities and country as a whole. In this situation, it encompassed all of the above and on scales and reaches of power I could not even begin to imagine.

I was simply doing my job, involved in a process of helping to solve problems. I very much enjoyed both the responsibility and opportunity and savored this moment in a lifetime of what had seemed endless struggles and losses and stolen opportunities. I was doing something that mattered. Life was good and everything would continue getting better.

3
THE DEVIL'S FIRST MINIONS

My first real hint that not all was right with the world came some two weeks or so later when Amy Selen, Clyder's supervisor, stopped by my desk and asked me what exactly I was working on that required extra hours and conversations with my supervisor. At this point, I still did not know what Clyder had or had not shared with her or what he wanted to share or not share with her. I explained the issues I thought I had found initially, not knowing what (if anything) Clyder had shared, and wondered if this were some kind of test. She asked me if there was anything else and, while I had, in fact, begun getting a greater sense of some possibly pervasive problems in materials management and tracking, something in her demeanor made me think better of sharing any specifics. I just answered with what was an honest enough response, i.e., that it was still too early to tell what I had found or what it could turn out to mean.

She listened to me speak, her gaze off to one side as though weighing what I said, with thoughts she most definitely was not sharing. When I finished with my brief summary, I instinctively added (for reasons that did not fully occur to me until later) that everything was in the reports I had given my supervisor, and I underscored that all was as public and pre-approved and re-approved as it could be. She nodded to herself, digested it all for a moment, then looked me in the eye and flatly said, "Well, I want you to stop."

As Selen turned away and stepped across the small corridor that separated her office door from the entrance to my cubicle, it would not have occurred to me to question that blunt instruction directly. Aside from a respect for the position (if not the person), getting my head torn off did not seem a great tactic, most notably since I already felt a little exposed in terms of having a broader view than normally allowed. That said, I also did not think it wise, for the benefit of the company or for me, to quit looking into things, so I immediately went to Clyder's office and knocked on the door. There was nothing to stop me from questioning the instruction indirectly and it seemed wrong to just stop.

It is important to note here that my contact with Amy Selen actually began sometime earlier when I had moved on from working as a technician in the Test Manufacturing Lab and had begun working in the Environmental Test Lab in late 1985 where I helped in writing up test procedures and monitoring. At that time, I did some work with her on special projects under the larger umbrella of Product Assurance, which was her responsibility. I formally transferred from the Environmental Test Lab in 1987 and from that time forward, worked under the supervision of Clyder, who answered directly to Selen.

Clyder invited me in and I shared the exchange that had just occurred with Selen who, in all fairness to her, was responsible for a very wide swath of quality assurance and privy to issues, processes, and hidden procedures we would never know about. Clyder asked me very specifically what I had told her and what I thought it might mean. He asked what, if anything, she gave away in terms of reaction other than a flat instruction to stop. Oddly, he did not ask me whether I thought it was important to continue or not, or if I personally wanted to stop. Clearly I was concerned. Selen's instructions trumped his by a full pay grade.

Clyder pondered the exchange only very briefly, and then in a tone almost as flat as Selen's, said we would continue for the moment as is. The only proviso was a casual suggestion to be discreet. The discreet part went without saying, but, given that it had been mentioned, I reminded Clyder I was in an awkward position: not following her direct instruction could be taken as insubordination in a climate in which layoffs were already occurring. Clyder just calmly reminded me that *he* was my immediate supervisor and I was thus to follow *his* instructions. Anything else would be his call in relation to me and would land on him.

Given Selen normally passed by my open cubicle, which was close to her office, Clyder moved me into the cubicle area somewhat closer to his offices, but more specifically, farther removed from hers so that I would not be under her immediate observation. In some ways, continuing to pursue investigations she had wanted stopped felt uncomfortably clandestine and awkward as, up to that point, my working relationship with her had been both open and stellar in spite of her volatility and abusive interactions with others. By contrast, I also felt more protected, and that this had been the appropriate thing to do.

Beyond that, however, this new space felt like yet another move upward. The new cubicle was contained in a much smaller and more private area than my last workspace. It had only one additional empty desk in it as opposed to four. And it was not as though Selen could not easily find me if needed, though she would have to come through a closed door separating the space from the rest of the building and maneuver through several mini-corridors to reach my cubicle. Obviously this served Clyder as well as me, and would later prove critical once the real clandestine work was to begin: when I found myself in the position of a secret federal informant.

I wondered, of course, what Clyder had or had not shared with Selen relating to her instruction to stop. More to the point, now I wondered how he was going to handle whatever we found from this point on. On one hand, I felt reassured that I was doing the right thing, dutifully following proper and authoritative instructions, and my back was covered if any questions came up later. I have to admit I also felt somewhat relieved to know I *could* continue looking for what had gone awry and that we could continue looking for ways to find immediate, long-term, and systematic solutions for the prevention and early detection/correction of anything similar in the future. Most of all, I was pleased I was looking out for the company that was so good to me.

Although I believed that the corporation itself was the potential victim here, I also believed it may have accidentally created some of its own problems with inept procedures and fragmented tracking systems. This belief was deepening as I gathered important additional information in the couple of weeks since the first meeting.

All in all, what I began unraveling continued to perplex me and troubled me a little more at each step. But with each step, I became more and more convinced that something needed to be addressed, and more and more comfortable in the importance of what I was doing.

I cannot say it coincided perfectly with my regaining the feeling my job was secure and I was safe continuing the research assignments, but any temporary sense of well-being and related expectation of clear sailing was quickly shattered. My life was about to spin on a dime.

It began with one phone call from Northrop security:

"This is Joe Costello of Northrop Defense Systems Security. Dan Quealy and I would like to see you in his office. Now."

I knew that Dan Quealy was the head of internal investigations at Northrop. Beyond that, I knew very little about that arm of Northrop and would have been quite happy to have been able to leave it that way. What could they want with me? Surely not to tell me I was laid off, as the only appearance security staff normally ever made in those cases was to show up at your desk with a box to clear out your things, and given a personal escort out the door. That most decidedly did not require the head of security. This was something else altogether. But what? And why now?

As I hung up the phone, my mind raced over everything that had occurred and/or that I thought I had found or even just suspected, leading up to and then following my meeting with my supervisor.

Should I touch bases with Clyder to see if he knew anything or put him on alert? Should I go straight to Selen and see if this had anything to do with her wanting me to stop working on what I was working on? Was I just being laid off and handled differently than others because they need to do more than cut off my computer access? Wait. Computer access still worked. What could this be?

I gathered my nerve, picked up a writing tablet for no particular reason, and headed not just for the security offices, but the office of the head of internal investigations for all of Northrop. Oddly, the question that did not occur to me yet was whether or not I had stumbled across something I really should not have and somehow now knew something I should not. Then again, I did not know what *they* knew.

It did occur to me that they may have heard about what I was working on as I looked beyond the day-to-day aspects of our product assurance monitoring. I had been very discreet and had also made sure that, to the extent possible, the additional investigations occurred in overtime hours only. What had Clyder shared or not and how much of that had been to or through Selen? And why security anyway? Surely the initial problems I had found were relevant for management in general—quality assurance, human resources, and even accounting in particular. Why security? Was I one of many being shown the door? No, that still did not make sense. My computer access still worked. And if it were any of these things, why hadn't someone else come to me before? If it came down to Selen being angry about my continued exploration after telling me to stop, it was not like her to let someone else have the pleasure of reprimanding someone, to let someone else feel the power of watching them squirm and determining to what extent they were subject to reprimand.

I am sure my mind could have spun on and on like this for some time, although it was already spinning. There just was no piece of information I had that made sense of security needing to speak with me, let alone the head of all internal investigations for the division.

I arrived at Dan Quealy's office and knocked on the door. Part of me was eager to know what had prompted them to ask me to meet with them, most especially right at that moment rather than scheduling a meeting at some other time. On the other hand, I would have been happier not having to be there at all or having this impending encounter put off indefinitely or, preferably, never. I raised my hand to knock a second time, but the door swung open. Without a word, I was gestured in.

The man closing the door behind me was Joe Costello, the person who had called me. Quealy himself rose and thanked me for coming on such short notice and gestured to a chair for me to sit. To make matters even stranger, he asked me if there were anything they could get me. Coffee? Water? Permission to leave was the only thing that came to me, but my answer was, "Nothing. Thank you. I'm fine." This last part was not quite true, of course, but I had to believe they took it as a polite nicety and not the beginning of a conversation around an untruth.

"You are probably wondering why we called you here today," he said, "especially on such short notice."

He gestured again for me to sit and I complied. I actually had an odd thought that very briefly gave me the slightest degree of relief, or at least allowed me to let go of the impulse to read their every gesture or nuance and tone of words. I was now in the "game room," as I thought of it, the place where normal rules of engagement were left at the door and literally every gesture and word was part of an ongoing ritual or game plan to disorient and manipulate anyone who sat in the very seat I was occupying, if for no other reason than to establish who had the upper hand and power.

"Do you have any idea why it is you are here?" Quealy asked.

My mostly true answer was, "No."

"No ideas, no guesses?"

"Nope."

Quealy gestured for his colleague to sit as well, again a subtle reminder of who was in charge, although that was never in question. Even less so as I found myself sitting across from the two of them in a strikingly dimly lit room, with what I imagined was an intentional positioning that blocked my access to the door. Interestingly, although they both sat opposite me, Costello was somewhat closer in a way that actually compressed the space I occupied while Quealy sat ever so slightly and most decidedly imperiously farther back. I actually had a moment in which I started to relax a bit more, thinking to myself, *This really is a game*, and, for whatever reason it began and went on autopilot. Mostly, I had a greater sense that I simply did not belong there, but remained on alert for why they might think I did.

Whether it was just for effect or he was genuinely trying to size me up—seeming to try to look past the surface and see right through me—he took several endless moments looking me over as though trying to think of what to say or how to begin.

His opening observation caught me a little off guard in noting that I seemed to have something of an unusual position here at Northrop. I was not quite sure what that meant. Clarification followed. I had a lot of unusual freedom to move around and look at things, to follow my interests where they take me.

Was that what this was about? They were just concerned that I might see the bigger picture of information and procedures others are generally blind to, as they only look for and see whatever is allowed in their respective project, division, or even job description box?

It was the nature of Quality Assurance, I thought. Where others operate in boxes by design and security necessity, we had to operate with a somewhat more global view if for no other reason than that the acquisition, handling, and ultimate disposition of materials moved somewhat fluidly between projects and across compartmentalized boundaries of strictly enforced secrecy. It started to dawn on me that my being there might not be over anything specific I had done or found, but that the very range of my job and access to information, by definition, made them a little nervous in terms of procedure aimed at secrecy and keeping one hand from knowing what the other was doing.

Before I could answer, Quealy continued, accepting a folder from his colleague, glancing inside, then closing it as though trying to grasp the meaning of what he just saw he finally spoke.

"Here's the thing," Quealy continued. It had come to their attention that I was reportedly seen leaving the building, then observed stopping my car in a gas station not all that far from Northrop, where I then allegedly opened my trunk, removed some boxes—much like some storage boxes he pointed to on the floor nearby—which I then passed along to someone else who put them in their trunk and drove away.

I was struck numb and very nearly dumb.

"That is not possible," I finally offered.

Quealy did not respond to my protestation, and moving on instead, he wondered if there were anything I might be working on, might have come across or uncovered, or maybe even just suspect that I had encountered that could prove . . . *embarrassing* for the company. This question should have given me more pause on its face, but I was still stuck on the totally fabricated information that I had been seen taking materials out of my car and passing them on to anyone.

"Who was it who suggested I had done this?" I asked. "Who said they saw me do this?"

"That is not what is important," was the response. What mattered was what kind of employee I was and whether or not I was to be trusted. After all, as was noted, I did have access to potentially sensitive information,

information that, by its very nature was, if not top secret, was for select eyes only and only on a need-to-know basis.

Quealy reiterated his curiosity as to whether or not there was anything I was working on that could be—there was that term again—"embarrassing" for the company.

"You know . . . " He dangled the next point. " . . . Something that could be misunderstood or misconstrued by outsiders."

This, of course, had been my concern all along. What was it they had been told about my monitoring or reports? Who would have claimed to have seen me pass documents? I could not imagine having any reason to take documents out of the building, let alone being able to get them out.

"Yes," I answered, "but only if it were looked at out of context and by someone wanting to do harm to the company." I could have offered more, but in shock of such an allegation, all I could really think about was second-guessing who could have possibly made that up and passed it on to security.

Perhaps it was a preemptive strike to my credibility if they were among those who might be incriminated, or at least shown as incompetent, by my findings when officially passed up the organizational ladder. It was disheartening to think Quealy and others in authority could even entertain that my looking at the information in question was for anything other than protecting the company. I think I may have missed part of what Quealy was saying and do not remember if I interrupted him or broke some silence, but in my daze, I still felt the urge to clarify reality.

"You know I did not do what you said I did. I've never taken any documents or property of any kind outside of the building, let alone passed it along to someone else. I did not do that."

The response was chilling. They did not say that I did do what they said I was accused of doing. They had said it had been reported that I had been seen doing it. Who would do this to me and why? And was it possible my standing and thus my job could be jeopardized or done in by a rumor? A patently and horrifyingly false one at that? I wondered what it was they actually knew or thought they knew, and wondered how much of this was information gathering and how much was test. My unspoken questions were not helped by what they asked next:

What exactly it was I had been looking at in recent months and what did I think I had found that was out of the ordinary, and what had I passed along to my supervisor?

I waited for more and had enough of my senses to take note they did not mention Selen or her instructions for me to stop looking or doing what I was doing. That was it. The only question on the table at the moment—the whole issue of who had falsely accused me being clearly sidelined—was what I had been looking at, what I thought I had found, and what had I reported to Clyder. The problem here, I thought, was not so much that what I had found or thought I had found was out of the ordinary, as they put it, but that it might *not* be all that out of the ordinary. It may have been out of the ordinary that it was found at all. And could it be made to embarrass or make the company look bad?

I gave a fairly detailed account of what I had discovered and what I had shared with Clyder both in conversations and printed reports, comforted by the fact that I had, to the extent required, shared and documented virtually everything. What I had come upon and what we were doing to get a clearer picture of how to understand and, if necessary, to correct these problems was discussed, but only in the narrow confines of my supervisor and no one else. At least in that sense, it was aboveboard and in the open for those with need to know.

My head was spinning with all of this, most especially with questions about and possible implications of the allegations against me. I could not imagine who would have said this. The information I had been gathering could not yet be known by those who could be implicated in wrongdoing by it. Or could it? Was all this just some kind of fishing expedition to assure themselves I was, in fact, a trustworthy employee whose necessary access was a bit less restrictive than they might have preferred? What would happen to my job if they believed it or even entertained it as being true?

After I finished my summary of the facts as I knew them in regard to the question on the table, I came back to the accusation. My mind just could not let go of it.

"It not only did not happen," I offered. "It could not have happened."

"And why is that?" they wanted to know.

My answer: Aside from my being a particularly loyal employee who would not do such a thing, it could not have happened because I did not normally drive alone. I carpooled with a fellow worker who will remain forever nameless. If I was being followed for some reason, I suggested, they would already know that.

No one said I was being followed, was the reply. Was there some reason I should be?

No. Once again I said it could not have happened as charged because I carpooled with someone else.

"Maybe you do," came the vague response. "Maybe on that day you did not."

"No, on that day I did. I definitely did."

"How could I be so sure?"

"Because I know."

"Good. That's good," was the patronizing response. "Do you think, by any chance, you could provide us with copies of those reports you gave your supervisor?" they wondered.

The answer was, "Of course." I pointed out there was nothing really secret about them as far as their existence or what was in them for those authorized to see them. There were copies in binders at my desk, for which I knew they had keys. And everything I had found I had given Clyder.

"I do not know who he might have shared them with," was my answer to one of their last questions. "But yes," was my answer to the last one, "I can make copies for you."

They would appreciate that.

"When would you like them?" I asked.

"We'll wait. Oh, and Jim."

"Yes," I answered. "Tell no one of this little meeting we've just had."

As I rose, I realized just how powerfully this had all hit me. My legs were shaking and it was almost as though there was some kind of time delay between my willing my body to move and it following my command. Just the limited distance to the door felt like one of those horrible dreams in which your body will only move in slow motion even while you are trying to get it to move more quickly. I reached for the doorknob, now aware that my hands were sweaty and shaking, feeling their unwavering stares at my back as the door closed behind me.

This could not be happening. My only concern had been for the company and in a matter of minutes it seemed that had all turned on me in some Alice-through-the-looking-glass nightmare in which the best of intentions got turned into suspect behavior and motives, and a loyal protector of the company was seen as a potential enemy.

The words *tell no one* still echoed in my mind.

I went directly to my cubicle to gather the agreed-upon documents. Then, as I made my way from my cubicle and past Clyder's office to head toward the centralized copying center, I was more aware than ever of the omnipresent eyes of security everywhere—most notably the glass-bubbles that tracked my progress through the halls. I suddenly imagined someone sitting at some wall of monitors watching my current twists and turns through the labyrinth corridors of the facility trying to look normal. Unaffected. Unconcerned. Making sure I told no one.

When I handed the now-substantial stack of papers to the clerk, I got the usual question verifying what I wrote on the request slip.

"That is one set of copies?"

I paused, took the slip back, and made a correction. As I passed it back, I said out loud what I had just put on the page, "Make that two."

In what may have been one of the most significant ironies in a long string of them, it was the accusation that I had taken any documents out of the building and the warning to *tell no one* that suddenly convinced me I should. For the first time, I wanted copies for myself, regardless of the dangers that created or the protocols it violated. For the first time, I was truly on guard and stripped of that wonderful cocoon of trust I had so cherished up to a very few minutes ago.

I still did not suspect the company itself of wrongdoing. But clearly I could not trust being mistrusted. Just as clearly, I suddenly had no idea whatsoever who it was I could trust, or who it was I needed to fear. When asked when I needed the copies by, I repeated those last words that still rang in my ears and sickened my heart:

"I'll wait."

My mind could not stop reeling. Who would have made such fabricated allegations if, in fact, anyone did? And what implications did that have for my job?

And in the middle of all this, the only thing I could think about was *What about my job?* I could not afford to lose my job. And there were those invisible eyes behind glass bubbles staring down at me even now, directly behind me and from both ends of the corridor. There really were eyes and evidently spies everywhere. Whom to trust?

I took the completed copies and originals and started my trek back to Quealy's office. I stopped by my cubicle and for the first time ever set aside the copies of the reports I now planned on hiding for my own back-up and protection, even if at that moment I could not imagine what I was going to do with them. For now, I just looked around to see if anyone were looking, put them in my desk drawer, and locked it. I then completed the journey back to Quealy's office with the requested copies in hand. I was stopped at the door by Costello, who took the reports but blocked me from entering again. Quealy looked at me from farther inside as he moved behind his desk and sat down.

I was still not sure what they were after or concluding from any of this, but I intuitively and, perhaps even to test, offered, "You know, if there is anything about any of this you would rather just handle yourself, I would be happy to just turn it over to you. After all, you have much more access and perspective of these things than I do." To underscore the real message, I would be happy to step out of it and let it go. "I just want what is good for the company."

If I had been looking for a clearer picture or relief, it was not forthcoming. Instead what I got was a largely inscrutable and possibly slightly mocking, "That's good. That is what we want, too. Oh, and by the way," they added, "remember what we told you earlier. Do not discuss any of this with anyone."

I assured them I normally did not discuss anything about my job or the things I was looking at with anyone. Not my coworkers, not my friends outside of the building, not even my wife and most immediate family. It was just protocol, after all, in a facility charged with protecting secrets that affected governments all over the world, always on guard against espionage and threats to national security that could follow from any breaches.

That was all fine and good if true, they said with that hint of suspicion still dangling in the air. But I had misunderstood. It was not just that I was never to discuss what it was we were discussing here today. I was not to ever share with anyone that the conversation ever happened. Regarding anyone outside of that room at the moment, I was not to divulge that we had even spoken at all.

I was not sure what to make of this or what point they were trying to make. Perhaps they were concerned I would go looking for whoever suggested they had seen me passing documents in some gas station.

Then the truly disturbing part hit, if anything could be more disturbing than the suspicion I might be taking secret documents out of the building and passing them on to persons unknown: I was not to even speak of having met with security with my supervisor or his immediate supervisor. Why would they want me to keep that information from them and how was I to proceed without sharing it? I suddenly felt more alone than ever.

By this time, I had a major dilemma. Above all else, I wanted to keep my job, ideally with the recent boon of overtime or raises from continued promotions, for the added security and well-being of my family. But to even go through the motions of doing my job meant dangling in the wind in the crosshairs or crossfire of . . . someone. To really do my job, it meant finding still more information that might make it seem the corporation was misbehaving or, in some cases, committing scattered instances of outright fraud. I really could not see any good way through this and I found myself wishing above all else—in one particular moment that will stay with me forever—that it would all turn out to be a mistake or series of mistakes, a simple glitch in procedure that the corporation would appreciate having had identified and thus, would just as gladly correct.

The problem was, in simply continuing to do what I had been doing day to day (documenting noncompliant materials through their entire continuum of acquisition through use or failure, tracking them across discrete stages of research and production, and monitoring them across project boundaries), I continued to find even stronger and more inexplicable problems. Inexplicable, that is, if one wanted to believe that these errors were unintentional systemic or company anomalies and unknown to anyone in authority.

It all had to do with a number of projects ordering substantial quantities of parts and materials that could be correlated to a spike or massive temporary buildup of inventory, which were sent back to vendors shortly thereafter. This would make sense as an accident or unexpected delays in a project making the parts and materials not yet needed, or just inefficient management if it were isolated and unusual. Worse and even more inexplicable in any terms I could imagine, this even included re-purchasing parts that were known to be bad in a way that inflated inventory already bloated with known and unusable parts and materials.

I kept expecting (subconsciously) and hoping someone would tell me to stop doing my job as it had evolved, or at least cut me back from the tracking and analysis that allowed me to see patterns others would not. I struggled with what to make of this in light of my having been told not to talk with my supervisors about the meeting with security, or the allegations that had been made against me. I was really beginning to wish I had not come across or recognized any problems or anomalies in what was supposed to be prescribed protocols and practices. I was even beginning to think a cutback in my still-existing overtime an acceptable price to be free of the stress and growing concern over how I was seen and not knowing whom I could still trust. I had to wonder who, if anyone, above Quealy had been informed of the allegations against me or of our meeting. This made me wonder who, if anyone, had been informed about the possible ramifications of what I had found and reported, let alone the transgressions in materials handling and billing.

But I continued to dig for answers concerning new issues of the possible inflation of inventory numbers. Finally I accumulated too much information to ignore and came to a point where I really felt I needed to find some kind of trustworthy touchstone, an assurance that there was still someone I could trust.

I decided to raise the issue with my supervisor. Surely he would be concerned over this strange handling of inventory, most especially the strange prevalence of reordering or restocking inventory with known bad parts.

As we met in his office and I laid out what I had come across, I watched for some kind of "tell" as to what he was thinking. I especially wondered what he might know about the meeting with security. Were we both sitting there knowing what happened while avoiding acknowledging that it happened?

The answer to the inflation of inventory was not one I wanted to hear. This was standard practice at a time of year when programs and projects had to meet milestones to keep billing the government, and having the noted flow of parts made it look like they were on track.

This gave me an unbelievable feeling of nausea and a sense that the earth had just opened up beneath me. This was a known and common practice to mislead the government and, worse, my supervisor knew it and evidently did not think much of it. As my supervisor and the person who was my closest and only immediate ally in examining the kinds of problems I had discovered, this left me feeling suddenly exposed and confused. What were we doing in finding problems if there was no real interest in fixing or preventing them? Why was he supporting my developing tracking reports that were becoming trusted documents among higher-ups? Had there been any more allegations made against me and were there any other meetings or monitoring going on I did not know about?

I tried to wrap my mind around this double discovery and carry on, to at least go through the motions of doing my job while I figured out what it meant and whom to trust. It was in that sickeningly dizzying mindset that I encountered Quealy walking toward me. The corridor seemed suddenly to shrink in size and made passing without contact impossible. I really wanted to believe the problems I had brought to him were already being corrected. I savored the idea I could relinquish any concerns on behalf of the corporation. Mostly, I wanted to become invisible. We passed with only slight eye contact. I felt a churning in the pit of my stomach I had not known before, and I tried to force myself just to continue on.

I could not. I stopped walking.

I turned to face Quealy's back, words coming out of my mouth as though someone or something else had taken over my body.

"Excuse me?" Dan did not slow and I repeated more loudly, "Excuse me."

Dan stopped walking and looked back at me, waiting to hear what came next. I stepped forward, as if controlled by some irresistible force. I had to know.

"What happened with the issues and the reports I gave you about the cables?"

I could tell Quealy was not pleased with being asked, but in company protocol I was pretty sure it was within my right to ask, having been brought in for discussion and having provided written reports.

Quealy stared at me for what seemed a very long moment, as though pondering what to say or how to say it. Maybe he was pondering if he was going to say anything at all. Finally, he just shrugged.

Nothing had happened with them. He had been instructed not to file a report regarding our discussions or the reports I had given him. Evidently, some engineer working on a specific project no longer needed the cables for his program and issued a stock sweep to remove and dispose of the cables from the stock system, unaware that the cables were needed for follow-on contracts, spares for similar projects, and equipment. Engineering then wrote a change for the last three numbers on the parts and reordered them to replace the ones that had been removed from stock and disposed of by accident.

I suspect my disappointment that it had not been handled differently (or handled at all) was probably clear on my face and I did not know what to say, nor did I feel safe asking how that could be. Quealy then added, as if in defense from my unspoken thoughts, "We handle hundreds of millions in business here. These cables were only around five hundred thousand. I was told not to file a report."

Quealy waited a moment, decided we were done, and went on his way, quite possibly a little concerned about what I might do next. I did not have any notion of what to do or what was any kind of "next." What I did know, in the pit of my sinking stomach, was that I no longer believed the corporation was the innocent and well-meaning victim. What I knew was that I would never see the place or the materials management problems the same way again.

As I arrived at my cubicle and sat down at my desk, the space itself seemed to shrink and close in on me. I realized the irresistible force that had taken over was simply the need to know what was really going on, and to find some course of action. Some hint of control over what was going on. Some notion of whom I could trust.

Though I cannot remember for certain, as the growing stress turned the experience into a bit of a blur, I think this may have been the first period in which I not only lost my unquestioning trust of the company as a whole, but woke up to a gnawing fear of becoming a fall guy and actually going to prison for the actions of others. If nothing else, some idea of what was coming and from where I needed to be watching for trouble was beginning to take vague form. I realized at that moment just how totally alone and adrift I was. I realized how any step in any direction to discover or handle any information I found to help the company or myself could only put me farther out on my own with no one to confide in who would cover my back. I was coming to realize that quite possibly there might be no one at all. I *had* been told to speak to no one.

I believe it was during this time I remembered some long-ago news of an audit wherein an engineer had been called into question. He had claimed to have been asked to sign blank authorizations at Northrop for electrical tests, and/or sign off for use. The audit had cost the corporation some major fines at the time, but he was the only person in the whole affair who was convicted and sent to prison. It *was* his sole signature on the paperwork, so he alone went to jail while those in charge—the ones who had allowed the abuses through neglect or orchestrated it for profit—went untouched.

For reasons going far beyond failing my family and leaving them bereft of support and my presence, I could not even begin to entertain the notion of prison. Some of the worst horrors of my fairly horrifying childhood came rushing up from depths where they had lain in hiding. What mattered at the moment, on my drive home, was just how completely at risk I suddenly was.

I was lost, adrift, with no plan of any kind or any real notion of what to do next.

I found myself wishing I had someone—anyone—I could talk to, someone who would have an idea of what to do. Better yet, someone who could come up with a plan and *tell* me what to do.

As the saying goes, we should always be careful what we ask for.

4
THE HANDLER & THE ABYSS

It was now January 1988 and several weeks since my disturbing encounter with Quealy in the hallways of Northrop. With my immediate distress having faded ever so slightly into a fragile combination of wishful thinking and denial, life had settled into a strangely familiar but subtly disturbed kind of on-the-edge normalcy.

If this sounds like a crazy contradiction in terms, it is. It was also the faint beginning of what my life and my family's lives would look like—and progressively worsen—for the next seventeen years. It was all but impossible to know whom to trust, what to make of anything and whether it was observed, imagined, or feared, or to know what to do or not do next. Every moment loomed as a challenge and double-edged sword.

It is difficult to convey the sometimes-nauseating disorientation and constantly draining stress this betwixt-and-between state creates for its holder directly, and for his or her family indirectly. There is or can be, however, an ongoing and inescapable state of fatigue to outright exhaustion, and a disruptive to debilitating hesitancy that goes into literally everything you think and do. You find yourself paying just a little more attention to others at work; they stay in your peripheral vision and at the edges of your mind. You wonder if perhaps they, too, are seeing something out of the ordinary or of concern as well, or you wonder if they are now possibly taking you in through their own peripheral vision and thinking of you as somehow different or suspect.

Perhaps the strangest part of all this, at least in these earliest stages, was the concern that I might be misreading or over-assessing things, causing un-intentional and unfair harm to the people and organization, even though they seemed just as likely a possible danger to me in all kinds of ways. In either case, any hopes I had of convincing myself I had overreacted or of ridding myself of the nagging sense I had stumbled into something I would need to deal with no matter what, was shattered with a single phone call that would, by every measure, change my life forever. Not just because of the call itself, but because of what I ultimately did with it.

The call came one evening when I was having a particularly difficult time shutting off the internal dialogue about my work. I found myself se-riously pondering the odd balancing act it put me in. I dearly loved my work and the freedom of movement it gave me in an organization that, in many ways, did not even tolerate, let alone promote that kind of move-ment. I loved it both for the challenges it offered and the opportunities it provided for me to stretch and grow professionally. Moreover, I had carte blanche to follow literally any line of tracking problem or discrepancy.

The irony here, and the balancing act I had come to recognize, was that the very characteristics about the job that made it fulfilling and of greatest service also meant if there were other problems out there worse than those I had run into already, before I knew it, I could very well find myself knee-deep in something I might even prefer not knowing about. I could be suspected of knowing about any number of things if anyone thought about it. I had not run into it, but easily could have. These were the thoughts that ran through my mind all that day at work and on the drive home, though I attempted to set them aside before I arrived home.

As I pulled up to our house, all I could think about as I sat in my car and stared at it was how stable and good we had it now financially be-cause of my current position and how much my family, most especially my wife, Mary, had already gone through not that long ago from the errat-ic behaviors related to my then still-active alcoholism and escalating drug use. I knew I owed them a great deal. I also felt quite grateful for their still being there and the chance to make up for lost time. It was with the latter thought that I chose to do better than simply put on a good face and try to leave my thoughts at the door. I decided to be as present and thankful as possible as my family continued its adjustment to having me fully in it.

It was still light out and dinner was not quite ready, so I settled in to watch a little television with my five children coming and going, paying varying levels of attention to the shifting gathering in the living room and whatever they were doing in other rooms. It was one of the most relaxed and settled moments I had let myself slide into in weeks, so I thought nothing when the phone rang in the kitchen and Mary called out that it was for me. I had no idea who it could be as I took the receiver from her and she returned to the stove nearby.

"Hello," I answered, probably somewhat absently as I continued to take in the room around me and the family I loved, and absently spied the waiting TV program in the next room. Thinking it was another telemarketer or bill collector and ready to hang up, I said again, "Hello."

The voice on the other end said, "My Name is Richard Zott."

. . . *Zott?* . . . *Zott? I do not know a—*

"I am a federal agent with the D.C.I.S. The Department of Defense Criminal Investigative Services for the Attorney General's office."

"Excuse me?" I responded, my entire universe spinning on a dime.

"My name is Richard Zott, and I am a federal agent with the Department of Defense Criminal Investigations for the Attorney General's office. I understand you may have information on some irregularities or problems in practices at Northrop Corporation, where you work. We'd like to talk with you."

It is unbelievable how many thoughts can explode in the human brain all at once, not that I was at all functional otherwise. Who did he say he was? All I could remember was *federal agent.* How did he know I might know anything? How did he know about me at all? Who else must know or suspect something to have passed anything along? Who and how many were aware of me and my work and who would suspect anything? Mary was now looking at me in concern, clearly detecting that something was wrong as I tried to collect my thoughts and find my voice.

I took in her look, glanced at the rest of my family going on in happy oblivion, and realized that if nothing else, I needed some privacy. "Excuse me," I said to the voice on the other end of the line that, with those few words, had just placed a fork in the road of my life. "I need to take this on another phone." I held the receiver out to Mary and told her I would take the call on the other phone and let her know when to hang up.

"Dinner will be ready in a few minutes," she reminded me as she took the receiver. She could see something was not just wrong, but possibly quite terribly wrong.

My thoughts were reeling, but at least I understood that for her, the first concern was that this might be bad news about family. I managed to shake my head no and made my best attempt to reassure her with, "It's nothing."

I crossed through the living room to the small anteroom where the other phone sat on a small table, and picked up the receiver. I called out to Mary to go ahead and hang up, then backed into my oldest daughter's bedroom. I took in the otherwise blissful sight in the next rooms, but found myself strangely alone with quite possibly my worst nightmare waiting for me to get back on the line. I closed the door over the phone cord as the voice on the line filled the empty space.

"Mr. Holzrichter, are you there?"

"Yes, I am here. What do you want?"

"As I said, we would like to talk with you."

I yielded to gravity, which already wanted to get the better part of me, and I sat on my daughter's bed. My ears were ringing and my body was charged with adrenaline.

"Yes, I heard you," I responded, trying to make myself grasp that this was real. All I could think of was that my life was spinning on the point of a pin. My thoughts were searching through weeks and months of events, trying to get a fix on what they may want to know or talk about, and who could possibly have sent them my way if they were in fact real. My worst thoughts were questioning if they were who they said they were at all, or if this was all a trick or ruse on the part of Northrop to trap or test me. Memories of my meeting with Quealy and the false accusations of passing on documents to someone resurfaced.

I managed to take one focused breath after another to overcome the overwhelming urge to crawl out of my skin and to disappear and magically be somewhere else. By any measure, this was serious stuff.

The voice, neither threatening nor reassuring, repeated, "Mr. Holzrichter, are you there?"

"Yes, I am here. What do you want with me? How do I even know you are who you say you are?"

He answered in a slow, steady, inscrutable voice, "As I said, my name is Richard Zott and I am a federal agent. We would like to talk with you about a few things to do with your work."

In the kitchen, Mary went through the usual motions of getting everyone together and to the table, daughters helping with getting the food together, sons absently abusing each other. Her thoughts were only partially on the closed door, her every movement and expression very much in the here and now, the eternal hub in keeping things together and functioning in the moment. At some level, she wanted to believe this call that so unnerved her husband was just some routine problem from work. At some other level, which always lurked in the not-quite-fully-conscious background, she also imagined it could be some sinister danger of her husband's necessarily secret work finally showing its face, the perpetual danger of working in a facility of secrecy and weapons of death, always on the lookout for leaks or dangers to itself.

On one hand, she was curious. On the other hand, she maintained her disciplined focus on family and immediate practicalities, as this was her chosen role and nature. She essentially shut off the part of her that would question knowing more as a possible safeguard to her family should it ever be the worst, and she needed to be a survivor. She stayed focused on each minute task in front of her, then the next, and then the next.

Back in my daughter's bedroom, I fumbled to find pen and paper to take notes, to get the information down, to take this in with the same orderly and detailed orientation with which I did my job.

"Why me? Why my work? Who told you to talk to me anyway?"

He answered, "We can discuss all that when we meet. It is just a formality. We just have a few questions you may be able to help us with."

I found a writing pad and pen and placed the pad squarely next to me on the bed, my thoughts now playing out several simultaneous possible scenarios for what was happening, and gauged my responses for all of them at once.

"How do I know you are who you say you are, and what if I don't want to talk with you even if you are?"

"As for proving who we are, we can provide credentials when we meet. As for not talking with us, I am afraid that is not an option."

Not an option. There was something both intimidating about those words and strangely reassuring. They were definitive, off the fence, inescapable.

I said, "For all I know you could be some kind of spy trying to get information from me and pretending to be federal agents and I don't know what makes you think I have anything to say to you or anyone anyway."

Of course, I did not explicitly state my greatest fear, that this person and whoever else was part of the "we" he referred to were actually minions of the long-feared and vaguely defined dark side of Northrop internal investigators, or hired spies from the outside pretending to be federal agents setting me up to see how I would respond.

"We are who we say we are and it will not take much of your time," he answered. "You really do not have any choice here."

"I tell you what," I finally offered, really struggling to keep my thoughts in order and consider possible ramifications of anything I said if this were a setup or some kind of fraud. "Let me report this to my work, to Northrop, tomorrow and when they verify you are who you say . . . "

Richard Zott gently cut me off and said, "I am sorry, but that just is not going to happen."

Deep breath. Continue. "Look, I have no way of confirming who you are or what you want, so it would be best if I reported this at work first and then once they confirm who you are and approve my talking to you—"

I could not even finish the thought as we both knew that if he was who he said he was, Northrop was going to do anything but give its blessing to meet. Then I would be squarely on high-security radars I did not want to be near, let alone on.

Richard Zott let the silence hang in the air for a moment, then he continued. "As I said, that is not going to happen. The first thing that would occur would be that you would be instantly surrounded by Northrop Corporation investigators and attorneys, and they would both grill you to find out what it is you may or may not know that puts them in possible danger and they would most definitely convince you not to talk to us and that just is not an option."

Again, this closing out of options and closing in of action.

"What if I just do not want to talk to you?" I asked. "What if I refuse?"

"The alternatives are simple: You either talk to me now or at some point, I will put you in jail."

Boom. Concrete, nonnegotiable, simple.

So I said, "What time can you be here tomorrow?"

As I opened the door to my daughter's bedroom and came out to join the family, now halfway through their dinner, Mary took in my expression as I sank into my chair at the head of the table. She rose without a word to fix my plate, her curiosity still matched by unshakable resolve not to ask and her preference not to know. There were a thousand things I would have liked to have said or expressed in kaleidoscopic confusion and a real need to talk with someone, but we had a shared and unspoken knowledge it was best not to speak or share what was possibly in motion.

She set my plate in front of me and surprised me to some extent by asking, however casually she tried to sound, "So, who was that?"

I paused, with a fork of food suspended in the air, trying to judge how well I was doing at keeping my hand from shaking, and answered, "That was a federal agent. They want to talk with me about work."

I knew she was not going to ask anything more. I could see the thoughts on her face as she looked at the chaotic details of life and five children surrounding us. She was wondering if our income and life were in any kind of danger.

"They are coming to see me tomorrow."

There it was. I had her attention now in a different kind of way. Whatever unspoken fears she ever had about my work and the people I worked for and whatever had been weighing on me for some weeks now, it was about to show up in human form—federal agents no less, and in her home. In typical Mary Holzrichter fashion, her gaze wandered over me and the space around her. Her mind gauged the situation and assessed the need for practical action.

"We have to clean, and you are going to help. No video games."

With no further comment, Mary went into cleaning mode, pulling the day-to-day disorder of a family of seven into the kind of order she preferred the world to see.

Nothing more was said. I could not bring myself to eat more than a few bites of food that normally would have been the highlight of my day but now tasted like dust in my mouth. I put my plate on the sink.

As the children dispersed into their respective play or distractions, Mary and I cleaned with purpose. Time seemed strangely slowed down or suspended. As she became aware of the actual time and read my unstated thoughts, that I needed some kind of grounding and routine to deal with what we were not discussing, she said, "Go ahead. I will get more done now and we can finish in the morning."

In the first five years following my stay in rehab, I never missed a day of attending Alcoholics Anonymous. If ever there were a day I needed a meeting, this was it. However, as I drove the short distance to the meeting, it occurred to me just how alone I was in my current situation, how little I could share with anyone, and how much I felt the need to be able to talk to someone . . . anyone. I found myself looking in the rearview mirror to see if anyone was following me. I took note of the faces and attention of almost every other driver.

As I stepped into this meeting that was both a familiar touchstone and a daily life preserver for me, for my sobriety, and for my family, my eyes scanned the room for anyone who was new and unfamiliar, anyone who just did not seem to belong there, or anyone who was suddenly more attentive to my presence. More than ever, I was aware of just how much the nature of my work and secrecy of the facility where I worked meant I could not talk about any of it. In a room full of people, I felt alone. The drive home was even worse, my super-heightened senses and anxiety taking in every detail of the drive I normally would not notice, the path and directions of all other headlights, the glance or lack of a glance of any other drivers I could see in the now-darkened world that led home.

It was late afternoon the next day when Richard Zott and his partner Elizabeth arrived. I had called in sick to work, which was not much of a stretch by any measure. From the window, I had already looked out from a thousand times that morning, I could not see the license plates on their vehicle as Richard Zott got out and put on his gun, then a tan coat that had been draped over his seat. I would learn later that I would not have seen any kind of government plates anyway because they never wanted to give their identity away. Their work was ultra-secretive in worlds defined by secrets. All I could think of as I watched from the window was how I could not fail my family, how I could not, under any circumstances, bear going to jail, and how much I hoped beyond hope they were who they said they were.

Mary, taking her cue that their arrival was imminent, rounded up the kids to go into another room to watch television together and draw or play games or anything that would keep them distracted and unaware. The door to that room and everything that mattered most to me was already closed when the gentle but distinct knock sounded.

As I opened the door and Richard Zott politely said, "Mr. Holzrichter."

It struck me that as noninflected as the words were, it was definitely not a question but an acknowledgement. It was a reminder that this man and possibly both of the people standing on my doorstep—the threshold to the sanctity of my home—knew who I was on sight and probably a great deal more. And I knew nothing about them. *How much did they know*, I wondered, and *what is it they want to do with it?*

Whether reading my thoughts or just out of the kind of strict procedure we were about to follow, they offered their badges and identification without comment, discreetly glancing to make sure no one on the outside would be able to see the movement or gesture, eyes glancing inside to take in the situation they were about to step into.

"My wife and kids are watching TV," I offered, looking over my shoulder, already noting this encounter was going to be a strange combination of communication on the unstated and very careful stating of whatever was communicated. I also knew they were the real deal and that I was going to answer whatever they asked and do whatever they asked me to do.

As I guided them into the most private space I could muster, I noticed a subtle but decided shift in the sickness that had taken over my stomach since the phone call. It was more tolerable, and even an excited feeling of butterflies or hopeful anticipation taking the place of the previous anxiety and dread. *The cavalry is here*, I thought. As much as I feared where all this could go, I finally had someone to talk to, someone I could tell my story to and shed some of the heavy load I had been carrying. In truth, there was a part of me that suddenly found all this kind of exciting.

We settled in almost without a word, coffee served and politely accepted all around. We had that brief moment of sizing up and waiting for the other to make the first move in what I thought must almost be a ritualistic kind of beginning to this kind of encounter. Not quite ready to show any of my cards first, I finally asked what exactly they wanted and how they got here in the first place.

Richard simply said, "Tell us what you know or any concerns you might have of things not just right at Northrop."

And, of course, I related the series of events that came most readily to mind: The incident with the cables that had been scrapped and destroyed by accident to the tune of half a million dollars, then replaced under the pretense that the replacement parts were something new and different, even if just slightly so.

I asked him again, "Why me?"

"We can't actually say what brought us here or you to our attention." Before I could respond, he deftly deflected the question to come with, "So, this scrapping of parts that evidently are good is normal?"

"Yes," I answered, not quite ready to tell him there was potentially much more to that. "But the scrapping itself I do believe was accidental. It was the reordering that bothered me, because the change of inventory numbers had to be on purpose and—"

"They knew they were the same parts but were just hiding that fact?" Richard asked.

"Yes. I thought there was no reason to change the part numbers on paper other than, I assume, to hide the fact we were ordering them a second time and billing the government for what should have been our cost as a result of that error." There was a good deal more at issue that I did not yet have any clear awareness of or evidence of, but this definitely had their attention.

As I would come to appreciate later, this one incident alone embodied much of the kinds of problems we would encounter later on, such as having surplus parts, which meant Northrop had ordered in excess of what was needed, demonstrating they did not have the basis for accurate estimating they claimed they had. Then it looked like they were removing the evidence that they had bought the parts in the first place. In falsely removing what they thought were unneeded parts and thus excess inventory, they cheated the US government out of the refund or credit that theoretically should have been issued for that contract and those theoretically unused and over-bought parts.

In the case of these cables, though, they had been scrapped in error and were needed to support spares and repairs of units in the field. The solution found was to have engineering come up with an authorized request for replacement parts that were exactly the same, but looked as though they were different and the project required some newly altered version of that part.

I would discover much later that these kinds of maneuvers at Northrop were not unknown to my enigmatic guests. They had originally been called into action with Northrop for other reasons that were in their own ways related to Rex Robinson, my future co-litigant, after he had contacted the FBI with his own separate concerns. While the FBI is the investigative arm for the Department of Justice (which has both a criminal side and a civil side), they determined at the time that it was outside of their jurisdiction and turned it over to the Defense Department, which then assigned it to the Defense Criminal Investigation Services of the Defense Department's Office of the Inspector General. Prior to their landing on my doorstep, these two agents had already been exploring alleged time card fraud at Northrop in which projects that had run out of money, but needed to keep working, allocated their employee hours on that project to some other project that still had money.

At this time I did not grasp all these implications myself and had no idea what they thought of what I did know and shared. If they had come here because of any reporting related to that incident or its successive steps, I could not read it in their faces.

"So what happened then, after you reported the problem to your boss and got called in to speak with . . . ?"

"Dan Quealy," I tossed in. "You mean besides having the fear of God and losing my job put in me . . . nothing."

"What do you mean nothing?"

"I mean nothing. I ran into Quealy sometime later, a few weeks ago, as a matter of fact, and asked him how the investigation turned out and what they decided to do about it."

"And?" Richard Zott asked.

"And nothing," I answered. "He said it was for an amount of money hardly worth bothering about, I mean half a million dollars, and that he had been told not to file a report."

This was the first hint of a reaction from these two as they exchanged the slightest hint of a glance and Richard Zott leaned ever so slightly forward. "He told you he was instructed not to report his findings?"

I felt for the first time there was some kind of better contact here. "I'm saying he was told not to even report that the issue of the cables, that I brought to his attention or my initial reporting of concerns ever came up."

Richard Zott sat staring at me for a few moments, as though running scenarios through his mind's eye. I was not sure I wanted to know. He looked at his partner and then back to me.

"You do know, don't you, that he is obligated to report any investigations he conducts regardless of his results or findings to the government?"

"No, I didn't know that," I answered with visions of prison creeping back into the picture.

"As an investigative employee of Northrop Corporation under federal government contracts, he is bound by contract to file his report not only to Northrop but to the United States government. He violated his mandate of reporting internal investigations at Northrop to the customer."

Suddenly the scale and stakes in this game and conversation exploded in size and imagined dangers. "Well, I'm okay, right? I mean my boss told me that since I reported the problem to him . . . "

"Technically, you did your part initially. But the truth is, once you know of wrongdoing, like this Quealy guy who did not file a report or notify the proper authorities . . . "

Suddenly a whole host of horrors descended on my brain. "You mean I could have been in trouble . . . "

"I am telling you that even if you report it to your superiors, then you find out nothing was done to correct or report the problem to the customer, meaning us, the government, of a possible felony being committed, that could be construed as committing a felony yourself as well." Richard Zott let that sink in and timed his next question with skill. "So, what else do you think you know that you would like to tell us?"

I thought about this for a moment, and realized I really needed to draw them a picture of what I did at Northrop in tracking problem parts and not only their disposal and status in inventory but the tracking of those steps. "Excuse me for a minute. I need to get something that might help me to explain it a little better."

I left them sitting there waiting until I left the room to whisper to one another, if they even did, and entered the room where my family was watching television and where I had a white board stored that would serve well now. As I maneuvered it through the crowded room I put on a nothing is out of the ordinary demeanor, even though the contrast of what was sitting in the next room, so close to my loved ones, was indeed palpable.

As I set up the white board to literally draw a picture of how intentionally compartmentalized Northrop was in terms of departments and projects, I began to explain virtually the same thing I had laid out in the prior meeting with Quealy. It was much the same strange experience of not being able to detect or second-guess what they did or did not know, and trying to gauge what they thought of what I told them. I showed how sometimes parts purchased for and left over from one project could be used for another with the government contract charged for the parts on the subsequent project that were not needed, as stock was in hand. I showed them how perfectly good parts could, at least on paper, be wiped from the system and destroyed, to the tune of millions.

They could tell there was something I was dancing around or avoiding in drawing this picture and discussing the details of the problem I had come across and reported. I finally had to tell them my real concerns: It appeared that the very lack of tracking and continuity between projects could potentially mean that it was commonplace to wind up double, triple, and even quadruple billing the government for parts that were brought into inventory, falsely scrapped in the system, but had actually been moved around, with gaps between tracking and their physical existence so they could be used somewhere else.

This was all significant and troubling for all the obvious reasons. The difficulty was in being able to tell if it was general sloppiness or intentional and institutionally orchestrated, something I still did not want to believe.

They could tell by my discomfort that there was still something more, a something I found most troubling. With only a little prodding, I told them about the inflated inventory. There was no question of sloppy tracking versus intention here. The ability to continue billing for the contracts in question required the milestones of ordering and thus presumably using or being ready to use parts and materials specified in the contract for that phase of research and development or production. There was no getting around the fact that it was substantial, intentional, and totally false to the point of being construed as actual fraud.

They asked me what I made of that in terms of possible abuses or even fraud and what it was I had documented or knew for certain. My thoughts, of course, went to the very copies of documents I had smuggled out of the facility to protect myself from becoming a scapegoat. The documents were in reference to regarding the cables, but I chose not to share that with them at this time. First, because they were the only copies I had. Second, because they were right there in my home. But mostly because I had not yet decided how far I trusted them.

It had become common knowledge back then that the government, in some cases, recruited the assistance of whistleblowers to make a case, only to turn on the whistleblower themselves, bringing the full force of not only the organization they challenged, but the weight and might of the US government crashing down on their heads.

Almost as though reading my mind, Richard Zott asked me if I had found concrete documentation for and if I had any copies I might have kept for myself relating to the incident with the cables.

"Yes," I answered. I had made backup copies for myself in that situation, but I volunteered no more information as to their whereabouts. "Are you asking to see them or have copies for yourself?" I asked.

The answer was a calm but emphatic "No." They could not, as active federal agents, make that request of me. What they could do, should they become my handlers, would be to guide me in hiding them on Northrop premises where they could be found in the event of an official raid should things come to that.

We were done. It was a huge disappointment, the anticlimax not worth the level of tension and anticipation leading up to the meeting.

"Is there anything else?" they asked.

I was more than a little disoriented and even disappointed (though a little relieved), but I answered no and we prepared for them to leave. While waiting for some hint of what happened next, I was stunned at the answer to the question I did not ask . . .

"We'll be in touch."

I had expected that after this meeting, life would be more clearly re-defined and hopefully safer for me and my family. But it ended with *We'll be in touch?*

As I watched them get back in their car to leave, once again it came crashing down on me just how alone I was and how precarious my posi-tion. I closed the door as they chatted and started their car. I turned back inside to look at the white board on which I had drawn my life and situa-tion, only to be told, *We'll be in touch.* Not only did I feel let down be-cause the sky had not opened and the path to all things appeared, I was utterly and totally alone.

But I was *not* unknown. No, definitely not unknown, but by whom? And now I was possibly even more exposed and at risk. What really came home as I stared at the lines crisscrossing the whiteboard (much as my own job crisscrossed secret lines at Northrop), was how inescapable it would be for me to avoid finding more problems—problems I now knew had to be reported to Northrop. And after my meeting with Richard, I knew I had to also tell the government it contracted with or be in the situa-tion of committing a felony myself . . .

After wiping the board clean, I turned to tell my family they could come out of hiding.

On entering the room and taking in the TV-and-play-distracted chil-dren who had no idea the hell that was on its way, I realized how easy it would be for me to be accused of knowing about things I did not know about. I casually told Mary they had left and evidently would be in touch, a fact that seemed a little odd even to her. It was just now beginning to dawn on me to what extent I was a sitting duck, an easy patsy to take the blame and the fall for things Northrop and its employees did, for which they could claim ignorance and pin on me.

As I watched the kids disperse, I was now more than ready not to be held hostage to that limited space. I could not even begin to know just how prophetic that last thought would turn out to be, or just how much my life was about to be turned upside down. I had become, in effect, a spy in the devil's own house, for a government and agencies I was not certain I could trust, that would be both the key to my survival and instrument of my demise.

♦

It would be many years later before he told me, but something happened for Agent Richard Zott that day. It was important to this case for him and would grow into a lasting friendship between us.

It was me and my family, of whom he had only the first inkling.

Part of the discussion he and his partner had as they drove away was in taking their usual measure of the potential resource they had just interviewed. The first two criteria of whether or not I was credible and honest I seem to have passed with flying colors. They already knew I had access to potentially important information from an unusual perspective and level of access. This was confirmed in spades by the information I presented in my little impromptu whiteboard presentation. And it seemed clear to them from the outset that I was not just honest, but wholeheartedly sincere in my concerns over what I was sharing. As he was to tell me only recently in the process of writing this book, what was so striking and moving for them was very specifically my sincerity.

Theirs is a world of dealing with deceit and the amoral to immoral. For them, as it turned out, this encounter was a potential goldmine of practical information. They had not so fully expected the fact that I would be so systematic and critically organized in looking at things, or so able to decipher their possible implications and problems. It was an encouraging, if not yet inspiring, breath of fresh air. Unbeknownst to me, they had actually been moved by my apparent lack of calculation for self-interest, and genuine concern for righting a wrong. My only apparent calculation was my very real concern for my family.

I share this here as a reminder that many of those who come to serve in government and elsewhere do so out of a genuine desire to serve. In the case of those like Agent Richard Zott and his then-partner Elizabeth, who would later become his wife, it is with a desire to protect and serve. But on a more personal basis, it is very often out of love of country and a desire to assure that we all have the opportunity and the safe playing field to be the best we can be. Theirs is a drive, and even a need, not so much to chase down and punish bad guys, as to be the best they can be in supporting the good guys. In so doing, they endure the oftentimes despicable actions of many people, organizations, and even nations. That day, as he now tells me, they got to drive away feeling good.

I asked Richard what kept him going, most especially toward the very end when things had gone on so long and seemed so endlessly difficult. His answer was that for him as a federal agent and representative of the government, he could not fail me or my family. More than that, he felt that if, after all we had suffered and endured, he and his team failed in supporting us when we were trying to survive and make things right, they failed as a government. He felt that to abandon me and my family would be to fail as a country. His most encouraging philosophy was that to rally and succeed was to be worthy of who and what we claim to aspire to as a nation. He believes that he and everyone who became involved in this case are better people for it, and for having known and helped me and my family.

This is humbling and gratifying, but it is only the slightest preview of the good souls who came to rally around this case and this cause. What is most important about it, I believe, is not what it says or does not say about me, but what it says about the people in government and elsewhere, whom we so often mistrust and even disparage, who only really desire to do their jobs and do them well. It speaks to how important it is when we ourselves suit up to make it possible for them to do their jobs and to invigorate them with the reminder of what calls them to their work.

What Agent Zott and his partner drove away with that day was a reminder that sometimes they could serve in doing what was right without having to second-guess the motives of the person they were dealing with. What they drove away with was the sense they had a partner they could trust and who would match their commitment to do their job and do the right thing just because it was the right thing to do.

◆

All of this was unknown to me at the time, however. I had no idea they were giving any of what we had discussed any real thought at all. I was still feeling pretty deflated from the lack of an immediate plan and the ambiguity of *We'll be in touch.*

What I did know was that I felt even more alone than before I received that call, and even more lost as to what to do. It would only be some time later, much later, that I would discover this is all part of the initial handling and testing of a potential asset and that however much I could not see it at the time, my life most definitely would never be the same again, that I was in fact being handled, and that what was now in motion would define and threaten to obliterate my life and family for almost two decades.

The sense, if not complete reality, of being more alone than ever unfolded fully and settled in that evening. This even had its first full rumblings with Mary. She had always been less trusting than I of my employer's goodness, even if she also appreciated the stability of the job and income in taking care of our family. However much I downplayed this visit by federal agents to discuss issues I had not discussed with her, the visit set off red flags for her that this was significant and as ominous as it seemed, and that our lives would never be the same. It solidified for her that she did not want to know the details of my job—as insurance—so she would still be around to take care of the family if something happened to me. Amazingly, that meant she put up with my stress and growing withdrawal, not really knowing what was going on, in a state of what for others would have been unbearable free-floating anxiety. Even more amazingly, she put up with this state for almost two decades, with a host of other people parading through our lives and our slightly delayed and shared unspoken fear that my very life was in danger.

My decision concerning what to do with all this would take some days more. In the meantime, I took out the twelve-string guitar I had played years before as a drinking-and-using entertainer, and sat down with my kids before bed to sing to them—a challenge, as my heart was very much in my throat. Then I left the ever-reliable Mary to begin the nightly ritual of baths and bed. I left for my more-crucial-than-ever AA meeting, knowing full well I could not discuss any of what had just happened and what may or may not have been about to happen. On this particular drive to my meeting, I was as attentive as before to other cars and possibly tailing headlights.

In a life that was just coming together with the stability and hope I had not known my entire life, and had even threatened myself for a time with my alcohol and drug use, I was now staring into the immediate and quickly disappearing future that just looked and felt empty and black. I discovered the initial experiential meaning of the phrase that when you stare into the Abyss, the Abyss stares back into you. Even then, I somehow knew or was at least beginning to grasp there was no way out but forward. I knew I did not want to go to jail. I knew I would do whatever they wanted. I had to find my way through this nightmare. All I could think about clearly was the question, *How do I take care of and protect my family now?*

It is difficult to explain, but with the sense of things so completely out of control, I felt as though I was surrounded by actual demons, with ominous and overwhelming deep feelings of trepidation that the Devil himself was now my back-seat passenger, malevolently staring at my back, and that I was his hapless prey.

Looking over my shoulder, I found myself reaching over my head and turning on the inside dome light.

5
INTO THE DEEP

From March of 1988 to December of the same year, I continued exploring how things worked and did not work under the roof of Northrop Corporation, or rather under its many roofs—its multiple facilities in the Illinois area. After reporting internally problems I had identified, I gathered and placed the information that might prove incriminating when officially collected by federal officials if it came to a raid or subpoenas. I did things like taping documents to my body to smuggle them out of the building for copying, and, with an eye toward survival, made my own set of copies. In a life that seemed to have become defined by ironies, I was the most unlikely candidate for the secretive work I was doing, but doing it well because of how I look at and go about handling problems in a very progressive and systematic way. To a great extent, no one seemed to notice the risks of my perspective.

In many ways, I was serving the company better than I ever had before, or in certain key areas, better than anyone had served before, particularly in terms of the tracking systems and reports I created to be on top of things (and cover my ever expanding fact-finding and data gathering). And because I was providing invaluable information for many very high-level people in the company who *wanted* the official information I was providing, I was a major thorn in the side of Selen and a few others.

Their official jobs were things pertaining to quality assurance and accounting, but their *un*official tasks and responsibilities seemed to include distorting, hiding, and/or eliminating inventory and information from the computer system and, as we alleged, facilitating a massive shell game in materials acquisition and management directly tied to false tracking and billing.

On the legitimate management and tracking side of things, there are several things to understand and keep in mind as we go forward.

First is that when a defense contractor like Northrop bids on and wins a contract with the US government or foreign governments for which it does equally top-secret work, it is based on some kind of projected estimates for the reasonably anticipated costs of research and development, as well as for the inclusion of production where provided, the maintenance of replacement parts where needed, and spares. When possible, these projections and proposals are based on some kind of relevant historical record derived from the actual experience and demonstrated performance on analogous projects in the past. This allows the bidder to convey an air of reliability for both their proposed numbers and to demonstrate and ability to deliver, while also allowing them to do realistic and competitive bidding up front. Clearly, you do not want to overestimate your costs and cease to be competitive just as you do not want to win bids that turn out to be more costly than expected to fulfill and deliver.

The payout for these kinds of contracts is not necessarily based on actual delivery of a product or even stages of actual development so much as demonstrating measureable progress or best efforts to make that progress vis-à-vis predetermined milestones to be met or not met along the way. Among the latter is the ordering of inventory to indicate that progress is being made on schedule. After all, the next rounds of parts and materials are ordered and on record as in inventory.

Part of our theory, you may recall, was that the inventory was contrived, temporary, and a sham simply there to meet these milestones for a progress payment, and in reality unusable. Some auditing (beyond that normally conducted internally by contractors themselves) is conducted on an ongoing basis by external government quality assurance monitors and fiscal auditors, some of whom (in the case of Northrop) actually remain on premises. The key issues here are the extent to which a great deal of all tracking was indirect, the ways information was compartmentalized, and the willingness to fudge the numbers to the advantage of the contractor and detriment of the customer, meaning the United States government.

What is next worth noting was that within days of my meeting with Federal Agent Richard Zott, I was making double backup copies of documents (keeping all originals in house) to sneak out of one of the highest security facilities in the world by taping them to my legs and torso, and walking them out the front door. One set went immediately to Agent Zott and one set I kept for myself. On one hand, I simply wanted sets of all data safely outside of the building for future backup in case I was exposed and/or anything "happened" to me.[4] On the other hand, I had increasingly little confidence that any incarnation or version of data would necessarily endure for long before it was potentially adjusted, reinvented, or lost. Aside from the first-time experience of becoming an information mule and now officially a federal informant, the first encounter delivering copies of information to Agent Zott made its own indelible impressions. Make that several.

We were scheduled to meet at a large hotel in the lobby, which in retrospect was rather public and exposed. The expectation, no doubt, was that it was too early in my working as an informant for me to have generated any attention or suspicion. Then again, nearly a year later when I had potentially stirred up suspicion, Agent Zott informed me (while smuggling me up the back elevator of the Dirksen Federal Building in Chicago) that the precaution was not about me being under suspicion. It was a precaution to keep agents of Northrop from becoming suspicious. As he explained, there were too many employees at the many Northrop facilities to be able to watch them all. Northrop's alleged solution was to watch the federal agents, as they were vastly smaller in number and, to my shock and horror, had been identified and were known to them. *They* were not safe.

In any case, it was what happened on my first handoff of documents to the federal agents that impressed upon me that my life did not remotely resemble normal. As we met and Agent Zott directed me to a chair to be more comfortable, a bright flash went off and lit us both up. In a fraction of an instant, he had pushed me to one side with one hand while he had

---

4 While it was outside of his authority to request that I smuggle information out of the building, Agent Zott was more than happy to receive what I was voluntarily providing. Otherwise all he would actually have in hand was whatever information I provided to him in my own writing or verbally and knowledge of where to find all other materials should the investigation turn into what would essentially be a raid on the premises.

his gun very nearly drawn with the other quickly asking me if I recognized the person or if he looked familiar. It was amazing to see just how quickly he took in the situation and the entire surroundings. Happily, it was just an oblivious tourist who was now snapping still more pictures that had nothing whatsoever to do with us, which made it clear the previous shot had not been of either of us. Agent Zott, seeing my shock, said flatly (but reassuringly) that it is illegal to take photos of federal agents in the performance of their duties and especially when meeting with a CI (Confidential Informant), and that anyone knowingly taking a picture of me in particular would have been a seriously bad omen.

As he watched the tourist walk away and he took in the still-concerned look on my face, Agent Zott casually nodded in the direction of the departing tourist and said, "I can still shoot him for you if you want me to."

It took a moment to grasp that he was kidding and actually putting me at ease. I let him know that would not be necessary, and we sat to discuss and pass along some of the first documents I had secretly photocopied, intermingled with other innocuous paperwork I had gotten out of the building.

Over the course of the almost eighteen months that followed, my undercover work was now, in some strange way, part of my regular job duties at Northrop. There were some close calls, endlessly stressful yet increasingly routine acquisitions of information, corresponding smuggling of documents out of the building, and meetings with my handler that painted an ever more frightening and grim picture.

Frightening because of my inability to determine who knew what and who was actually pulling the strings.

Grim because it was all so far-reaching, strangely and almost schizophrenically institutionalized, and decidedly intentional on the part of some invisible set of someones beyond the handful of middle management people like Selen, who appeared to know all of what was going on and whose job it was in part to sustain and hide it.

It was in relation to Selen that my greatest sense of risk continued to grow, and the schizoid nature of the company became confusingly apparent. It was most apparent around a specific report I developed that enabled me to delve ever more wide and deep in both the monitoring and secret investigations I was doing. It became a highly valued and essential tool to many and threatened to expose things that were to remain hidden by a few. The craziest part was that Selen would get in trouble when some problems surfaced that were partly bad management, but were also symptoms of the larger and later alleged widespread corruption.

It was impossible to tell who the ultimate puppeteers were on the abusive-to-fraudulent sides of things. It was equally difficult to tell where my immediate supervisor, Clyder, fit in all of this, which was both encouraging and disconcerting at the same time.

Encouraging in the ways he seemed to want to know the truth and supported certain reports continuing, even at the aggravation of Selen.

Disconcerting because it was never clear what he really did know or not know, and to what extent the axe really would fall on him rather than me; I followed his instructions without knowing with whom he was sharing or not sharing information and what his real intentions were.

In terms of my working relationship with Clyder and the continued expansion of the work I was doing both aboveboard and undercover, we continued expanding our working relationship by exploring the issues together. He even accompanied me on visits to other facilities beyond our home base of Rolling Meadows. The purpose of our journeys was not so much to look for new problems, but to see how widespread the ones I had already uncovered were. They were pervasive and found at every facility, existed in every department, and occasionally seemed to be part of very nearly every project. It was in my own continued investigations that I went deeper and into more detail to see not only how widespread some problems were, but what others existed, and who and what procedures were involved.

In contrast to our joint travels and investigations, I looked for minute details in my individual explorations to find just what happened, step by step, in the acquisitions, physical handling, tracking, and accounting of parts and materials, to find what went wrong and where. They went well beyond failure rates. It was in this more detailed and system-wide investigation that I both served the company well and became exposed to certain risks at the hands of still-unknown manipulators who would have wanted these practices to remain in place. My research and investigations systematically captured when and where the problems occurred.

This is to say that the reports I generated, if analyzed correctly, demonstrated patterns of error or abuse, along with a glimpse of who would have had to have been involved or known about the cases, as pre-authorizations were required for activities or events that should not have occurred. My greatest risk in the long run was that I was not just looking for the where or the how of these regular occurrences that suggested either a breakdown in systems or surreptitious systems within systems, I was also looking for a means of identifying who was both immediately responsible (even if coerced) and who was involved at higher levels. Still worse for those involved, I was also trying to find ways to document it.

Intentions and specifics aside, it is very important to note that any and all reports or information I provided to the government via my handler were also provided to agents of the corporation itself and a growing plethora of higher-ups who insisted on receiving the systematic reports I had developed that, once again, had become intrinsic tools for those who at least appeared to be on the up-and-up as managers and corporate agents.

The reports were also a thorn in the sides of those trying to hide both anomalies and abuses.

As a particular example of the latter, there was a problem that emerged (somewhat late in the game) in the handling of returned items that were swapped out or bartered for other items. These other items, however, were not part of the contracts of the returned items, but a different category of parts and materials (though roughly the same value), with some discrete units allocated to the contract and others placed in inventory to be used as needed. This wreaked havoc at the end of the day when trying to balance the contract accounting with actual parts that were used to complete the contract.

When the reports that captured this were provided to Murray Snow, who was the Vice President of Product Assurance and Selen's boss, the hammer of reprimand came down on Selen with distinct instructions that however it had occurred, it was not to occur again. This problem had later ramifications in what could have been a massive cover-up I was nearly drafted into. But it did, in fact, occur again with Selen instructing me to omit certain higher-level executives from getting copies of my report which, by then, were expected on a regular basis.

This, also once again, brings up several aspects of my situation and means of surviving that were significant both to immediate security and all subsequent survival. The first point being, I still had no idea whom to trust or how to tell the difference between those who wanted the information I was providing for legitimate and effective management and those who could be revealed as transgressors of protocols, contracts, and/or federal laws that were required for eligibility for ongoing billing. Legal and criminal issues aside, this eligibility proved to be crucial later. Our attention at the moment was on documenting likely fraud. The investigations and reports themselves could not reveal the real underlying issues I was finding and most especially the fact and reasons that I was looking for them. I even more especially could not risk it becoming evident that what I was compiling could be and was intended to be used as evidence. As a result, my reports were worded with excruciating care only to be exceeded by my growing stress and sense of impending exposure in providing them.

Ironically, it was this careful wording that could have led anyone paying attention to at least look in the right direction to discover and connect the dots for the problems I was discovering, that was used later to accuse me of intentionally setting up the company with false allegations. If anything, I was being deliberately vague to maintain plausible deniability should anyone accuse me of pointing out real problems. They were as detailed and as carefully worded as they were so that when government action did occur, no one could claim I had not provided the information needed to recognize and correct the issues.

My ever-present concern was in not getting caught, but it was my secret hope that someone would read my reports, get the big picture, and simply fix it without suspecting I understood the ramifications.

The great irony was that the more analysis I provided and the more information I accumulated, the more exposed and at risk I felt. In fact, as we neared the eighteen-month mark of my clandestine information gathering, I became more and more an emotional wreck, withdrawing from my family until I was almost completely absent.

Early on in my work in Product Assurance, I took note of how the process of monitoring and documenting performance and failure rates was too fragmented and piecemeal to use for effective management. I also deduced (correctly) that this had to have had significant impact on the traceability of material, from affecting the ability to make bids on new and future projects based on an accurate history, to how and when material would fail, be consumed, and/or be transferred or shared with more than one project.

What I put into place were expanded systematic procedures to build a comprehensive statistical model that could calculate competitive bids and assess the effectiveness of materials management and product development on an ongoing basis. It would do this by holding accountable those whose materials management and/or failure rates were out of and/or above the norm. Ironically, the expansion of duties that pit me against this corporate behemoth occurred, to a great extent, because I wanted to generate some overtime to better support my family.

The unique nature of my position threatened those hidden behind the curtain of compartmentalization and intensified my growing opinion of "trust no one." As I said, the first incident of physical destruction of inventory that I noticed did, in fact, turn out to be the acts of a specific purchasing agent and as-yet-unknown allies, triggering concerns that would reverberate throughout the process.

It was also tied to some of the external investigations already coming down on Northrop I did not know about. In this case, those investigations resulted in the on-premises arrest of the purchasing agent by federal agents who disregarded the corporation's insistence that the arrest not be public or on the premises.

The problems were these:

a) How and why could parts and materials be purchased then disposed of on arrival without being proved defective and returned to the vendors for credit or refund?

b) In such an ostensibly controlled system, how could this kind of purchase get authorized or even occur?

c) How could this happen without the system catching it and setting off flags and alarms almost the instant it occurred?

And, of course, my more personal concerns were who was involved, who could be affected by my reporting of the problem, and who would possibly be in a position to inflict harm on me. At truly key points of these transgressions, someone in multiple levels of authority, including my colleagues, had to have provided some kind of authorization or at least look the other way.

Prior to meeting with my supervisor, my initial concern was about bringing unwanted and unfair attention to any fellow employees who had not committed any transgressions or been responsible for any significant errors in procedures. My concerns over possible retaliation began to grow soon afterward, however, and really came to a head when I was called into Quealy's office and accused of taking documents out of the building to pass them on to someone else. It was my belief (and only slowly diminishing hope) that the problems I encountered were isolated and not reflections of wider corporate involvement. Thus, the early discovery of the destroyed cables and apparent cover-up of an initial error, compounded by falsification of new requisitions added to my disquiet. I didn't know what was or was not tolerated from above, so I did not know whom to trust with the information or that I was passing it along.

The discovery that Quealy was told not to report the cables issue made the ground I was treading shaky, and my every step threatened to reveal more. Further, because my own supervisor (who instructed me to continue my investigations) was well aware of, but apparently indifferent to, the seemingly fraudulent activity, one can sense how unsettling the situation was and how precarious my own position became.

By the time DCIS Agent Zott and his partner Elizabeth arrived on my doorstep with news that the DCIS, the FBI, and other agencies were already watching Northrop for alleged transgressions they would not share, I was already feeling overwhelmed, alone, and lost. Once I committed to gathering more information for them, information I was also sharing with my higher-ups as I discovered it, I dug so deeply that some could question if it was part of my job. The more I tried to do what was right to help Northrop clean up its act, the bigger threat I became to the corporation and anyone involved in bad management (at best) or possibly fraud (at worst).

Then there were the close calls at work. One in particular prompted us to take an ill-fated course of action:

I was stopped by security and asked to remove my shirt. What was particularly lucky, but seriously unsettling, about this close call was that, unlike the day before, I had nothing on my person. The day before, however, I had left the building with documents taped to my torso. Having documents found on my person would have spelled my instant exposure and demise. Thus, I sensed time was running out on the ever-present possibility of discovery. The likelihood of getting caught was greater and my ability to endure the neverending stress of it all was fading.

What is perhaps more important here, at least in my eyes, was the toll it was taking on my family, and most especially my wife.

As time and my investigation progressed from March to December 1988, I was already nearing my breaking point in hiding this unbelievable stress from everyone. The effort to hide my distress and keep the information secret became a heartbreaking and ever-growing wall between me and those I loved. I could not discuss any of what now comprised my work life.

My every waking moment was in many ways a nightmare. My every waking moment around my family was a challenge not to inflict my worry on any of them. The increasingly draining and futile effort to hide my distress made me more and more distant and withdrawn, and at times actually absent. If it had not been for the daily AA and NA meetings I had attended for years, even without being able to share the details of my situation and challenges to my sobriety, I can say without doubt that I would not have made it a fraction of the time the investigation and subsequent trials lasted.

At a time during which it took much of what I could conjure just to keep my head and focus together, I found myself being less and less sensitive and responsive to the needs of my children even for the most mundane attention. Mary, who appreciated something of the stress I was under without knowing the details, wisely and intuitively did not want to know. In her ever-present wisdom that has been so much of my rock to survival, she feared for my actual physical safety even before I did. Even though she did not know and did not want to know the facts for her own safety, she hoped for assurance that if something did happen to me, she would be spared in order to take care of the family.

Ultimately, I felt isolated, alone, and on the verge of drowning in this investigation. It seemed to have grown into a vast ocean beyond my vision or control. In contrast to the line in AA that "the farther away you are from your last drink the closer you are to your next," I feared that the farther away I was from the innocence with which I had begun this journey, the closer I was to inevitable—and devastating—discovery. As my investigations began to create a clearer picture of the seeming abuses, the numbers seemed to constitute a massive and elaborate shell game. How could it be managed, given that without some breach, some people had to know while others clearly did not? I later learned there were sporadic reports that could not come to fruition, because of compartmentalization and incomplete or imperfect information.

In some ways, my every step and new bit of disturbing information raised the question again and again of who knew what, along with questions of who genuinely did not know, versus those who did not want to know and thus just looked the other way. This led me to look at how data was managed on the largest scale. This act would create for me a dynamic that would become a perfect storm, concluding with my exposure and demise as a secret informant.

An entity like Northrop exists to invent and manufacture things that did not exist before, or to improve things that already exist to perform different specific functions. This includes designing things on a drawing board for how they would theoretically work, then creating or purchasing the pieces, then putting them together to see if and how they will work, or if and how they will fail. They will be improved upon or corrected along the way. Some of these component pieces are built by outside vendors by request while some may just be preexisting parts and materials from cables to gold solder (gold being a great conductor of electricity). Many of the "parts" or pieces of the final product of a given project (say, the Stealth Bomber) are made up of progressively more complex parts until you have a machine that functions or does not function as a whole. It may have specific components that are still less than ideal when all is put together, prone to failure, or just open to improvement in performance or durability.

All of this also requires corresponding equipment for testing that may also have to be designed and built from other parts. In some cases they may already exist and can be purchased as a functioning unit. The first key thing to keep in mind here are that many of the pieces used to build and/or test ever larger and more complex units are incredibly high-tech, sensitive, and extremely expensive. It was not unusual for component parts the size of a pack of cigarettes or smaller to cost thousands to hundreds of thousands of dollars each.

The second thing to keep in mind is that in research and development it is expected and actually planned that many of these parts will be exhausted in various stages of development and become unusable. They may underperform or fail and have to be redesigned or replaced. Part of the trick in bidding large projects accurately, competitively, and profitably is knowing in advance, as much as possible, when, how, and at what part of the process units will become unusable, fail, or need to be redesigned and replaced. My job was to document rates and phases of failure.

The third thing to keep in mind is that in the high-tech and high-security world of a defense contractor like Northrop (which served governments all over the world and faced espionage of all sorts), tracking these parts and materials throughout the phases of a single project could be challenging. It was even more complicated to track the status, location, and even the existence of these parts and materials, if and when they actually moved in physical inventory and working assignment to a different project, and/or were purchased in part or in whole. Once again, this was a universe that operated on the endlessly applied criteria of need-to-know and compartmentalization of information.

So, in brief, what were these practices I uncovered? In reality, they were very detailed and difficult to discern with absolute clarity in this byzantine system, most especially as I learned just how much of it was at least known, if not intentional, and part of alleged massive cover-ups for errors and sins already committed, and to protect those to come.

The problems were partly known to the DCIS by the time Agent Zott landed on my doorstep. What was not known was the massive effort made by someone inside the corporation to alter, bury, or erase data.

The problem was, simply, that the government was billed for parts that were never purchased, was billed for an exponential number of parts that were purchased, and was frequently billed for parts that reported scrapped but were not. Much of this was possible because of a false belief (or deliberate charade) that viable historical data and tracking existed at all.

For example, say there is a project that has gone out to bid and a contract has been awarded. This contract claims it will need one hundred units of something. It may be that, based on actual history, only twenty are likely to be needed. But until I initiated statistical models, tracking, and reporting, there were no such historical records, data, or working models.

Say this contract legitimately requires twenty-five units on hand for development. Some will be used up, some will have to be replaced when they fail, and others may be defective. They order the full hundred they anticipate, for which the government agrees to reimbursement. If they already had a full hundred in stock, they now have a surplus on hand. If some have not been delivered, they have a pending supply they do not need. In the case of the latter, they could cancel the remainder and be issued a credit or cancel the order. In either case, they now have an overage of seventy-five units versus what was projected, based on nonexistent historical data. If this were the end of it, they would owe the government a credit for the unused and unneeded parts. However, this was generally not the end of it.

In many cases, this excess inventory can actually be taken off one contract and physically moved to another, which becomes an accounting wash to the government. A problem arises if the second contract claims to have ordered the same parts, but hasn't, and applies those nonexistent purchases against its estimated costs and justifies its billing unreduced. This has some risk because there is a traceable record of forwarding the parts from the first contract to the second. What is more common is for the first contract to claim consumption of more parts than actually were, with some or all of the excess inventory being "wiped" from the system even though they still physically exist in inventory.

These parts can then be used by the second contract, which does not need them and will not purchase them, but will claim to purchase them anyway, thus keeping the funds.

Further, what makes this shell game all the more offensive is that the parts on the first contract that were fictitiously wiped from inventory are now fictitiously wiped a second time while the parts in physical inventory are moved to a third project.

Each successive project reconciles and justifies its budget by claiming to have ordered and paid for parts it had not, since it already had real physical inventory on hand and paid for. They may even claim a third time to have scrapped parts, which will get forwarded again, qualifying for an allowed markup per unit. This is known as a forward-pricing scheme.

There is a similar abuse in the purchase of testing equipment needed for research and development. For example, let's say one hundred black boxes are legitimately estimated, purchased, and actually used. One box is used in many tests, but actually appears "on paper" as having been consumed in one test. Instead of buying and using one hundred, only a few are needed, with the overage being a falsehood.

In this scenario, the government pays for contracts that scrapped out and destroyed parts that never should have been ordered to begin with and which were neither defective nor used up in any way. It pays for parts that were never purchased at all or that were purchased once and subsequently claimed to have been purchased again, sometimes repeatedly, when they were not. At each step of the way, the government also pays an acceptable profit margin on parts that may or may not exist in real new purchases. It also pays out hundreds of thousands to millions for test equipment that is not needed but generates a profit margin.

All of this had to occur with authorizations that should not have been granted. All of this happened against contracts that did not warrant payment at all. And quite often, all of this supposedly occurred against contracts for projects that were faking their progress and milestones to keep their cash flowing.

The reconciliation of data on the page with the reality on the ground has implications in four ways:

First, there is a government requirement and working assumption of an accurate tracking of parts and materials from request to final disposition.

Second, there is a government requirement and working assumption that demonstrations of milestones for ongoing billing are truthful and accurate.

Thirdly, there is a government requirement and working assumption that there is an accurate and viable system in place to keep track of it all.

And finally, there is a government requirement and working assumption that all existing and future contracts and bids are based on complete and accurate historical data.

We said that, for the most part, none of these conditions existed as required and assumed by the government, that they were obstructed in practice by the extensive fragmentation of projects and data, and that they were covered up in ongoing manipulation of data and records by those who were in a position to see the bigger picture in ways Northrop employees (and even most auditors and onsite government monitoring agents) could never and would never see.

My problem with all this was getting details without getting caught, and finding ways to document bad faith practices that had clear and undeniable intention. The problem with *that* was being able to distinguish between sloppy or bad practices versus intentional mishandling of parts and misrepresentation. Unfortunately, it turned out that there possibly ongoing and increasing practices in data management, or mismanagement in the facility, that systematically altered all records and data faster than I could get to it. This was a double-edged sword.

On one hand, this data manipulation was the clearest possible demonstration that someone in the company knew of the kinds of problems I had been finding and trying to document. It showed clear knowledge and intention. On the flip side, its very existence was already altering the data landscape in massive ways.

When I asked Petra Schiller, one of the most key data handlers, how all this alteration of records could be occurring, I was told there was also a memo in existence authorizing it all, and the memo itself would be destroyed once she was finished changing the data on the system. The only thing that was not a surprise was that Selen and a handful of cohorts were at the helm and guiding the whole endeavor. What I did not know at the time was that when I shared this information with Agent Zott, he soon recruited Schiller to be a federal informant, too.

This was all too much, all too big, and all too amorphous. The data and records were in constant change. It was like trying to capture a fixed and provable picture of sand dunes in a sand storm. Proof of anything I could try to identify and document was morphing into something else or disappearing in rapid keystrokes altogether. I was exhausted and felt horribly exposed. My efforts to capture information, let alone worthy documentation, seemed more impossible and most definitely more dangerous than ever. I felt overwhelmed, helpless, and mostly hopeless. I just wanted it all to be over and go away. I continued to wish, well beyond anything rational, that someone would just come along and fix it.

I wished that I could do it myself.

By this time, I knew I could not continue much longer without getting caught. The reports I had developed for the corporation put me as much at risk with those they threatened to expose as they did in good graces with those who saw their legitimate value, if not their full implications. The very act of converting to the new data system wreaked havoc on the means by which many abuses had gone undetected. And all of this was happening at a time when the government was cracking down on fraud and billing abuses in the defense industry, particularly in light of the public outcry against the infamous $900 hammers. It was also a time during which a number of films were screened that featured informants (in far less dangerous circumstances than mine) who were abused and killed. This left me obsessing not about the *what* of all possible worst case scenarios, so much as the *when*.

If "they" knew what I knew and/or was continuing to uncover (even more so if they knew what was being done with it), I had no doubt that someone in this war machine would not hesitate to take me out and make it look like an accident. Worse, what I was discovering should have, by all rights, gotten the entire place shut down, putting thousands of colleagues and coworkers out of a job—many of whom were already fearful with others being laid off by the thousands. This thought on its own brought the weight down on me even more heavily. What was I going to do to support my own family if and when I got caught or when all those to whom I was reporting decided it was time to take action? Beyond the anticipatory guilt and concern over that, there was the additional possibility that one of those very friends and colleagues I cared about would feel the need to take revenge and take me out on their own. I was afraid to the point of nonstop anxiety and paranoia. My relationship with my wife and family was stressed to the limit.

I had passed the point when I could not imagine going on when I had the close call mentioned above. It was a gift, of sorts. Security guards did stop me on the way out of the building and did ask me to step into a side room and open my shirt. It was a stroke of sheer blind luck that it had not been the day before, when I *had* had documents taped to my torso. It was a moment of great angst as they searched, and I wondered if my good luck would hold. Time, it seemed, was really running out, along with all the steam I had ever had to give to the task. Whether I got caught, laid off, or just collapsed from the stress of it all, the efforts to date and the data inside the building would be wasted and lost.

It was against this backdrop in January of 1989 that Agent Zott and I came to the unanimous, if grudging, agreement that I should find someone inside the company I could trust with my informant status and serve as my replacement in guiding the government to the location of hidden documents if I should be laid off, or if something more dire were to happen to me. The problem was who I would look for, let alone choose. Agent Zott asked if there was anyone already working on site as a government product assurance monitor or financial auditor I trusted.

In contrast to so many unknown, invisible, and irreversible lines I had crossed to date, this was perhaps the first since consenting to become an informant in which I could see the line and know it for what it was. It would be yet another step into additional risk and another point of no return. As was so often the case in this long journey in which there really were no good choices available, this seemed to be the best choice or at least the least bad choice available to us. It was truly important to safeguard the work done so far and any hope of successful resolution in the future.

By this time, my fears had reached levels of uncontrollable, albeit well-founded, paranoia. Getting anyone other than my handlers involved (and the added risk of exposure they represented) made the situation that much more nerve-wracking and the choice more crucial. The choice we all made as to the specific individual to approach proved to be almost immediately wrong, and not just a little bit wrong. In the span of only a few hours, it appeared likely to be disastrously and very nearly terminally wrong.

What was to follow was a storm of converging events that would cast me out of the questionably secret protection of the frying pan and very much into the fire.

6
AN INVESTIGATION AT RISK

It seemed reasonable enough to me and Agent Zott to protect my efforts to date and any possible subsequent discoveries. In other words, someone else on the inside would need know where information could be found in case of a raid, or turned over to federal agents if I were either discovered to be an informant or I was laid off for other reasons. At Northrop, the options were not just limited but, for reasons I found very discouraging, it was nearly impossible to find someone I could trust with my secret, let alone with being responsible for accessing the information I had gathered.

The reason for this concern and spirit-crushing discouragement came from the fact that the Department of Defense (DoD) actually has multiple teams of assigned monitors on site for auditing and product assurance, whose very jobs and reasons for being there were to watch out for the kinds of errors and abuses I seemed to have uncovered. The problem was not just the extent to which the government's own watchdogs missed seeing anything. It was the degree to which some or all were passively or knowingly complicit in overlooking the kinds of problems I was uncovering. As Agent Zott shared (both before and after what was to follow), he and some other field investigators from the DCIS had concerns that some of the internal monitors placed on site to be government watchdogs were more than a little too chummy with those they were supposed to monitor.

More specifically, there were a few too many (as in, more than zero) shared fishing trips, courtesy tickets to sporting events, and other gifts meant not to look like or be taken by the outside world as gifts for comfort. Unfortunately, this reached all the way to the very top of those placed in residence by the United States government and was as widely pervasive as it was also widely suspected. Agent Zott's concern made it difficult to choose an individual from this group whose job was to look out for the government's interests, but choose I must.

In my mind it came down to just one person. In what to this day I still believe was the best (and in many ways only) choice if we were going to take this distressing but necessary measure, I offered the name of George Williams. He had been placed on site by the DoD Defense Cash Accountability Systems (DCAS) as part of a team of on-site DoD monitors. The reason we chose Williams was as frighteningly simple as it was simply frightening: It was as much a calculated process of elimination as it was a matter of trust. If there were anything I had been challenged to do thus far that required a leap of faith, this was it.

Some of the other auditors and monitors on site were eliminated immediately as I specifically did not trust them. Still more were removed from consideration as I did not know them well enough to have any idea to what extent they could or should be trusted. In the normal processes of doing my job and conducting my research and investigations, at least I had experienced a number of encounters and conversations with Williams that suggested to me he was a good guy who, most of all, was genuinely concerned with protecting the government from abuse or harm. I still believe this to be true. As it was to turn out, however, this one person became more problem than solution, putting me at incredible risk within hours.

I was very much on edge as I approached Williams at work and, as casually as I could, asked him if he had a few minutes to chat. Though I made my best effort to appear nonchalant, fortunately, there was nothing unusual about my conversing with any of the onsite government monitors, as many of them were on the distribution lists for the audit reports I had developed and now routinely circulated. Similarly, there was no particular need to fear that conversation with him would raise the attention of any Northrop employee. Still, I took a quick glance at the hallways as we stepped into the DCAS offices and his cubicle. It was now approximately 10:30 a.m.

I remember this awkward moment of suddenly wondering how to begin, and decided it was best to just keep it simple.

"George," I said, "I have something to tell you and something to ask."

There was a slight shift in his attention and demeanor. He became more attentive and attuned to the fact that whatever I needed to share was clearly important to me. I think I managed to keep some appearance of calm that did not reveal the fact that my heart was very much in my throat. We sat down. He asked what I needed. I swallowed hard and told him that first I had to let him know that I was a federal informant and had been for some time. Because of his job he instantly understood what this meant even if he did not yet know the particulars.

In retrospect, I have to respect the extent to which it suddenly was his turn to wonder what, if any, eyes were on us. He seemed to brace himself to appear as little rattled as he could, although given what followed he was probably already sorry he had agreed to speak with me. Likewise, he probably wanted to abort this moment and find a way to pretend this conversation never started.

Now he swallowed hard and asked me why I was telling him, and what I wanted from him. I told him that it was best that he did not know what I had been looking at and/or how I came to be a federal informant. I also told Williams I had given his name to Agent Zott from the DCIS. He had been vetted and chosen to be the person I would approach. My only need was for him to know where documents I had compiled were sequestered internally, and to request he pass them along to federal agents when they needed them if something had happened to me. With the wheels turning in his own mind and wondering what that all had to do with him, I repeated I needed him to be my backup in case I got laid off (or worse), and to turn the evidence I had gathered over to my handler and any other federal authorities who might be involved in a raid on the facility.

He looked as one would expect when a bolt of lightning has just shot through your body and, with your mind reeling after regaining consciousness, trying to think of what to say or do next. His response was he needed to run this by Roger Steele, his own supervisor, which would have been any reasonable person's first impulse, to ground himself and, perhaps, escape this sudden and unwanted responsibility and risk. It was the standard response, after all, of anyone who had worked for the government for any length of time: *Not my job*, and then kick it upstairs. I told him that for reasons I could not tell him that would be a very bad idea.

He seemed to be doing his best to take in what I was telling him, and said he would do it. To this day, I do not know quite what did or did not stick, but I do remember telling him I could not go into all the details. However, once he agreed to perform this duty, I filled him in as best I could. After giving him a brief nondescript summary of the kinds of information I had compiled, along with a shorthand communication of where it was all located, I left.

I do not remember now whether or not he asked how imminent the possibility of a raid might be or how sweeping its scope. What I do know is that I left that meeting believing he understood and accepted the responsibility. I also left that meeting knowing no one else could learn of this. It was bad enough that even one other person inside Northrop knew of my situation and status.

Oblivious to what was headed my way, I returned to my cubicle and my duties, somewhat relieved that the encounter was over and that backup was in place should the unthinkable happen to me. I spent an hour trying to reorient and focus on what still needed to be collected and secluded, against how little time might be left before I was either laid off or discovered.

My nerves were just starting to calm down from having taken this drastic step. I was not prepared for what happened next.

My phone rang. It was Williams, and he asked if I could come to his office right away for a few minutes. He needed to talk to me. After the situation I knew I had just put him in and the terrible isolation it created, I could hardly refuse. He was a very good guy, after all, who was now placed in a very stressful situation with no advance warning or support or time to think it through. As I stepped into his office, however, it was my world that was about to spin on a dime. His supervisor, Roger Steele, was sitting there staring at me with an expression that immediately told me he knew all and was not pleased.

I could not believe my eyes. And I remember my heart pounding in my chest and my ears ringing. I knew I was finished. It was as though I had been revealed to the world. Part of my mind tried to stay focused on the immediate encounter, while still other parts went reeling with visions of the worst possible case scenarios. Now, not *one* but *two* people within the walls of Northrop knew of my status and endeavors.

They insisted that I should not be offended or worried, as there were protocols and chains of command that needed to be followed. From Steele's tone and body language it became immediately apparent (at least to my thinking) that I was a threat to their competence and commitment. What I had uncovered, documented, and shared with federal agents had been going on under their very noses. It was embarrassing and cast aspersions on their job performance.

Steele was somewhat more insistent than George in wanting to know exactly what I had been looking at, what documentation I had collected and where I had put it. I once again suggested that it was better for the safety of the investigation and me that they not know. When I gave just enough ground to let them know it had to do with financial reconciliations, Williams acknowledged that he knew there were some problems going on in that area but he gave away nothing more. Steele, on the other hand, cut me off and said curtly that he had recently had a meeting with the "Attrition Committee," run by Selen, that brought up some issues tied to the term "financial reconciliation."

I am sure the expectant expression on my face suggested the pending question, *And?*

Whether it was in answer to my unasked question or just finishing his thought, his next words cut me to the heart. He said when he heard what they were going to be discussing, he threw up his hands, said, "I don't want to know this," got up, and left the meeting. This struck me as being even worse for my immediate dilemma. It appeared he did not want anyone to be able to say that he knew about the issues in general or, worse, in detail.

Before I could fully wrap my thoughts around the implications of this unexpected event and the horror of another person knowing my confidential informant status, Steele cut off the conversation by telling me that Colonel Lambert, the top level DoD authority in residence, wanted to see me. Now.

My first reaction was shock, then disbelief. I thought, *Are you kidding me? You cannot possibly be serious.* They were, as they say, serious as death.

Now I was very much aware of who might be observing my contact with these two government monitoring agents while they jointly escorted me to the offices of the highest ranking among them. We were greeted by Colonel Lambert himself in the anteroom to his massive office. He clearly was not pleased by whatever had already been passed along. As I was guided in and placed in his intentionally intimidating gaze, he commented that he understood I was the holder of information they would be interested in and, by his opinion, should have been informed of long ago. This was somewhat strange, as all three of these men knew what it meant to be a federal informant and that not having informed them was a matter of protocol.

The whole point of being a secret informant is obvious to a child: *It's a secret.*

Given the progression of things, this was a status I did not foresee lasting too much longer. The reality was, these players were already on the audit report distribution lists that should have already set off flags for them.

When I voiced my discomfort over anyone knowing my status, let alone now three, Colonel Lambert offered the following:

He was not only the highest-ranking resident representative of the United States government assigned to stay on top of the contracts and projects at Northrop, he was, for all intents and purposes, and as far as it concerned me, "the government on premises." Therefore, he should be informed of any and all problems, as it was his right and responsibility to know what went on pertaining to quality assurance and accurate accounting or (and then getting an angry expression on his face and loudly saying), "Everything!"

Before I could complete my next thought of *If they had been paying attention . . .* I was stopped dead in my tracks by what I saw through the open door to his conference room. It appeared that virtually every government monitor and financial auditor assigned to the facility was sitting there staring at me. By the looks of it, they were either circling the wagons or lying in wait.

It turned out to be both.

When pressed to share what I had been doing, looking at, and documenting, I again protested that as a federal informant, my anonymity and secrecy were not only essential but protected by law, and that I had been advised by a federal criminal agent to not divulge it. They cared little for that and immediately went on the attack, with a combination of defensive challenges to what little I offered, and outright aggression to the most cursory answers I could give. They turned on me, ganging up with dismissive and bombastic challenges such as, "Just who do you think you are, anyway?" and "Where and how could you erroneously imagine you had uncovered and documented even what little you shared?"

The line of attack had two recurring themes. One, that what I was saying I had found (however cryptically) could not have occurred because if they had, each of the respective persons present would have discovered and dealt with that in their respective projects and territories. This was patently false. I tried pointing out to them repeatedly that I was not placing blame or suggesting they had not been doing their jobs. It was the narrow field of vision needed for security reasons that ensured none of them would have a broad enough view to detect the problems.

"For example," I said as I pointed to one of the auditors, "do you oversee every program at Northrop or are you assigned specific contracts with their associated purchase authorization numbers?" He said he oversaw at most ten P.A. numbers. I then pointed to a second and then a third auditor asking them the same question the both responded they each oversaw ten numbers.

I said, "Exactly. I see them all, and what it looks like they did was put some under yours and some under yours and some under yours," pointing to each one of the auditors. "By doing this they kept it from raising any red flags that something was wrong and attrition numbers far exceeded acceptable numbers. As far as you each independently knew everything was fine but overall it looks like there is a problem. And this doesn't even take into account excess inventory."

The very suggestion that the system was designed in a way that none of them really knew what was happening in their assigned domain was far more disturbing than reassuring. It turned their confident (but in practice, incompetent-by-design) worlds upside down and inside out.

This prompted the second round of dismissive accusations, which were ad hominem attacks against me as a credible investigator. *They* had advanced degrees and training, MBAs, CPAs, and the like, whereas I was, by virtue of my lack of formal credentials and job title, little more than a clerk. A puke. The fact that I had developed systems and reports the entire company had come to rely on seemed of little consequence.

My body was so charged with adrenaline I could barely control my shaking hands or find my way to the chair waiting for me without swerving slightly in shock, on weakened knees. To my surprise I was no longer feeling debilitating fear but the first rumblings of rage.

I thought, *How dare you!*

Even as I tried to grasp the implications of how many people now knew my secret, and gauge what I was willing or able to say, I could foresee any number of them setting out to look for what I was alleging, to actually investigate as if it had any basis or merit in fact, or to just prove it and me wrong. Worse, I could envision any number of them walking down any number of hallways and sharing the information with whoever in the company they were too closely tied to socially, or with whom they might feel the need to cover themselves down the road. I was already imagining one or both scenarios occurring within minutes of the end of this increasingly cacophonous, brutally contentious meeting. My mind's eye could already see that, within hours or days at best, my body would be stuffed in some trunk to disappear forever from the lives of my children and my wife, never the wiser of where I went or what happened to me.

If any or all of them suddenly altered how they did their jobs to verify or disprove my claims, this could expose me. It did not matter whether it was true or false; either way, they would catch attention. Their sudden concern would cause Northrop to scrutinize how and why that shift was occurring. This scrutiny could potentially expose me and the work I was doing, if for no other reason than I had been the source of the data, and had been providing it to everyone all along. Whether by suddenly digging deeper into their respective areas and/or by suddenly wanting to see what happened from project to project or even between forms of tracking, it would be a disruption to a system already under duress, traceable to me.

As for any of the dozen or more seriously distressed government personnel, my secrecy and any hope of safety would be over as fast as telephones could be picked up, dialed, and answered. Unbelievably, an action taken only hours earlier to assure the safety of the data I had risked everything to gather had turned on itself, and, by all appearances, was on the verge of threatening me and all my nerve-grinding, soul-crushing, family-damaging efforts to make the data accessible to my handlers before it was destroyed.

When it became clear they were not going to hear what I had to say, however generously I let them off the hook, my anger momentarily outgrew my fear. I took it upon myself to announce the meeting was over.

I am certain my reactions were fueled by the horrors I imagined befalling my family, and the pressing need to consider what could happen in the next minutes to hours.

Most of all, I just felt unadulterated rage. How dare they! I had really had enough.

This entire conversation, let alone its scale, had not had to occur at all. I reminded them all once again—most notably Colonel Lambert and Roger Steele—that while my investigations involved their areas of concern, they were not privy to the unfolding of a federal investigation. And more to the point, they were not in a position or allowed by law to interfere with it. Still more to the point, the conversation that day had begun at the instruction of my federal handlers, to find and arrange for someone within Northrop to be able to locate and hand over documentation in the event of a subpoena or a raid. As politely as I could, I reminded them that this chain of events was not only unnecessary but against protocols—and they knew it. We ended with Colonel Lambert agreeing to allow Williams to be my assigned inside contact.

As I made my way back to my cubicle, I could not imagine how to contain the exposure of my informant status, and keep my areas of investigation from further exposure. In my usual problem-solving way, I tried to find a way to get ahead of it. All I could think about was, *How long do I have before the axe falls and from where will it come?* I did not have a clear thought so much as reeling calculations ran amok, seeking some grounding and a conceivable plan of action.

Then a vague notion took seed: The only possible way to get ahead of this disaster was to find a way to prompt others into honestly addressing the issues, even as others geared up a small army to hide and perpetuate the problem.

As was not often the case, I reached Agent Zott immediately. When I did, he was, for the first time in our acquaintance, clearly and overtly furious. He did not, however, have any magic answers. For him as a federal agent, the case was starting to shift from being his paramount concern. His concerns now became my protection, the data's protection, and holding the corporation's officers accountable, in that order. In that, I discovered him and the others to follow to be good human beings. The case had very human faces to it and very real consequences. He would have to think about it.

But I did not have time to wait. I had to find some way to make something happen. I decided to take one last desperate run at trying to protect the corporation from itself.

The questions were how I could influence someone in any way that mattered, how much time I had before the axe fell, and from which direction and from whom it would come. And I wondered what would happen to my family when I was suddenly out of a job or possibly gone altogether.

Agent Zott never did come up with any magic bullet after my encounter with the small army of government officials that day. If anything, I think he and all the others working with me were praying for some kind of magic smoking gun to appear, one that would give us clean, irrefutable documentation of the transgressions, one that would allow them to sweep in and take action before the Sword of Damocles came down on my head.

In the short term, the only thing more surprising and unsettling than my rapid exposure was that nothing observable was immediately forthcoming other than our collective sense of urgency.

It was also the first time that the issue of witness protection came into the discussion.

Perhaps the most interesting thing here for many readers is that I still did not believe the corporation itself to be inherently evil, incapable of correction, or beneath redemption. The most remarkable thing for me is that in my newly ramped-up state of desperation and feeling that I was about to be crushed between a rock and a hard place, I still held out hope for the company that had given my life such promise, that it would want to live up to the standards of its *prima facie* reason for existence—the protection and well-being of our country and the values it stands for.

All it needed to do was create a clean, integrated system for tracking materials and accurately reconciling accounting procedures, admit errors or transgressions that had occurred in the past—whether by accident or by accidental design—and commit to making sure they would not happen again beyond normal and acceptable human error.

Could it really be that simple?

7
DESPERATE MOVES

As I returned to work to ponder what course of action to take next, the irony struck me just how much my current situation was the result of a series of seemingly unconnected events, accidents, and coincidences.

My secret status and activities had been only temporarily secret, so my situation at this point could only be described as tenuous, at best. If I were going to do anything to stave off impending doom and destruction, it would have to be fast and concrete.

As unlikely as it was to hope, in any rational world, that I could do either, I opted for the latter. I could try to take action that would help the problems get corrected, making the larger of them go away or at least become manageable. The quandary was whom could I find that I could trust?

The people I would need to persuade to do something proactive to fix the problems did not do what they did out in the open. They did everything off the radar and behind the scenes. This suggested there were still those within Northrop who did not know about the things that were diligently buried, being destroyed, or getting hidden. By contrast, it also meant there were those who (so I thought) would want things fixed. I needed to find those who were unwittingly mixed in with those who would turn against me.

The problem before me was finding a way to incite positive and proactive efforts to highlight and address problems (rather than scrambling to hide and even perpetuate them) while taking into account the complexity of the issues, the deliberately designed narrow fields of vision, my unique position in being able to see across those fields, and my status as a secret informant. And now I did not know if my secret was still intact or about to expire. It made the question of what to do a challenge of strategy, timing, and risk of exposure at every turn when exposure might cause me to be done in by some unknown person or entity, or become a government or corporate scapegoat.

The dangers were in not knowing how events would play out and how to do both. The task of trying to get things to work was too large, too broad, and too diffuse, with little or no time to do it in. Not only that, but I had to get my already-collected information out of the building before getting caught, *and* I still urgently needed to gather more information. My desperation took up my every waking thought.

It may seem to some that my efforts to prod certain Northrop personnel into doing the right thing could be seen as a betrayal of the government's investigatory efforts, of which I had been a part for now almost eighteen months. At the very least, it could have been a waste of time and might negate all the suffering my family and I had been through.

To that I remind the reader that the goal was for the company to openly acknowledge its problems, to hold it and those within it accountable, and commit to work with the government to correct them. Arresting past or continued offenders was always a possibility. Agent Zott was very clear on this.

I never wanted to do harm to the corporation or the many people who worked for it, and my belief (however naïve) that the corporation would be willing to fix its problems was supported by the data I gathered and analyzed. This was in part to cover myself. Since I reported everything to Northrop (albeit with the hope someone would connect the dots), I could never be accused of setting them up. But because I reported everything to Northrop, if they did nothing, the data would serve the government's case if and when it went on to criminal and/or civil prosecution.

Viewed from a distance, my desire for Northrop to step up, take it on the chin, and do the right thing was equal parts desperation, determination, and delusion that can only be born of such extreme circumstances and high stakes. It was also a reflection of the fact that I wanted the company to survive and thrive instead of closing its doors and sending a good number of people to prison. I certainly did not want to be one of them. As much as I wanted to help Agent Zott and the others in making their case, I was never fully convinced I would not be one of those to take the fall.

There was no possible way I could entertain going to prison. I also did not want to die or face the wrath I felt coming my way. Mostly, I hoped that if there were any chance of coming through this and still having a job, a career, and a life, I really had to succeed in persuading someone to do the right thing. And I needed to do it quickly before I was formally outed or just plain disappeared. The challenge, aside from getting any information out the door, was getting information out that was clear, credible, and irrefutable. Pursuing my tandem goal to help the corporation help itself was just as challenging, especially considering its scope.

The solution came somewhat out of the blue, when, in 1989, 63 very high-value traveling wave tubes (TWTs) were scrapped. That mishandling and its related financial reconciliations were specific, concrete, and prototypical—and it landed right in my lap.

This problem, with this specific part and related tracking problems was good news, potentially bad news, and possibly devastating news.

The good news was, it was handed to me by Northrop and, by its very nature, genuinely had to be handled or face dire consequences. The bad news was, it meant bringing the issues out into the open, thereby identifying myself as someone outside the control of those who already knew about them.

If I could get anyone to respond in a positive way, this was my chance to do it. If it went badly and was perceived as a threat, one with which I was visibly associated, I may have been tying my own noose regardless of what came about with revelations of my eighteen-month status as a spy for the United States government. It seemed to me there was no other choice. The question was, could I pull off provoking and promoting a shift to fixing problems without turning it into self-inflicted professional suicide, and could I do it in time and on a scale that mattered?

When a related issue of another case of scrapped 405 TWTs was brought to me, that scale seemed greatly enhanced. The parts had been scrapped the prior year, 1988, in ways that perfectly revealed alleged faulty tracking, accounting, and inflated builds of materials. It was in the tens of millions of dollars, but, as it turned out, that was the tip of the iceberg.

The big question was whether or not I had any time at all before being revealed as a federal informant by one of the government personnel who had witnessed the impromptu inquisition in Colonel Lambert's office. The options seemed clear, if ridiculous: I could wait and do nothing to see if I was revealed, or I could go all out on the off chance I had time. I chose the latter.

I continued to gather information across the board and to smuggle copies of documents out of the building, as always. The 63 TWTs that had been mishandled along the supply chain and associated accounting took on special focus. It was a somewhat ideal snapshot of problems reflected more diffusely elsewhere that were too important to ignore and too widespread to ignore, erase, or bury. What I needed was a large enough sample and broad enough picture to take to Selen and anyone beyond her in order to present a coherent and convincing picture of the existence of these problems if not their solutions. This, I believed, would prompt more proactive efforts.

The problem that first caught my eye in looking into the scrapped 63 TWTs was that reports I pulled for related projects where they had been scrapped appeared to have vastly more parts of many kinds being scrapped than had ever been purchased by and delivered to Northrop. This would have been significant even on a much smaller scale of possible simple human or data entry error. These added up to millions in projects that already used "component" parts (i.e., parts made up of many parts that are then used to make still larger parts up to and including final deliverable units). As it turned out, looking for the answer to this mystery revealed a number of interconnected problems in the supply chain that reached well beyond these specific parts. These were precisely the kinds of problems that needed to be fixed rather than hidden because of how widespread they were.

When I brought this to my supervisor, Clyder, he was as perplexed as I was: How was it even possible to scrap more parts than were acquired? He suggested that I needed to talk with Don Mazurkiewicz at the Northrop Electronic Tube (NET) systems in Arlington Heights to determine how this was possible.

When I went out to the NET facility, I presented the screen printouts from my Rolling Meadows office and expressed my confusion as to the discrepancy. His first reaction was to shrug off the fact that I was looking at those screens at all, and his shoot-from-the-hip response was that they were all wrong anyway. The second response was still more surprising: They kept their own tracking system on site at Arlington Heights for more accurate materials management. As it turned out, there were two interrelated problems that each caused more problems.

We only addressed one of them at the moment—failing to update records when smaller component parts of any given larger component part were salvaged for re-use without adjusting the record for that part.

When a large component part fails, it is scrapped and all subparts of them are scrapped as well. It is only when they have been removed, retested, and put back in inventory that they can be physically used again. But since every component part built by Northrop has a list or "build of materials" (i.e., what it takes to build that component), re-using one without re-entering it into existing inventory means the computer will assume it must be a new part. This affects billing in all sorts of convoluted ways. Any subpart might be scrapped as part of a larger component only to be salvaged and used again any number of times. They thus have to be tracked in Salvage Transaction Reports (STR) with the corresponding credits tracking back to the proper programs and ultimately back to the customer.

Upon further investigation, with my supervisor Clyder coming along for the ride, this failure to complete STRs turned out to be extremely widespread, not only at Rolling Meadows but also at Arlington Heights and the Elk Grove facilities. It was the other shoe to drop and had even greater implications: The builds of materials were also seriously out of date, listing parts that were once used to complete deliverable units. This means that when there are revisions and or improvements to an assembly, the build of material must be modified to reflect this change. This also means when different parts are used or fewer of one part are used, they should be zeroed out so as not to charge when items or subassemblies are scrapped or charged. Thus, any time a component at any level of development or complexity was scrapped and wiped from the system, the central computer at Rolling Meadows would also scrap it on record and in its reports. The result was that it scrapped possible phantom parts and could be passing the nonexistent cost for the part on to the customer.

The implications of this were huge, though still unknown to me at the time. There were entire final reports for the prior year of 1988 that clients were refusing to sign off on because the numbers made no sense. While the additional 405 TWTs under consideration were included in reports that had been signed off on, they were indicators of just how far off those reports and associated billing had been. By still further implications, they were also indicators of just how far off current bids were, because they had been based on existing histories.

Considering this was also the period in which public sentiment was coming down on contractors for cost overruns, failure to deliver product, and $900 hammers, and you have something of the picture that exceeded my own knowledge at the time. Northrop was an organization already under extreme scrutiny and pressure.

Selen had actually been called to task more than once by the Vice President of Product Assurance, Murray Snow, for specific instances of discrepancies in inventory on hand versus what was on record, and the official billing process. When the problem recurred, she instructed me not to provide my reports to key people on the distribution lists, whom she did not want informed on such matters (meaning Murray Snow). The implication of such dual and potentially dueling recordkeeping raised serious questions. It created unique documentation of the chaotic or systematically error-prone aspects of tracking, even if not necessarily intentional. They presented clear and documentable evidence of misrepresentation, faulty materials and data management, and indicators of intentional fraud by manipulation of the records to cover it up.

Clyder joined me in the field once again, and for an extended time we looked at how widespread certain dysfunctional or deceitful practices and violations of protocols were occurring. My own reports expanded to take in more details. I had to be discreet, but there was almost no level of management I did not have access to, and I interviewed everyone from acquisitions to top management, from all areas of recordkeeping and data entry. It was in the latter area I discovered that there was already very widespread and systematic data alterations occurring that were far more actively focused on falsely altering or reconciling all related records than on addressing the causes of the discrepancies. In so doing, rather than protecting the data integrity, it was erasing evidence of error or wrongdoing.

Petra Schiller, as mentioned earlier, was the most central data entry person. She shared with me that there was a memo authorizing the data cleanup, and that the memo was to be destroyed once the purge had been completed. While I had no idea at the time that she had been recruited and was also a federal informant, I accepted her explanation at face value. Entire computer programs were being created to run through data coming into or already in the new system and remove or adjust whatever did not fit or would present problems 1) in justifying past billings or 2) as a basis for future bidding and projections. In some cases it involved re-allocating materials and related billing between projects and programs. In other cases it removed records that were false or improper.

It was very strange that during this time nothing seemed to have come out of my encounter with the onsite monitors and auditors under Colonel Lambert's watch. It was almost as strange that the ongoing reports I generated and distributed did not set off alarms for those who would have cared. The biggest surprises came when I took my compiled information to Selen, hoping to initiate a correction of the problems.

When I asked to meet her in her office to discuss some matters I thought needed her attention, she already looked overwhelmed, worn out, and haggard. Clearly her mind was on other things, and anything I might have concerns over would just be that much more she did not want to deal with. When I laid out what I had learned, and most especially about Don Mazurkiewicz having failed to update the STRs, she just went pale and stared. Then she went quite nuclear.

As she called Mazurkiewicz, with me sitting there, my immediate concerns were what to do with the 63 scrapped TWTs from January and February of 1989 as well everything they were connected with. When Mazurkiewicz answered the phone, she asked him (with a few expletives added), "Do you have any idea what you have done to me?" Her larger problem was that they had just sent out the clients' yearly reports and final billings that were all massively wrong. I had no idea how wrong they were. Further, these clients were already clamoring that the billings and reports made no sense and suggested incompetent or even unscrupulous behavior by Northrop.

I cannot say I have ever sat through or witnessed quite such a reaming, and thought it was probably a very good thing for Mazurkiewicz that he was not there in person.

With my own future hanging in the balance, I could not ascertain how this impacted Selen other than upsetting her greatly. My hope was that she was only this distressed because she was trying to conjure how to go about fixing a disastrous situation. When she finally looked in my direction, though her internal gaze was somewhere else, I managed to ask, "What do you want me to do about the TWTs?"

She thought for a moment, stood, and said, "Come with me."

I followed her out of her office and down the hall. She said she was bringing me with her to the Attrition Committee meeting. Before I even had the chance to gauge what we were doing or the tone of it, she began explaining in a very matter-of-fact way that she wanted me to share with the committee exactly what I had just shared with her. I thought taking the information to her was my big moment, my great hope that something better and different would take seed, though I had no idea what to expect. There was no question of whether I felt ready to share anything with them.

As we entered the room, there were some glances suggesting some of them took note of my unprecedented presence there. But as we swept in, Selen greeted them all with my name and the warning that they were not going to believe what they were about to hear.

It has been suggested, in retrospect, that perhaps I should have been more unnerved by my sudden spotlight, that I should have felt more than a little exposed by what I was about to share because it did, in fact, expose much about my unusual perspective. It exposed the things I had been looking at with such efforts at maintaining secrecy. It revealed to those who would be concerned about my knowledge (as incomplete as that was) some of the most dangerous and damaging information I did know. But, in contrast to the meeting with Colonel Lambert, to which I had been led like a sheep to the slaughter, I was introduced here with the clear message that what I had to say was both important and big, and its far-reaching implications concerned them all. I still did not know what my purpose here was or what the reaction would be, but as I spoke, Selen checked with others now and then, asking them if they got the implications of what I was saying.

I felt heard. I felt important. I had the first glimmering of hope. Maybe, just maybe this was going to matter after all. Maybe Selen and her crew were going to rally to all this and do something about it and fix it.

When I finished, I felt relieved and genuinely encouraged for the first time I could remember in what seemed forever. Selen turned to the room and asked what they thought we should do.

As for the 63 TWTs from the current year for which no damning information had yet gone out to the client, the consensus was that we would back them out of their status as scrapped, have Mazurkiewicz update and correct all the necessary documentation that had been neglected, then scrap them out again. Nothing huge, but they were at least starting out by correcting erroneous information properly. No word yet on what to do with the 405 TWTs from the prior year. There was minimal discussion about the larger implications, and to tell the truth, I was lacking some context in order to get the full implications myself.

They then moved on to old business led by Ken Chapman and Sue Licata, without asking me to leave, as though I had been attending these meetings for years. I was fully tuned in to what they were saying for a brief few moments. I was feeling great, if not exactly elated, but my meeting with Selen had been a pivotal moment in my plans and hopes for any kind of future. It was the moment I had been aiming and hoping for to help the company help itself.

Mostly, I thought I had made a difference and I cannot tell you how much that mattered. What I had risked so much to find would be put to good use, even if not discussed in detail that day. These people seemed to have cared about what I shared.

Then I started paying attention to the conversation going on, much of which I did not understand. Some of it raised the hair on my neck.

There were words like "excess inventory" jumping out at me, and others words and phrases like "purging data" and "hiding any likely discovery" of the excess inventory by allocating materials to closed contract billings and contracts that thus would not be looked at again. Of all the things that caught my ears and kicked me in the stomach was the plan to generate what they called "phony purchase authorization numbers" in order to beat the system and to move this inventory and other records where they would not be found. In a corporation like this, excess inventory is a sin of many consequences, and purchase authorizations are sacrosanct. This conversation was beginning to sound ominously *not* like the great shift I had hoped for or helped create. Quite the contrary. The old business for the day was the recent discovery that there was roughly $11 million of excess inventory discovered above and beyond any acceptable records for it or any possible allocation to currently active contracts or projects.

The concern, much to my sudden dismay and sinking hopes, was to make it disappear.

"Where is this entire inventory?" someone asked. It was all in the office of Robert Schilling, one of Selen's peers—in a high-tech setting like this where a TWT could be worth $120,000 and components the size of a pack of cigarettes worth infinitely more.

It was bad enough that Selen or anyone else in that room was comfortable having me there, but I started wondering what it was that Selen actually thought of me. Did she think I was just so much part of the team I would not care that I was now hearing about overt and intentional fraud? Was this some kind of test to see what and where my loyalty really was? Had they heard something about me from the government monitors? Was there any way I could now get through this without being considered an accomplice? And how was I going to handle whatever happened next, after having revealed so much about what I knew?

As my brain started to conjure my worst fears of being dragged off to prison (a more horrifying thought than not being able to care for my family), I heard the next words, which caught my attention and froze my heart.

The data entry and multiple layers of alterations for making the excess inventory vaporize was going to be incredibly time-intensive with no currently matching resources. Out of nowhere, Selen popped up and said not to worry, that Jim Holzrichter could help with the work. After all, I had most of the needed clearance and familiarity with the system and it could be argued (although it was not) that the report I had given demonstrated I could understand and unravel complex problems. I supposed that by reverse implication, then, I should be equally adept at covering them up.

Everyone rose to leave and headed in different directions as though the most matter-of-fact meeting ever had just been adjourned. Selen was out the door before I could find my voice or get her attention. I rose as quickly as I could to follow her, pleased to discover that, after what had just occurred, I had solid legs even if my stomach was doing flips. I exited the room just behind her and caught her striding down in the hallway.

She finally responded to her name and turned to face me, asking what I wanted. It suddenly hit me that I had no idea what to say. In new record time, my life had gone from one set of intentions and expectations to something utterly, completely, and destructively opposite. Worse, I thought I had just been assigned to be complicit in committing undeniable fraud against the government.

What came out of my mouth was, "What about the 405 TWTs from last year?"

"What about them?"

These were scrapped TWTs with the same tracking and accounting problems as the 63 scrapped TWTs from the current year. The only difference was the former were documented and had been signed off on. They were not prone to a second look. I repeated the question.

The first part of her answer was bad enough. Her terse reply was, "Let sleeping dogs lie."

The second part put a stake through my heart: "What the government does not know won't hurt them."

Selen turned and walked away, leaving me standing in the hallway frozen to the ground. Dumbfounded. Nearly immobilized. My brain was trying to conjure something to do next beyond put one foot in front of the other, to go somewhere other than here, left behind and alone in an empty corridor except for the ever-present black fisheye of the security monitors.

Only a few minutes later I was knocking on the door of Clyder's office. I had ceased trusting him completely the day he told me inflated inventories were standard operating procedure. Then again, I had no other real place to go at this moment. He listened to my story about what had just transpired and thought for a few moments without comment. It

occurred to me that in all the time he had supported me in my official research and reporting, and had even gone with me on fact-finding missions,
he had never once used the information to take corrective action.

Finally he looked up at me and said, "Don't worry about it. You've
reported the problems to Selen and to me, so you are covered."

I knew, of course, I was not covered. Whether I had correctly reported the problems or not, as far as I knew and understood, I was about to be
party to overt and actual fraud in hiding them.

I was incredulous at the cavalier aspect of the answer and apparent
disregard for addressing the outright wrongdoing under his very nose. I
took one more shot at making an impact and pointed out that what we
were about to be doing was flat-out illegal and asked him point blank,
"Why can't they just admit what the problems are and give the money
back?"

Clyder displayed no thought or emotion whatsoever and answered
flatly, "You are talking about over a couple of hundred million dollars." In
what was probably a response to the look on my face, he added just as
flatly, "They can't give it back. It's spent."

I went home that night, my mind in the worst distress since leaving
the meeting with Colonel Lambert and expecting security to be waiting
for me at my desk. It had always been possible for the government to turn
on me in my capacity as an informant. It actually happened all the time.
Now that I would be engaged in behaviors they could even more easily
put me away for, I had less confidence in my situation than ever. There
had to be a way to step up the visibility of the problems and what was going on so those higher up, those who would care and want to fix the whole
situation, would know what was going on and intervene. At the same time,
it had to be clear to those who wanted to hide and perpetuate the problems, that this whole mess was just too massive and dangerous to the life of
the corporation to go unaddressed.

The question was how to do that.

The answer did not come to me until I was driving to work the next
morning. In the meantime, I left that question behind or at least slightly at
bay and went to my daily AA meeting. For that day, then four years clean
and sober, I did not drink or use.

I corralled Selen fairly early the next morning and asked her if it was not better to just correct these problems rather than try to bury them. I am not sure if her look suggested she thought I was mad or not, but it certainly was the face of someone trying to assess something she did not expect.

"What do you have in mind?" she asked.

"Perhaps, if it is too big a risk to call in the government or outside auditors, we could use Northrop's internal auditors and keep the situation's full assessment and the problem-solving itself inside."

Yet another look as she no doubt tried trying to grasp what I was after or thought could be accomplished by this move. What I could not tell her, of course, was that it would take the whole process and all the problems out of her hands. It would move it way up the ladder to those who might have a very different attitude about what to do if only they knew.

I would discover years later that would have been pointless, as Northrop's internal auditors already knew, as did the highest-level executives. Even more troubling, in depositions taken some time later, Northrop revealed it had already hired an outside accounting firm to look at its systems, which issued what would have been a damning report. It would have been a smoking gun except for the fact that they had not been hired directly by Northrop Corporation itself, but through their legal representation so as to protect whatever they found under attorney-client privilege.

At this moment, however, though I did not know that, it was probably weighing heavily on Selen's overwrought mind and shoulders. Her only slightly delayed but furious replay was, "Just who the f--k do you think you are, you g-d-mned son of a bitch?! We aren't the g-d-mned Northrop police, you know. Get out of my f--king office!"

I was so upset from this encounter and the overall state of things that I came up with a reason to leave the building for a while. I went to a public and therefore unmonitored pay phone nearby to try and reach Agent Zott. After multiple attempts with no success, it occurred to me to call Chris, a US Attorney I had been working with. Agent Zott had taken me to meet him at the Dirksen Federal Building in Chicago, where they had sneaked me in the back way and up a freight elevator. I reached him fairly readily and filled him in on the situation. His main concern at the moment was that he wished I had been wearing a wire. I did not know that Agent

Zott had pondered it before deciding I was too honest and transparent to pull it off. Chris said he would try to track Agent Zott down and promised to get back to me in any case.

He did not find Agent Zott, but he was good as his word that he would get back to me. Unfortunately, and to my utter disbelief, he called my desk telephone at work the next day. Northrop, being Northrop, would monitor all calls and one from the Justice Department no doubt set off more than one bell and whistle. All I could think of, aside from security already being on its way, was how he could possibly not grasp what he was doing to me here. I tried to act like I did not know him and gave a few probably incoherent responses to greetings. My heart stopped very nearly dead when he asked if I would wear a wire to the next attrition meeting. I stammered something about not knowing if I would be invited back.

Frankly, the rest of the phone call is a bit of a blur. I did manage to bring it to an end somehow, wondering all along who might have been listening and what was already stirring into motion. This was a top-security defense contractor. He had to know that every telephone in the place would be monitored and, in all likelihood, recorded. As ridiculous as the thought was, I even found myself briefly wondering if he had intentionally set out to expose me. There was no rational explanation for his calling me here at my desk. And asking me to wear a wire at the next Attrition Committee meeting over an open recorded line? I felt as though any and all security I had managed to hold onto for all those months had just been stripped away in a flash. Now my every nerve was on alert for what would happen next.

I was truly alone and scared.

I wanted to maintain some pretense of normalcy, but all I could think about in terms of action was to somehow get to Agent Zott, first as some kind of touchstone or reconnection to reality after that surreal moment. Second, I needed to put whoever I presumably had at my back on very high alert. Lastly, I needed some idea of what to do or expect next. Beyond that, my overall impulse was to go home, pack my family up, and run. As it turned out, that last part would be an option briefly entertained by my handlers in the first real discussion of the option of witness protection.

It was also about this time that I heard from a man named Rex Robinson, one of the future key co-litigants in the lawsuits that were to come. He had been laid off from Northrop, ostensibly for reasons not connected to his quite vocal complaints about his discomfort with some business practices. He had heard from one of my friends that I, too, had concerns and wanted me to have the number of an attorney if anything should come down on me. At the time, neither he nor my friend knew what I was concerned about or that I was an informant. I finally gave in and took the phone number and put it in my wallet.

When I did finally reach Agent Zott, he was unmistakably furious. I appreciated his response, because I felt there was still someone on my side and that I was not crazy. Unfortunately, it was too late to matter. The proverbial cat was now out of the bag—or about to be—and I was vulnerable to what would soon be confirmed as a very dangerous world, a world already on high alert for its own survival. I imagined that, at best, I now had perhaps days before being out of work, unable to support my family, or even be around to care. I tried not to think about what was about to come my way, given the recent movies about whistleblowers stepping up and meeting their own demise.

I wondered how my family would do with me gone.

As I sat in my daily AA meeting desperately needing any kind of familiar ground, I imagined all the possibilities of what could happen next. I found myself praying to my own higher power for guidance and support in preparation for a sudden inability to take care of my family and a tsunami of retaliatory acts by Northrop. There was a part of me that simply wished to cease to exist and for it all to be over. There was some other, and much more enduring, part of me that simply had to find a way to care for my family, to find a way through whatever came next. It all seemed impossible and about to come undone.

That said, in this first or second week of March 1989, for one more day and in the midst of all of this, for the sake of my family as much as myself, I did not drink or use.

8
AN AWKWARD DANCE OF FOES

It had been strange that nothing really happened in the month or so between the meeting in Colonel Lambert's office, and my more recent life-changing meeting and volatile reaming from Selen. It was equally strange that on returning to work the day after the call from Chris that the world had not changed overnight, as I had half expected it to do. Everything appeared to be normal, or at least as normal as it can be when your life is nothing what it seems, when you are leading a double life. No one seemed to have heard anything. No one acted any differently. Whatever the time delay from my phone call being flagged to something happening, I had no doubt that Northrop's omnipresent security systems had captured that call and would soon take action. I had been revealed as a confidential undercover informant and they would have overheard the AUSA actually asking me to wear a wire to get evidence against the company.

The first clues, which came within days, were the subtle adjustments in my work assignments by my supervisor. I was not asked or assigned to help with the data entry manipulation decided upon in the Attrition Committee meeting.

A greater clue came when Selen asked me to step into her office and, standing face-to-face in the middle of it, told me out of the blue, "You know, Jim, if I thought there was anything going on around here I would be the first to go down the hall, and to the IG's office." This was a strange comment to make because nothing overtly immediate had prompted it and it was utterly ludicrous. It flew in the face of what we both knew: She was not only aware of things going on, she was in charge of and, by and large, executing them. Gathering that there was no more to follow, I thanked her for letting me know and turned to leave with her staring at my back. I stopped in my tracks when I saw that the whole perimeter of her office was lined with stacks of banker's boxes marked for shredding and destruction. Clearly she would have known I would see these. What was the point of her strange comment, then wanting me to see these boxes of data and records marked for destruction?

This was perhaps a week or two after the call from Chris, the call I assumed would out me for good, but it seemed so strange and self-contradictory that I did not immediately connect the two. I wandered back to my cubicle trying to imagine what her intentions had been and what to make of such contradictory messages. It was not until I was working on these pages of this book that her real intentions were pointed out to me. She was putting false words on record while making her point by her surroundings, just in case I was, in fact, wearing a wire. It was yet one more moment in the writing of this book in which the previously incomprehensible became instantly obvious. For that moment in April of 1989, however, I missed the connection and was still waiting for a clear indication as to whether or not my ill-fated phone call had been intercepted and was being acted on.

I was so twisted up in free-floating anxiety that I almost wished something *would* happen to show if I was in danger or somewhat in the clear for just a little bit longer. I was soon to have that wish answered.

The message came from security itself in mid-April, beginning with a phone call from Quealy telling me he would like to meet with me in his office right now. I braced myself, recalling the previous meeting there. It now seemed a lifetime ago. I remembered my angst at the time, wondering who, if anyone, had provided them with the then-false information that I had been seen clandestinely meeting someone in a gas station and taking boxes of documents out of the trunk of my car. In my current anxiety over what was about to transpire, I may have missed the irony. What had been so false in the first meeting had become not only true but the defining truth of my life, and it was about to be dealt with.

Quealy opened the door to his office and gestured me inside, to sit a chair with its back toward his desk, facing the doorway to his office.

Rather than sit, he stepped behind me and picked something up from his desk, keeping his back to me, then stepped past me to stand between me and the door, his back still toward me.

"We understand you lost this some time back."

He finally turned my way and held up a security badge. On reflex, I felt to confirm I was wearing mine, and realized he held one I had lost and replaced some time ago. Sighing in relief, I thought, *Could this actually be all he wanted to see me about?* But why had he said "we" found it?

I confirmed that, yes, I had lost it a month or two back and, through normal procedures, I had it replaced. I asked him where it had been found.

That was not what was important, was his response. The question was how and why I had lost it. This struck me as a strange response, and I had no idea how to answer. I was getting very uncomfortable with his looming between me and the door.

"Is there some problem?" I asked.

"Maybe, maybe not. It depends," he said. Where was this cat-and-mouse game going? Only slowly removing his eyes now fixed on the badge he asked, "Jim, do you by any chance know of any investigations that might be going on here at Northrop? You know, maybe by the government?"

He looked up from the badge and down at me in the chair facing the door, a fraction of his height, a slight smile in the corner of his mouth. Boom. That was it. They knew.

With something of a ringing in my ears and a pounding of my heart my brain raced for a way to accurately answer his question and not overtly tell a lie. I answered that I did not know of *any* investigations going on. I did, of course, know of *one*, not just *any*. I tried to look surprised and incredulous at the question.

"Why do you ask?" I queried, feeling I was sitting on a razor's edge.

"Because we believe there is an informant working here at Northrop," he answered.

"No," I again responded, trying to look as innocent and as surprised as possible just in case by some miracle this was not coming at me. I said, "Really . . . an investigation of Northrop by the government? And do you know who?"

"Actually, yes," he responded, "and he works in Product Assurance." I tried to look surprised, but he would have nothing of it. "We know we have a spy in our midst, Jim, and his name is James Holzrichter." I caught my breath. His next words pinned me to my seat: "In fact, we know it's you."

There it was, the first of many confrontations to come. Any move on my part would only make it worse. All I could think about was how badly I wanted to get out of there, to get out of that room, but he was between me and the door.

I couldn't get out.

I was trapped.

I was terrified.

What was he going to do to me? To pretend, even for a moment, that none of this had really happened was no longer an option. He wanted to know right now what I had passed along to the government agents and he also wanted to know who they were. I told him the agent was Agent Zott (he said he knew him) and that I had passed on the information about the original scrapped-then-reordered cables we had discussed the year before, along with the fact that Quealy himself was told not to report the discrepancies in protocols and billing, or even the conversation about them. I then told him I was not at liberty to discuss anything more and he could talk to my supervisors because they knew everything I had told the agents, because I had reported it all internally already.

He asked what was next and what I needed to do. I told him I thought I needed to see an attorney, which he agreed was probably wise. I said I needed to leave. He finally offered, "Yes, well, it is late. We'll take this up again in the morning." He hesitated. "You will be coming into work tomorrow, right?"

I agreed, but all I really wanted was out that door and access to a secure telephone off premises. I think he took in my distress with no little satisfaction, but he opened the door to let me out, perhaps to let me know that was within his power to grant or deny. I left, stopped by my desk to pick up my thermos and a few personal items, took note of where everything was, and fled the building.

The phone number of the attorney Rex Robinson had given me long ago, the one I had only reluctantly accepted, was burning a hole in my back pocket. I managed to make my way through the corridors, past security at the front entrance, and fumbled with my wallet to pull out the scrap of paper. This attorney was about to play a major role in my life, and I had his number in my hand as I cut through the parking lot to my car. I got in and took a moment to try and focus. I shakily lit a cigarette. I looked at the phone number feeling desperate and desperately ill. As I pulled out of the parking lot and looked in my rearview mirror at the facility shrinking in the distance, I knew I was looking at my future shrinking into nothing. The difference was, this time I knew: *What future? You don't have one. It's over.*

I stopped at the first gas station I could that had a public phone, possibly the very gas station in the false version of my passing along documents before it occurred to me. I tried to call Agent Zott first but he was unavailable. Surely he would have to know what just transpired. But I was on a bit of a mission here. The beast now knew who and what I had been even if it did not yet know what I knew. I needed an attorney and I needed one now.

I called Ron Futterman, attorney at law, and after speaking with his receptionist, Virginia,[5] she connected me to Ron. I filled him in on the general circumstances.

His instructions were reassuringly blunt and clear: Do not talk to anyone without him. He would be at my house in the morning. I was to go home, be careful, and if anybody followed me, I was to get the license number and call the police. Oh, and I was to try to get some sleep later.

When I arrived home, I tried to put on a good face for the kids, but told my wife. She needed to know right away that I had been caught, that Northrop knew I had been an undercover informant, and that I had called an attorney who would be coming to the house in the morning.

It is probably a testament to the level of stress we were both under and the ability of humans to block out anything so traumatic that, to our surprise when writing these pages, neither Mary nor I could recall anything more about that evening than that I told her the life-uprooting and spirit-disturbing news, saw that the kids were fine and in her amazing care, then went to my AA meeting.

Obviously I could not share any of this at my twelve-step meeting and

---

5 Over the years I came to appreciate her calm voice and true kind concern. She is truly a great lady.

part of me wanted to rush back home at its end more than usual. What I do remember was that in this sacrosanct place, I again found myself looking around for unfamiliar faces. When I left, I was on alert for anyone watching me as I had never been before. I found myself paying even more attention to the cars around me as I drove home, and most especially to every set of headlights from behind. This was to become a way of life, and at the time, I had no way of telling if I was or was not being followed. What hit me on that drive home was that there was nowhere left where we would be safe or where we knew who could be trusted.

Ron Futterman arrived at my house the following morning as promised, some time between 8:00 and 8:30. I gave him more details about the situation. I came to know a bit more about his connection with Rex and two other litigants-to-be, which included my friend and former carpool buddy. It seemed, from what Ron told me, they had all been laid off from Northrop, presumably not because Northrop had any issues with them, but as part of generic layoffs.

Rex and his friends had hired a different law firm to handle what they termed an age discrimination suit, but when that law firm heard some of the concerns about the company (vague as some of those allegations turned out to be), they suspected there was a possible federal suit well beyond age discrimination. This was, in part, because Rex and one of the other litigants were quite vocal about their suspicions that Northrop was involved in unscrupulous and illegal practices. The law firm representing their age discrimination suit thus brought in Ron's boutique law firm to explore the issues and possible filings in that arena.

This information made me understand what had prompted Rex to give me this attorney's contact information, even though my concerns were undefined and unexpressed. He explained to me that he thought there might be some merit in combining our cases should we decide to file a qui tam lawsuit.[6] Mostly he explained my rights as a protected federal whistleblower and advised me on what steps we needed to take next. That was when the phone rang.

---

6 A lawsuit filed for fraud on behalf of the government, originally signed into law by Abraham Lincoln.

I picked it up and said, "Hello."

It was Quealy wanting to know where I was and why I had not reported to work. After all, I had told him I would be coming in when I had left the day before.

Thinking to myself, *That was then, this is now,* I told him I had decided to take the day off and was conferring with my attorney at that very moment. As he listened to my side of the conversation, Ron took the phone at the point he felt Quealy became even the slightest bit abusive or threatening. After introducing himself and laying down a short but pithy set of ground rules, he said he expected them to be followed to the letter by Northrop, with the full force of federal law and whistleblower protections on my side regardless of whatever rights they thought they had on theirs.

It was only semi-reassuring to me that they were supposedly forbidden by law from any form of punishment or retaliation, up to and including firing me for being a federal informant, or so Ron told me. Since this was an organization I felt saw itself as above the law as long as they could get away with it, at that moment, I trusted nothing without serious reservation. That said, I have to admit that Quealy at least attempted a decidedly different tone when I took the phone back. I assured him that I would report to work the next day as usual, except for my now-customary two-hour early arrival. Quealy also agreed to follow the instructions Ron had given him to secure and protect all documents at my desk as protected materials and that they were now the subject of an ongoing federal investigation.

To Ron's credit, and with my enduring appreciation, he made sure I understood what my rights were and what to both expect and to accept from Northrop when I went to work in the morning. Most of all, I appreciated and continue to appreciate that he gave me an actual business card with his direct number on it and told me to call him immediately anytime if Northrop or any of its employees came close to (let alone crossed) any of the ground rules.

Having the rest of the day off to think about the state of things and what I might or might not encounter on my return to work the next day only gave me that much more time to worry. Then again, it was also some much needed time to brace for the unknown, most especially for what I encountered upon reporting for work the next morning.

As I walked to my area, no one would look at me, let alone engage me in the usual good morning salutations. When I turned the corner and entered through the doorway of my cubicle I stopped dead in my tracks, my mouth dropping open. My desk had been stripped clean of absolutely everything except for a keyboard and monitor, both of which were hard wired and not movable. After sitting down and pulling the keyboard to me, I discovered I was locked out of the computer system. On further inspection, I saw that even the phone was gone. All of my personal pictures and possessions, all of the document files and binders from my overhead compartment, and the file cabinet behind me were gone. The boxes of documents that had been sitting on the floor, some of which I had needed to get out of the building, were gone. There was literally nothing. Not even a paper clip in any of the drawers. When I tried to stop one fellow worker to ask him what had happened, he said several security officers had shown up the day before, threw everything in boxes, told everybody to mind their own business, and left. He went on to say it was like someone kicked over an ant hill and he did not want to know why. And, with a look of fear on his face, he backed away from me.

I imagine they had someone wipe my space clean immediately after my meeting with Quealy. I did not have much time to think about my plight because Eric Howell, the chief corporate attorney for Northrop, showed up at my desk in person and asked me to accompany him to the office of Murray Snow, Vice President of Product Assurance who, ironically, had been one of the people on the distribution lists of all the reports I had been generating for some time.

To me, having never met Howell, he was the immediate force to be reckoned with. Snow, who was himself normally a no-nonsense force, looked drained and ashen. He had always been respectful to me in our limited interactions and, out of empathy and reflexive kindness, I offered that he should not worry. I told him that the investigation had not been targeted at him and most of what was at issue had not occurred on his very recent watch. I could almost see the blood return to his face and his breathing return to something like normal, and both men gestured I sit in a chair in the middle of the room.

They began by stating what we all knew, that they could not fire me for having been an undercover federal informant. They did know and would honor my rights, no matter how disappointed they might feel for, as they put it, betraying them. They recounted some of the many benefits that had come my way by working there: The respect. The opportunities for work beyond my formal training and degrees. The help Northrop had provided with time off from work, as well as the insurance payments for my rehabilitation and treatment for alcohol and drugs. They left out the part about my creation of an EAP program for them that they then gave to someone else to run.

There was a part of me that wanted to protest that virtually all of my actions were aimed at serving the company, including a few high-risk Hail Marys, as last-ditch efforts to help them help themselves. It hurt to have such a fall from grace with Snow, as it would with others. I had taken great pride in my work and had looked forward to growing and doing more. I was not the bad guy here, so I bit my tongue. The one thing that was not going to work to soften me up was the blame game.

They then went on to admit that they knew that by law they could not ask me any direct questions about the investigation, at least not without getting in a little trouble themselves. But surely I understood, they said, that they could not afford to just let "the wolf loose among the sheep," so to speak. How I became the wolf in this scenario escaped me, but I continued to listen. The solution to a cooperative working arrangement, they thought, was if they knew what kinds of projects or data I could work on that would not compromise or embarrass them further. I was asked to provide an exhaustive list of what I could still do as soon as possible.

We all knew they were requesting a list they could use, by process of elimination, to determine what I had been investigating and/or found important. Thinking of what I could do that fit their criteria without tipping the government's hand, I said I could still do the pyramid charts and the hitter reports that Snow had become accustomed to getting every week. Howell asked what I needed from my records to do that and I told him the box of records that had been at my desk along with the drawings that were inside it. He said he would try to get them to me.

We all knew that, while they could not fire me specifically for being an informant, they could fire me for failure to meet performance standards, as long as the firing did not appear to be retaliatory. If they could meet that criterion, no matter how contrived, I could be fired at will. I agreed, however, to work on creating more of a list of things I could still do, as my refusal could have put me at risk of accusations of insubordination. I accepted their encouragement to let them know if I ever thought I was being treated incorrectly or unfairly and I was dismissed. With a large dose of skepticism and a slight touch of nausea, I went back to my desk.

When I arrived, my phone had been reinstalled. Within fifteen minutes of leaving Snow's office, Howell showed up at my desk with the box of drawings and other documents that had been taken. After he left, I peeked inside.

The most striking thing was that everything I had buried was all there in exactly the order I had left them. Were they stupid, I wondered, or were they just testing me in some way I did not yet understand? As I unpacked the boxes and put my work space back together, I wondered how long this little charade would go on and just how much they would really try to throw at me. As it was, I was now a leper in a workplace that, while secretive and a little invasive, had always been cordial. I worked with people who now would not look me in the eye or stay at any lunch table I joined.

After going to Clyder's office and telling him what both Snow and Howell directed me to do, he called Dick Cedarburg, who was in charge of setting up Product Assurances computer access to reinstate me. I was, for the moment, back online.

In the days to come, one of the ways they would torment me would be to give me very specific work assignments for which I suddenly would not have needed clearance, and I would frequently be "accidentally" locked out of the system altogether. With respect to the normal duties I had actually designed and developed, Clyder rapidly reassigned my duties to someone whose best-known qualification was her rumored penchant for adulterous relationships with coworkers, and her primary claim to fame was in having been sent home a number of times for unprofessionalism and scanty dress. As for any assistance Howell intended to offer personally, it came in the form of frequent and not necessarily announced visits at my desk to help refine a list of things I should not work on, and a corresponding list of what things would not be a problem. He also repeatedly requested I go and speak with Wally Solberg, the CEO at Northrop.

I will say that during this time, in May 1989, I managed to complete the tracking of the reverse and then re-scrap of the 63 TWTs that had been the catalyst for Selen to take me to the Attrition Committee. In combination with the 405 TWTs she directed us not to address at all, the change from the inflated bill to the corrected value, intended to be passed on to the government, was $15,000 – $22,000 per TWT, depending on the type. It changed what would have been an alleged incorrect billing of $945,000 to $1,386,000 for the 63 TWTs scrapped in 1989 alone.

If this is extrapolated out to the 405 tubes that were left on record as having been scrapped against the incorrect bill from the previous year, the difference between the real charges versus the correct charges ranges from $6,075,000 to $8,981,000. This was for one single part in one year, let alone for what was later known to have been used on the B1 Bomber. With many thousands of parts and components handled per year, the total amount is almost incalculable and incomprehensible. Due to the insufficient tracking and recording, as well as maintenance of the records at Northrop, they would never provide a definitive total either then or in the future.

In looking back after all these years, the most amazing thing to me is that I still managed to smuggle copies of the remaining documents out of the building to give to the government agents, even after Northrop knew I was an informant.

Fortunately, I still sat in a fairly private area and could sneak across the aisle when others were at lunch and on breaks and hide in the computer room, behind large mainframes, to look through materials and hide them on my person. When that felt too risky, I hid them in my thermos between the glass and outer shell, always curious as to whether or not they watched the same spy movies I did. As for making photocopies, I just mixed a few pages of a document at a time in other more kosher photocopying, after which I would remove and recompile the covert copies. I made sure to never take the original documents out of the building but I did take copies and I did secure the location of the originals, telling Agent Zott where they could be found.

All of this was taking a grinding toll and although I appreciated each and every week I had a paycheck and benefits, I really was not certain how long I could continue without destroying my health and/or having a breakdown in the process. All of this was made worse by not only my iso-lation from previously cordial and even intimate coworkers, their overall reaction to me on campus and off was one of avoidance, expressions of fear, and outright rage-fueled verbal assaults and implied threats of physi-cal attacks.

One colleague called me at home one evening after I had left him a message, and begged me never to call him again. His only explanation was that he had a family to support. Still another colleague cornered me at one point and screamed at me out of anger and fear, wanting to know who I thought I was and did I want to see them all out of work? I felt badly for them, of course, but had to remind myself that if they were that afraid of the company, they knew more than they were saying. They were actually showing the kind of fear they lived under at all times. And if the colleague who verbally attacked me actually understood that what I had document-ed could close the doors of the company, it meant there was much to which he had turned a blind eye. So-called friends I had sat with at lunch for almost five years would get up if I tried to join them, the whole table picking up their trays without saying a word or glancing in my direction. They would move to another table, sit down, and begin talking with one another again. All in all, any contact was getting more painful.

Northrop itself finally requested a meeting "just to see what's what." It was arranged and came to order at Ron's legal offices on June 5, 1989, in what, unexpectedly, was to be my last day on active duty with the com-pany. For a brief time, I thought it was also going to be my last day on the planet, culminating with Mary and several of our children in tow showing up at the hospital, where, by all appearances, I was having a full-on heart attack.

The numbers attending for both sides were not particularly large, alt-hough they were significant in composition. For our part, there was Ron himself and some of his team, along with a DCIS agent representing the government, and me.

For their part, it included their head corporate attorney, Howell, and Quealy, with a small band of high-powered attorneys from New York who were clearly in charge. I assumed they were attending in such numbers largely for intimidation value and dramatic impact. If nothing else, we were outnumbered and the intimidating entourage had its desired impact on me if not on Ron or the DCIS agent.

The presence of the DCIS agent, however, was a wrinkle Northrop did not expect nor like, because, in whatever we were to discuss, it would be a *prima facie* federal offense to lie to him or even in his presence.

For our part, we were not particularly interested in any real fact finding. The meeting was at their request, after all. If anything, we were curious as to whether or not they would admit to having looked at any of what I had reported to them in the course of my work and/or would acknowledge any problems or wrongdoing. For their part, there were three key concerns or areas of information and they wanted to see what they could glean from the discussion with me individually, and from Ron and me as a team.

The first concern, as expected, was what I reported to the government. The second and closely related question was whether or not we had filed a qui tam suit. The third and most usefully unsettling question was whether or not I had ever worn a wire.

As they asked their questions regarding what I had reported to the government, it was our repeated answer that everything I had reported to the government I had in fact reported to them. Not only that, I had been instrumental in generating entire systems of internal reporting that had been assimilated as ongoing reporting to the highest official positions within the division. In particular, I raised the issue of the original problems with the scrapped cables I had reported to Quealy at the beginning. We added the point that not only did he and they know about the problem, but that he had been instructed not to file a report, even though it was required as condition of the relevant contracts.

When Ron tried to cut in to ask any questions or request clarification, the opposing team cut him off with a stern reminder that it was they who had called this meeting and would conduct it in the fashion they saw fit. In some instances, they cut him off as much as they were able, insisting that as a continued employee with Northrop, it was their right to know. To this, we answered some questions in particular, always with the reminder that this and all information provided to the government had been provided to them as well. I sidestepped the fact that I had actually been hoping to prod them into correcting the problems using the sound data I provided that would have helped them do it.

It is difficult to imagine that they thought they would get any real new information on any of this. It was when they asked if we had filed a qui tam suit that Ron leaned in and bluntly said, "I am not going to allow him to answer that." They were not pleased with this but had no recourse.

They then asked me whether or not I knew of anyone destroying documents at Northrop, to which I answered without hesitation that Selen had. I added that she was destroying documents as fast as she could.

When the DCIS agent deigned to ask if I knew of anyone else destroying records or documents, they made the mistake of cutting him off. They sternly suggested his presence was a courtesy and he was only an observer with no official right to be there or allowed to ask questions. He was both unshaken and quick to correct them on both counts with a brief bit of haggling. When they got to their last and most perplexing question as to whether or not I had ever worn a wire, Ron let the question hang in the air for a moment and said once again, "I am not going to allow Jim to answer that." I think it was an answer and moment that gave him more than a little delight.

Not knowing if we had filed a qui tam claim was unnerving for them and, since those claims are filed in secret and under seal, getting an answer here would be the only immediate way to know if we had or were planning on filing.

Not knowing whether or not I had ever worn a wire was far more unsettling. It meant that they did not know for certain what we did or did not have, because it was the one record they could not access or manipulate. It was the one thing that kept them off balance.

When it came time for us to ask any questions, the level of absurdity became almost comical. With the DCIS agent in the room, they were not going to state or commit to anything. When the band of visiting attorneys jumped in, advising Quealy not to comment or answer yet another question, Ron nodded in his direction, suggesting that he was beginning to suspect that if he asked Quealy what his name was they would tell him not to answer. Without any apparent embarrassment, they acknowledged that probably was the case. There was little to no point in going any further or taking up more time. The meeting was adjourned with Quealy enigmatically tossing out that he would see me on Monday.

It literally made me feel ill.

In some ways the encounter had been good for us, particularly in establishing we were not just going to crumple in fear. Planting doubt as to whether I had ever worn a wire or not was perhaps the most useful result, and, in Ron's eyes, worth having the meeting. The DCIS agent agreed. For my part, however, this encounter was officially too much. To whatever extent their real intention was to give me a taste of being in no-man's land between the warring parties, it worked in spades and then some.

From the beginning of this saga, my health had already been in decline, which only accelerated in the following months, weeks, and days. On the heels of this meeting, I began to feel the pressure of the situation with major anxiety and chest pains the next day. I went into the emergency room where I was greeted by a physician who knew me and my medical history well. I told her she was not going to believe me, but that I had been an undercover federal informant for the last year and it was really taking its toll. While I could not share any details, I told her about the meeting the day before and my unavoidable feeling that I just could not go back into that hostile environment. I just could not.

It was probably a disappointment for the minions at Northrop that I did not die, that it turned out to be no more than an extreme and overwhelming anxiety and panic attack. It no doubt also served their interests (and possibly even their real intentions) in requesting the confrontation: The attending physician determined that it would not be safe for me to return to work in such a hostile environment and thus wrote a note supporting temporary but immediate medical leave. As a result, that meeting was my last official active working day with Northrop and an end to my undercover work.

It was, however, just the beginning of the battles and abuse to last many more years.

Because Agent Zott, the DCIS, and the FBI thought they had enough to move forward with criminal prosecution, the criminal side of the Department of Justice (DoJ) became involved in requesting the impaneling of a Grand Jury. Part of the motivation for initiating quick action was to get court orders prohibiting Northrop from distorting or destroying any more key documents or records, paper or computer or otherwise. This is not to say that Northrop would actually stop altering or destroying such documents or records, but they were under court orders and thus accountable should they be proved to have disregarded them. Their gamble was whether they would get caught or not.

While the criminal side of the case had been put into motion, the civil side also moved forward with the preparation and filing of a qui tam suit. We met to go over what documents I had managed to turn over to federal investigators, along with what Rex and the two other co-claimants had to offer as evidence. It was already evident that the two other co-claimants had little more than vague allegations without substantive evidence or details, but we were all four brought together as co-claimants.

On August 10, 1989, Ron formally filed the qui tam lawsuit 89C6111 under seal for initial judicial review and to see if the DoJ would choose to become involved in a civil proceeding.

Until the court ruled on the merits and/or the DoJ came to its decision, the qui tam filing was under seal and thus its content and filing were still secret from Northrop and anyone else. Unfortunately, it would also go into a kind of limbo while the criminal proceedings were under way. The Grand Jury was now impaneled and secretly reviewing and deliberating the evidence, so all civil investigations, actions, and collection of information through depositions, subpoena, etc. came to a complete halt until the Grand Jury concluded its investigations, completed their reviews, and came out from under seal. The civil suit would then be free to move forward for court review and approval, and for the DoJ to decide whether to get involved or not. Once the DoJ made a decision yea or nay, the filing would come out from under seal. The existence of the case would become public. At best, Northrop would be able to contest and counter and attempt to get the case dismissed. At worst, they would undermine it as much as possible. They did not quite get a dismissal, but they proved both determined and adept at undermining and decimating the case.

Once either of these parallel efforts went into motion, let alone the fact they were both secret and under seal, I was relieved in some ways and almost completely helpless in whole new ways.

As an undercover informant, some aspects of my life and risks were in my own hands. Now, everything to do with the case and the impact it would make on my life and my family's lives was in the hands of others. Worse, it was almost completely secretly in the hands of others

The only thing in relation to the criminal and civil cases that gave me any grounding came in the form of an extremely unusual request from Agent Zott. A month or two after those involved in presenting the case to the Grand Jury finally began to receive materials from Northrop, he called me at home to ask if I could come into the Arlington Heights office of the FBI to assist the DCIS, Defense Contract Audit Agency (DCAA), and the supervising FBI agents to review and make sense of the materials Northrop had provided. He also asked me if I could bring the documents I had removed from Northrop.

They specifically wanted help wading through the mountains of largely irrelevant data Northrop had sent in an attempt to bury them under an avalanche of useless information. They also wanted to know if what they had subpoenaed from Northrop would match up with the documents I had removed, and to what extent records had been modified or "lost." I let them know I no longer had any of those documents in my possession and had, in fact, made a point of turning them over to Ron. I announced that fact over what I assumed to be a tapped phone. I did not want the documents in my house as I did not want to give Northrop any reason to want to look there. Agent Zott asked if I could contact Ron, arrange to acquire the documents, and bring them with me to the Arlington Heights FBI headquarters. I said I would.

Ron was ecstatic over the news that I would be helping review the documents being prepared for the Grand Jury. It was the closest thing he and his colleagues would have to get a peek at the case's focus and workings in the ongoing criminal investigation. He wanted to know if I could come into his office in Chicago to pick the materials up. I said no, so one of his colleagues, Todd Thomas, an attorney whose law firm had begun working in tandem with Ron's office, called to tell me he would drop the documents off at my house the day before my meeting with the federal agents.

When Todd arrived, we chatted a bit about the importance of my being involved and somewhat debriefed him on the overall status of things. This was a relationship that would carry over later as aspects of the case moved forward. He would come to my house, sometimes bringing dinner, to debrief me and, I think, reassure me somewhat. Occasionally, these chats would be while fishing close to my home, sometimes right across the street.

As it turned out, my desire to keep the documents out of my house had been both wise and sound. That very night, after they had been delivered back into my possession, someone broke into my house while my family and I slept to find and, I assume, photograph what I had. Whatever disturbed my sleep at four a.m., I will never know. I rose to discover the front door propped open and the screen door locked open. When I entered the living room area where the documents had been left to sit overnight, I found a stack of them on the television, half of them already turned over and lying face down and the table lamp turned on. Upon hearing me stirring, the burglar did not get through the remainder, which still sat in the half-finished stack face up.

I called Agent Zott to let him know what had happened and he let me know that what I had just encountered was definitely the work of a pro. He had known what he was after and had, first and foremost, assured his path of escape before he set about his work. Agent Zott's next line sent ice through my veins. The pro had set up his exit in a way so as not to hurt anyone and, preferably, to get in and out without anyone knowing they had ever been there.

It would not be the first time the issue of witness protection would come up, but for Agent Zott, it was the first time it was taken seriously. He was sympathetic and supportive in a way that made me think this may have been a bit of a shifting point for him. He definitely wanted me to be on guard and to understand that when it came to some of the players involved, they would stoop to anything and stop at nothing. Later, he would share with me that this was the first time he really had more than vague fears for my physical safety. It would, however, be a number of years later, during the building of testimonies to really put some heat on Northrop, that someone would actually try to kill me to make a point. When that failed, then they may or may not have tried for my kids.

In giving the briefest consideration to witness protection, I had to decline the notion out of hand unless it became inescapable. Witness protection meant we would all be living a lie and living our lives on the run. The period of working undercover had provided its own reminders of the personal pain and costs of living a lie, and having to present yourself in ways that are incongruent with who you are, hiding yourself at every turn. Too, the progress we had made in our lives, the progress I had made in my recovery, was very much tied to working a program of honesty. I knew in my heart of hearts that we had to see this thing through.

At the moment, though, I could not have been more horrified. I had to come to terms with the fact that someone had been inside my home while my wife and our children and I slept. They could have done anything to us. They could have killed us. We would have become just another statistic to be recorded as a random act of violence. By all indications, the intruder was professional enough to have done anything to my family and me without anyone even waking up.

This was one of the most devastating moments of my life and the start of real fear. In spite of the fact that I could not rationally or factually come up with anything I did wrong, or even that I could have done differently, all I could do as I sat there in the dark trying to take it all in was ask myself: *What have I done?*

9
NOBLE EFFORTS—RAPID DECLINE

Over the next couple of months, I spent six or more days helping FBI Agent Kevin Deery and the DCAA's Dan Wish try to dig their way through a predictably useless and overwhelming landslide of documents. Almost none of the materials provided had anything whatsoever to do with what had been subpoenaed. In fact, Northrop would use this ploy of overwhelm-and-bury for many years to come.

This brings up what was characteristic of this case and almost all cases like it. While it may be useful to come across information that alerted us to Northrop's seeming misdeeds and malfeasance, what mattered was what could be brought into court and placed into the official record. In all the years that followed and to the very end, Agent Zott told me that they never did receive copies of some of the most key documents and records requested, with frequent excuses that ultimately would come back to haunt them.[7] During this initial period, in the aftershock of being caught and cast out of the lion's den, I felt I was of some genuinely crucial and beneficial help to the AUSA and the agents involved. I could at least partially put my hands on something concrete for what was to happen next.

This period of time was decidedly short, however. Once the evidence began to go to the Grand Jury, all those proceedings would be secret—

---

7 E.g., that they could not provide the requested material because they could not find it or because it had been "accidentally" erased or destroyed by parties unknown.

much like the interim periods to come. The case would remain under seal for a time after the Grand Jury ended its deliberations, while the federal government considered further criminal investigations and whether they would issue criminal indictments related to the concurrent qui tam suit.

This secrecy and suspension of all judicial action on the civil side would appear again much later, as the federal government issued a brief stay on the civil case to resume renewed criminal investigations. The key issues now were that, while Agent Zott and other federal agents could proceed in presenting the criminal case to the Grand Jury, my civil legal team and I were frozen out and left on the sidelines. As it turned out, this was as much a blessing as a curse. It freed my focus to deal with the extended financial emergency just beginning.

It might be difficult for others to understand how disorienting and debilitating it is for anyone who has been cast in the intense and dangerous role of undercover informant to shift so abruptly from the activities in which they are both a player and at-risk target to such a sudden and powerless limbo. I was cut off from any information on the content and progress of the case while it was under secret criminal review. However, the almost unimaginable speed of my family's financial decline was as bad as or worse than any of our fears of what would happen when the time of my departure from Northrop finally arrived. The depletion of what meager resources we had, and the decline in both physical well-being and emotional stability was swift and relentless. It took everything I could imagine in terms of effort just to keep from completely going under.

It is a surprising thing in life just how often you can discover and then rediscover that point at which you think you have done all you can, endured all that is possible, and used up all you have to give—then to find you are only getting started. You are challenged to come up with ever so much more strength and endurance than you ever imagined you could. It is worse when all your loved ones must also be challenged. In the case of my life and my family's, it was all that and more. While the next few years would be defined by the tenacious efforts of my allies who sought to hold Northrop accountable (in part by trying to decipher its byzantine accounting systems), my family and I increasingly struggled to put bread on the table and one foot in front of the other. It became a battle for the most basic necessities of survival. We went from proudly living in a nice home, albeit rented, to becoming homeless and having to stay in a homeless shelter.

In some ways, the secret Grand Jury proceedings protected Northrop from public scrutiny, which served its purposes. It benefited from the postponement of civil discovery into the allegations by giving them time. Even with the presumed wall of secrecy between it and the Grand Jury, Northrop was still able to flip undercover informant Petra Schiller, the central data entry person through whose hands most of the alleged data-related crimes had passed. She was the government's (and our) closest thing to an unequivocal smoking gun who, after being granted immunity, showed up with a Northrop-provided attorney to recant her allegations. She claimed the signed-and-sworn statements she had provided to Agent Zott had all been a mistake, and that he had misunderstood what she had told him.

Some of Northrop's sins we alleged initially were tied to intentional misrepresentations to the government for the purposes of inflated billings and manipulation to that end.

But in light of Schiller's about-face, there was also the potential claim that anything related to Rex Robinson's allegations was top secret[8] and not to be divulged for issues of national security purposes and could not be adequately defended by Northrop in open court.

Examples on Rex's portion of the allegations included the issue of falsifying timecards to allocate human resource hours to contracts that still had funds when other projects had used theirs up. A related item that would loom large throughout the case was Northrop's certification that the development of the device that would make the Stealth Bomber invisible to radar was complete and ready for production. Rex alleged that Northrop represented it was ready for Critical Design Review when it was not. Because of this certification, the Air Force allocated and released $254,000,863 in funds for production of an item that did not yet actually work. Two years later, after paying out these funds, the Air Force canceled the production contract because the device did not work.

We also alleged a different kind of fraud. In preparation for a walk-

---

8 At the time, no one at Northrop or the US government would admit the Stealth Bomber project existed.

through with Northrop engineers and officials and government auditors, Northrop adjusted its accounting of the physical inventory they knew the government wanted to look at. They adjusted the data system to match it so the data and tracking systems themselves looked accurate for the walk-through.

It was this dance around a faulty system that was most pervasive and would eventually dominate the focus of our case. At the moment, however, we were as unable to see through the smoke and mirrors as the government had been when initially looking at the reliability of Northrop's materials and accounting tracking systems.

With these and other stalling or distraction tactics, Northrop could outwait each of the successive grand juries that had to be impaneled anew and get a peek inside the "black box" by virtue of what was subpoenaed and whom the Grand Jury chose to depose. Curiously, the Grand Jury never called for questioning me or any of us who had filed the qui tam suit and/or provided the initial basis and my considerable documentation for the case. We were left on the sidelines, isolated and impotent in relation to the criminal case, and suspended in limbo and kept blind to the civil case until the Grand Jury had made its determinations to indict or not. As for myself and my family, we rode out what little remaining salary and brief disability I was able to get. We watched much of what few savings and resources we had drain all too rapidly while I tried to qualify for disability.

For the next three years, my family and I would have nothing but increasing poverty, declining health, and unbelievable strains and abuses heaped upon us. At the time, we had no idea how long the initial leg of the journey or nightmare of a court battle would last. While ignorance of how long and devastating the case would become was anything but bliss, full knowledge would have been unbearable. What was already clear, though, was that life as we had ever known it would never be the same. We had no expectation that I would be able to find another job like the one I had just lost. My lack of advanced degrees and credentials now stood glaringly in my way. It did not matter that I had envisioned and created something as innovative as the tracking systems I put into place at Northrop. Without Northrop as a positive and validating reference, we already knew it was unlikely I would be able to find another job with the same income.

I was now tainted with the label few seek and fewer still want:

WHISTLEBLOWER

I was a pariah.

I had not set out to be one. I never took on the identity of one. I was just a working stiff who found himself in a very bad situation that I had to find my way through—deemed by the government as eligible for certain protections *as* a whistleblower under existing legislation, which labeled me. I was equally damned by Northrop as an enemy, a threat, and a traitor. It is one of the many ironies of whistleblowers who often risk and generally lose everything for God, country, and the protection of the public that two of those three will turn on them and view them with mistrust and even malice. Throw in the company they may have been trying to help or save turning on them and you have the picture.

The only way I had to claim any kind of a new or renewed life was to make it through this case with an outcome that validated both my abilities and intentions. In trying to do what was right and required by the government, I was seen now as a threat and unfit for almost any kind of employment other than the most demeaning and menial types of work. What I did not expect was how unknown entities could make even the most unskilled and undesirable employment unattainable, or how they could possibly extend the inability to find a job to relatives.

After leaving Northrop and during the three years in which the case stayed in the Grand Jury, our lives went from the promise of stable middle-class life and a shot at the American Dream to a downward spiral that could fill a book all on its own. One of the worst moments my family and I had to endure was when we had to move into a homeless shelter. The stink of human feces and urine filled the hallways, and shortly after our arrival, someone wrote on one of the entry walls: *Six arrived, 5 will die.*

Fortunately for my family and me, Mary reminded me that what was happening to us now, and how we handled it, could benefit our children.

You see, who I was now was significantly influenced by my childhood (and hers too for that matter). We were forced to continuing the challenges and circumstances of my personal life saga. For the next twenty-five years, my greater life journey would color and shape much of how we successfully (or, at times, less successfully) dealt with specific incidents. It would be integral to surviving the case's seventeen-and-a-half-year first round up to its settlement with Northrop. It would be challenged by another five years of frivolous lawsuits against us by two of the initial co-claimants who dropped out of the case. Mixed in was some additional craziness, and in some instances, equally false and frivolous saber-rattling by others as I tried to work with several different whistleblowers as individuals and groups.

The importance of this will become clear to the reader fairly quickly, just as I believe and truly hope it brings home, once again, that this is not just a procedural or mechanical story about whistleblowers and whistle-blowing. It is a story about real people and real families trying to find their way through real life with the burden of becoming and being labeled a whistleblower—which is to say it is a more accurate perspective and true understanding of whistleblowers and whistleblowing.

The larger arc is only now coming to fruition as I come to terms with the damaged and, in some ways, stolen relationships with my recently deceased or terminally ill siblings. It is in the grander context of personally working out a larger history in which I continue to find a way forward with my family that I had so desperately wanted to protect from the instabilities of my own youth. My "children," of course, who are now in their late twenties and early to mid-thirties, were robbed of much of their own childhoods.

◆

I knew very little of my own father, and my mother seemed to be in a world of her own that, given my father's absence, left my siblings and me quasi-abandoned and on multiple occasions, cast away like unwanted baggage. Between the absence of sane and sound parenting when my siblings and I were together, and our experiences after we were split up and sent away, we learned little of what solid family life could look like, even as we each became determined survivors and damaged goods. We were farmed out to stay with relatives or friends or our parents, who did not like or want us. With greater frequency and harm, we were sent off to foster care and orphanages to fend for ourselves. Our growth was impaired, we accumulated the wounds that went with it and our own views of a world in which we had no welcoming home or place. We were forced to find our way through our challenges and choices without the requisite maps or tools afforded to those in stable homes. We were pushed back to divine and define our own personal compasses as we overcame or failed to confront our personal demons.

As for my father, he was as remote as he wished he were connected and caring. The massive scars that marked one leg and crisscrossed his shoulder from injuries incurred in the war were exceeded only by those you could not see. When he was at home, he was greatly subdued, even absent. While I do not remember the progression of his alcoholism or of anyone or anything specifically identifying it as such, it was very much tied to his extended stays in mental hospitals. This was the primary place, other than jail or the morgue, alcoholics found themselves in the early sixties. I loved him no matter what and he was at least physically present some of the time. To his credit, he was never abusive to me or my siblings in my presence. My mother, on the other hand, was probably never cut out to be a mother, or a wife for that matter, especially to someone like my father who was so subdued and simple.

My mother, who had been rejected and abandoned by her own family of origin (and was still treated as partial outcast) was drawn to the excitement and glamour of the night life and the life of a performer. To this day, I remember the contrasts of the fancy cars sent by mobsters to take her to clubs where she partied and performed into the wee hours, while my father sat in the dark with just the glow from his cigarette and the empty quarts of beer sitting by the arm of the couch as he waited for her to come home. She was as devastatingly inattentive when present as she was unintentionally cruel in her disdain for her circumstances and the burden of having a family. Interestingly, her own battles for a sense of place, value, and expression that came from her childhood set forth ripples of family dysfunction that not only shaped my childhood and early life, but in their continued reverberations and aftermath continued to impact and shape those of my own children. But as bad as this was at home, it was my journey and the journeys of my siblings into the world as children cast aside that would inflict the greatest direct injuries and leave the most blatant and long-lasting scars.

Several things came into play that affected my own addictions and demons, and then, later, my own fears and sense of failure with my own family. It came in part directly from my parents' respective absences to the fact they were never fully present when we were all together. They came into play even more so in the repeated and differing ways we were shunned and farmed out to relatives who wanted no part of us, and to orphanages and foster care more defined by abuse than by care. It was in these latter circumstances in which being rejected, abandoned, and, in several cases, tortured and sexually abused that made their worst and most lasting marks. Strangely, I felt my own siren's call in that direction, and became a singer in an equally unstable life so many years later. It was my father's absence and alcoholism I was to inherit, contribute to, and be forced to play out with my own children, who, I swore, would never experience the same.

As awful as much of this was and as much as it had to do with the course of my story, it still comes within the bounds of what many would just consider a bad luck of the draw: the parents my siblings and I wound up with, the kinds of hardships shared with many we just call life. Such dysfunction also creates a lack of perspective and the skills to create something different or better. The greatest injuries, needs and scars were created by the experiences of being sent off to orphanages and foster care. It was in these situations we were most terrified and alone. It was in these situations that we were most directly threatened and overtly abused by other children. And in our world, in which there were intermittent parents who only created more need for love and support when present, left us to inadequate, cruel, and abusive care of other adults. We were berated and abused by those charged with our care. We were beaten and, in my case, sexually abused in more than one circumstance. We were, to put it simply, cast off into worlds that were full of danger and harm.

My oldest brother, who, as a child and adult, showed up for me in important ways, is now heartbreakingly terminally ill. He had recently recounted the experience we had at the Ulrich Children's Home on California Avenue in Chicago, Illinois. When we arrived at the orphanage that first dark night, I can still remember the Charlie McCarthy dolls sitting on the night tables by the beds. We felt in particular danger, and our peers made sure we feared for our safety, if not our lives. That first night after the adults left us, both my brother, Mike, and I (being the younger) were stripped naked, beaten, and chased around the ward by the other children. Any adults on the premises responsible for our safety and emotional well-being were even more absent than our own parents had ever been at their worst. Another time, after several days during which my oldest brother could not find our middle brother and me, he discovered us hanging naked by our wrists in one of the bathroom stalls, beaten, in physical pain, and suffering great humiliation. In a heart that deserved to ensure its own survival by shutting down, his was broken by my childish innocent look that said, *Why? How can this be?*

Fortunately, my sister escaped some of this, as she was more acceptable to our grandparents and was taken in by relatives who found her more tolerable and perhaps more salvageable than us boys. What matters most at this point of the story, my family and my still-unfolding life is threefold:

First, in a life with an excess of emotional needs and dearth of resources and family ties, we were all left, to varying degrees, without a roadmap to adulthood or taught any skills for navigating, let alone creating it. In my own case, I was also left with an acute sense of being unloved and unlovable, inadequate and undeserving, and constantly undervalued, minimized, and dismissed. What turned out to be the most telling was we were all also called upon to find in ourselves whatever it was we continued to look for in the world and in life, whether as something to cling to in desperation, or in an act of truly blessed faith and grace.

No matter how much life battered me around, how inadequately I engaged it, or how simply unfair things seemed to be, there was a part of me that held to an innate sense that it *could* be better. What persisted for me was not so much bracing against and accepting the follies, foibles, and evils people are capable of inflicting on themselves and others (accidentally or intentionally). What always persisted was a hunger to believe that we could and should do *better*. That certain things in the world seemed wrong because they were wrong. That at some point and in some way, *better* was not only within our comprehension, it was within our grasp.

This will all have resonance for the continuation of this story, not the least of which has to do with getting through it at all. It will have a great deal to do with the conclusions I've drawn, and what I made of this journey and the unfolding future. What is most relevant here are the ways this shaped my own personal demons, tools, and compass in life, along with just how much family—and taking care of mine—mattered to me, especially in the wake of the harm from my addictive spiral.

What might be most interesting for many readers is the fact that as ill-prepared as I was for all that was to come, it was in the midst of this twenty-year maelstrom that I did my best to suit up, but gradually found the way to grow up. I overcame my alcoholism and drug addiction, and set out to make things right. It should bring home how much I wanted this job at Northrop to work and how devastating it was that it did not. I hope it brings home the importance of faith, love, and tenacity in getting through the worst of the worst. Had it not been for my family, there are so many ways I could have remained lost in life. Without their love and need to be able to rely on me, and Mary helping me to appreciate that it wasn't and still is not all about me, to build a bridge and get over it, as she would say. I am certain there are many times I would not have been able to find my way in life, let alone get through the challenges that befell us in our battle with the corporation whose own interest had little to do with ours, other than crushing and eliminating us where they were in conflict.

What matters most to me both in the present and in retrospect, and bears on understanding virtually everything in the remainder of this story, I hope the reader grasps just how desperately my wife and I sought to provide for and protect our family. The job at Northrop provided a seemingly unique promise of hope for and access to the so-called American Dream.

Its horrifying transformation into the nightmare it became put everything we cared about at risk. What I think should matter to most readers is just how much that essentially primary and primal drive to protect and provide for our family gave order to our world in which there was so little, and guided us so often to not only keep going, but do so in ways that inherently got things right. Put another way, Northrop ultimately lost its case because, in spite of their worst sins against us, I did not lose my family. Put in the simplest of terms, my family are the real heroes to me and my enduring inspiration for this story.

♦

Returning now to the present, two things were abundantly clear. Even if I had had the chance to go back and work at Northrop for a bit longer, there was absolutely no way I could have begun to think about it without a repeat of what had felt like a heart attack. We did not have the monetary resources for surviving for more than a few days, let alone weeks.

Mary and I had begun digging our way out of debt up to the point I was enlisted as an undercover informant. And, as stressful as it was and already damaging to my family, we continued making financial progress in the final eighteen months of active employ while I functioned as an informant. We continued to catch up with prior debts and began to get a little ahead even as the clock ticked down. When I went on leave and then disability, all Northrop-related income stopped.

The first jolt was the shocking discovery that there was a month-and-a-half waiting period for short term disability to kick in. The second jolt was watching what little savings we had and my 401(k) evaporate almost overnight while we waited. The third jolt was having to sell my beloved twelve-string guitar just to keep the electricity on. For me, at the time, that was the most traumatic. It was not just a reminder that we had no more material possessions to sell, even to be able to see in the dark or stay warm in the cold, it was the stripping away of links to my better-remembered past of singing to my children.

In that case, with back to wall, nothing else to sell, and no way to borrow, I told Mary the guitar was just a thing and we couldn't eat it. So I asked a friend who had expressed an interest in the guitar if he would like to buy it now. Perhaps only other musicians can fully appreciate the connection to such an instrument. It was also a reminder of my crazier days when I was still performing, even though I was drinking what income I did manage to earn from it or putting it up my nose until I had hit bottom. The heartbreak at that moment was the fact that in both the best and worst of times, I would pick up that guitar, often at the request of my children, and simply sing. I would sing for and to them as they sat at my feet and at their ease in whatever room we were in. The friend who bought the guitar from me so we could get the electricity turned back on generously paid more than twice what I asked for. To this day, I have not been able to bring myself to seriously entertain buying it back, so traumatic was that moment and the sense of loss.

It is in retrospect that the poignancy of this moment comes into a revised perspective for me. It turns out that the exit of that instrument and the joy that was associated with it broke the hearts of my children. It was not until the writing of this book that I discovered that my oldest daughter, who watched that night, broken-hearted at her own loss, felt she saw something in me break at that very moment and she did not know how to reach or repair it for me. As with so many lessons in the writing of this book, I was once again reminded that children see so much more than we think they do and that however much we put on a good face, they are just as marked as we are by those moments in which they see us harmed or injured in ways they cannot fix or help. It is a reminder of the ways those of us in similar situations find ourselves feeling disgraced and diminished in ways that cut into our very souls. At this time in the history of our country, this kind of experience is not remotely limited to those who find themselves in the punished and persecuted role of whistleblower, although it is very much a widespread consequence of it.

During our initial three-year period of rapid financial decline, it was probably both a curse and a blessing that giving any real attention to the case against Northrop was completely out of my hands, and that the qui tam case was in complete limbo. It meant that the one thing that mattered most to me, taking care of my family, now had my full, if seriously crippled, attention. It is interesting to me, looking back, that it did not occur to me to be angry with Northrop for what I saw as its sins, or dumbfounded that it could turn out the way it did. My heartfelt concern was for how to keep my family fed, clothed, and sheltered, all three of which were a growing challenge.

In terms of acquiring work to pay for anything once the disability payments ran out well ahead of the disability, it ranged from cleaning filthy toilets at a Moose Lodge tavern for less than minimum wage to buy milk and bread, to working for $20.00 a week at a gas station, where an accident left me doused in gasoline. This brought me a spark away from a literal burning hell to match the existential one we were in. Ultimately, my wife and I were working up to seven jobs at a time just to keep ends from getting farther apart, let alone getting them to meet our needs.

It took its toll in many ways. My children, who never once went hungry or were ever made to feel like a burden to us, were nonetheless embarrassed (as would be expected) by the obvious poverty they neither invited nor could control. They had to attend school in worn and patched clothing. They also did not have the money other kids did to participate in school activities and young life others take for granted.

This was all the more bitter to me because it was exactly this kind of poverty and the feeling of being outcast, less than others, that I had so profoundly wanted to spare them.

The direct and indirect human costs of this case knew no bounds. My wife, unbeknownst to me, took out a number of low-cost life insurance policies (a practice that lasted for years) as they came across our threshold, with double accidental death coverage. She was certain if I were taken out, it would be made to look like an accident. Hers was a troublesome dilemma, as the prospect of how she would take care of our family if I were completely disabled or gone was her ever-present unspoken worry. The immediate costs to my wife and me in not being able to provide more with no view of things getting better cannot be measured. It was exhausting to us both. Having to live with the fact that the pending case hanging over our heads meant that (as I found out later) when I came home from whatever work I was doing, my two daughters felt they had to make sure that all window shades were drawn and that I was not positioned for a clear gun shot through any window. Now you have a picture of our life.

I am certain we each had our private moments of despair, or events and circumstances that had great impact at the time, even if they were to be replaced at some later point by something still more embarrassing, painful, or just plain poignant. The most striking collective event that still stands out was when we could no longer hold onto our rented house even with government subsidy, had to put all our belongings in a friend's pole barn, and move into the homeless shelter whose tactile sensations I cannot forget. The stench of human feces and urine in the hallways and under the stairs was revolting enough. The message "Six arrived, 5 will die" scrawled in the entryway was its own special violation. It was a reminder that faceless danger and ill intentions were lurking with immeasurable and incomprehensible malice at every turn. It stood as an all-consuming assault on the heart and the senses, and seemed to have neither escape nor end. The most poignant irony occurred when we were finally able to qualify for and find subsidized housing to break free and escape. With hopes of getting our footing back, we were happy, at least for a while.

It was when we thought we were free of the homeless shelter that one specific moment stands out. It happened to my wife, and I was helpless to take her pain and loss away. When it came time to leave the horror of the shelter and move our meager things to our modest new home, a number of our friends had gone to the barn where it was all stored, packed it up, and delivered it. It was then we discovered that what belongings we still owned, furniture and things associated with making or having a home, were covered in mold, mildew, and shocking quantities of bird droppings.

They had been destroyed.

It was not that our friends had not meant well, or that efforts had not been made to keep things covered and safe. It was just one more reminder to us how vulnerable we were at this point. It was finally too much for my Mary, who sank to the steps of what was to have been our home and began to cry. All I could do was sit down with her. I had no magic words or moves to make it better, so I held her. It was one of the only times in memory that this bastion in my life collapsed in complete hopelessness and momentary defeat. Everything had been taken from us and there was no getting a home or our footing again. It seemed it would never end.

And this was just the first few years into the battle with Northrop that would define our lives for another decade and a half, then another half decade for residual cases until we could fully put all this behind us and move on with life. Even now, as I look back on these events and dark days, I can relive the moments as if they were yesterday.

All that said, it would be a crime not to add the ironic and paradoxical gifts and joy that came with it. Toward the end of this three-year period, I began the first and lowest level of employment with the newspapers that would later provide a better, though all-consuming employment. I had obtained work putting together thousands of Sunday papers at one cent per section. In ways only the poor can appreciate, my children would rally and we would stand together doing them, each of my children getting a penny per paper, which could net them several dollars. Only those in our circumstances can fully appreciate even this small gesture, to teach responsibility and a work ethic in extreme poverty. The affirmation of being able to do anything for my children at all that gave them a sense of contribution, control, and at least a few dollars to call their own was significant. No one who has not been in a similar situation (and certainly not most whistleblowers, who, by and large, lose their families in short order) can appreciate the closeness that came with the urgent need to work together. Even the isolation and marginalization my children felt at school and with other kids contributed to our bonding together, in some ways profoundly.

This very tenacity would eventually carry us through this case and a successful conclusion, but it took even more of my time away from the family. Once I took on the actual distribution of the newspapers, it wore me down with very little sleep for years. The wear and tear, the fatigue, made me more absent than I knew, even when I was home grabbing sleep when and where I could. But even then, there was some closeness with my children, who loved to come along to work with me just to be together and feel they had some power to be supportive and contribute.

What was perhaps most gratifying in the writing of this book was the discovery that all of my children grasped and appreciated just how hard their mother and I worked to provide for them, no matter how far short we fell, and against the ever-present backdrop of the case itself. My youngest daughter tells me now she was always looking under my car before I left for work each night to check for bombs, and Mary tells me she used to start the car with the door open because she hoped she would be blown clear if a bomb went off.

Finally, the federal Grand Jury investigation that had been convened several years earlier (and renewed once) was over. Finally, an end had come to its investigations and deliberations over whether or not they would issue any indictments to proceed with criminal prosecutions of Northrop and/or any of its employees. The unhappy conclusion was that criminal prosecutions were not going to be pursued.

Part of the reason is that for criminal prosecution, issues have to be proved beyond a shadow of a doubt and if nothing else, Northrop had been very adept at hiding things in the shadows and assuring that little if anything was ever clear. It would be some years before their maneuvers would come back to bite them, but for now, this meant the case was no longer under seal for criminal proceedings. The languishing qui tam suit that had been filed several years earlier could possibly go back into motion.

Since the issue of whether or not there were any crimes committed had already been resolved by the Grand Jury, all the DoJ needed to consider now was whether or not they would join in our civil case. Until then, it would remain on hold and under seal. Should the DoJ later decide to reconsider or renew pursuit of criminal investigations, as later turned out to be the case, the civil lawsuit would go back into limbo, and no formal action would be taken.

However, at this point the qui tam suit was taken out from under seal to go to the court for evaluation of merit, thus it was no longer secret. Northrop was served with a copy of the complaint and was then free to get in that game with its own filings, motions to dismiss, and depositions. It was free to launch its defense with our subsequent accusations of abuse.

Put another way, I was once again involved, so I became a potential danger. I also became the target of standard steps normally launched against any "problem" employees and most especially "whistleblowers."[9] Many of these had already been used in the first days of the discovery of my status as an informant. First, isolate. Then, intimidate. To the extent perceived necessary or expedient, undermine and discredit. If necessary or expedient, do everything possible to make the problem employee or whistleblower appear to be crazy or at least mentally unstable. To that effect, make certain they cannot make a living of any kind unless they yield, and in all likelihood, not even then.

What was not included in variations of the official government or corporate playbook, but existed all too often in reality: kill them.

Thus far, the only element of the game that had not been thrown at me was the latter, but as it turned out, the game was still young. As for the others, they were about to be subjected to a level of menace I only imagined in my worst dreams. But first we needed to deal with the DoJ to see if they were going to be on our team or not.

---

9 As laid out in a formal proposal under the Nixon administration and used as standard procedure since then in dealing with all persons of ethics and/or conscience.

Either way, short of renewing criminal proceedings, the qui tam could go forward to get the blessing of the federal court. The difference between having the US Department of Justice on board or not made all the difference in resources and clout. The benefit of it being pursued not only *on behalf of* the government, but with the authority, power, and support *of* the government was paramount to us. The case was still not only under seal, but its very existence was secret, and Northrop was presumably in the dark.

That said, if Northrop *did* know it was in motion, they would have hoped we would have to go this particular route alone. In the short term, Northrop got their wish, but how it came about was not only questionable but a bit of a discouraging surprise.

10

OF DEPOSITIONS, DISPOSITIONS, & BOULDERS UP THE HILL

It is now the fall of 1992, some three years since the investigations being conducted by the federal government were originally submitted to the Grand Jury. Gordon Jones, "Director of Commercial Litigation Fraud" of the DoJ contacted my attorney, Ron Futterman, with a request to meet with and interview the four litigants ("relators") listed in the qui tam action before he would consider recommending any intervention in the case by the government. Aside from wanting to review the case on its merits as submitted, it was reasonable that he would also want to meet those he would be treating as co-relators if the government opted to join the case.

These cases tend to be long and wearisome to all parties and this one was already several years old, having sat idle while possible criminal charges were under review by the Grand Jury. Gordon Jones might also have wanted to know to what extent we would be reliable partners in terms of credibility, integrity, and ability to endure. He might have just wanted to look us in the eyes. Whatever his intentions or concerns were, a meeting was set up at Ron's offices to interview me, Rex Robinson, and the other two relators, who would eventually be removed from the case and voluntarily dismissed with prejudice.

This was an action taken collectively by the attorneys, the government, Northrop, and those two relators without any consultation or communication with either Rex or me until several months, after it was a *fait accompli*. These two were deemed out of the picture and barred forever from re-entry or re-filing any of their allegations. And we, Rex and I, were barred by law from taking up even any portion of their actions or claims. They were to have nothing to do with the case at all.

They were gone . . . or so I thought. But I digress. Let us get back to the meeting with Mr. Jones.

This meeting was a very big deal on many levels. If we were to proceed with any hope of sustained effort, let alone success, it needed to go well and we needed to put on our best face and case. Rex and I did not, in our wildest dreams or worst fears, anticipate where or how badly it would go south or how fast it would get there.

The simple practicalities of the case meant we needed the involvement of the DoJ as much more than an observer. We could still proceed on our own with the qui tam suit even if Jones opted not to join the case (pending the court's and DoJ's approval). But to do so meant going up against a giant corporation with almost limitless assets with a team that did not have a fraction of its resources or clout. As it was, Ron's office had already involved other law firms in the case to help share the financial burden and risks and, depending on how this meeting went, would have to make some hard choices about whether or not it was even financially feasible to continue, even with the best-case scenario. Ron and his colleagues were looking at facing off with a genuine Goliath that, we would later learn, may have intimidated the DoJ into inaction this first time around.

Historically speaking, there is no second time around. Not ever. But that is for later, and came well after our discovery that this meeting, the one we believed would greatly influence our fate, may not have been what it appeared to be anyway.

Jones arrived for the scheduled meeting accompanied by James E. Bradburn, Special Agent of the US Air Force Office of Special Investigations (USAF/OSI). It was not a surprise to me that the Air Force had anyone in attendance as, being the principal government entity contracting for research and development with Northrop, it had an obvious interest in the case. This was perhaps even more pertinent because of Rex's involvement with the Stealth Bomber, the project that no one admitted existed.

I had, in fact, already met with Bradburn and his colleague, Daniel G. Smith, also a Special Agent of the USAF/OSI a month or two earlier at their request. It was at Ron's office, separate from the other participants in the case, to review what I had allegedly discovered as an informant for the DCIS.

For our part in the current meeting, in attendance were Ron Futterman himself, Aram Hartunian, Rex Robinson, the two other relators, and I. All seemed to be going reasonably well, or as well as one can hope, until they were nearing the end of interviewing one of the two who eventually left the case.

Out of nowhere—and I mean absolutely nowhere—one of the other relators leaned forward and asked the interviewers if they had heard of SETI (Search for Extraterrestrial Intelligence of the SETI Institute). There was nothing in the questioning that could have prompted the question and absolutely no context for it. When our interviewers responded with little more than perplexed looks, he went on to add that he believed there was other intelligent life in the universe and that it was arrogant on our part as humans to believe we were alone in the universe.

We who were there to be interviewed with the future of the case very much at stake, could do little more than freeze in horror and disbelief. Jones and Bradburn stared blankly, looked at each other, perhaps exchanging an already agreed-upon cue, and started collecting their things. Without a word they picked up their papers and tapped them together to arrange them neatly before packing up their brief cases. They had heard enough. The interviews were over, as were our hopes of being seen as credible witnesses and reliable co-relators by the DoJ.

As I can remember, none of us said a word, but the look on Ron's and Aram's faces said all that needed to be said. This was a pivotal moment in gauging their ability to bring this case to a successful outcome, and the key resources and allies they needed were leaving the room. It was not so much seeing an expression of anger or disbelief as seeing the expression of someone who had just seen hope slip through his fingers, and the weight of that descending on him. They left the room without a word or mention of what we would do next.

The two relators left together, seemingly oblivious to what had just occurred. Rex and I left together to return home on the train. I finally asked

Rex if he had seen the look on our government interviewers' faces, then Ron's and Aram's. He nodded yes and muttered something along the lines of just how bad our co-relators had hurt us and that we were screwed.

Nearly two months from that meeting we received official word from Jones, on behalf of the DoJ. They were declining to join the case and intervene, which in itself was not a total surprise to anyone with half a brain, because after what happened at that meeting, I wouldn't either. What was a surprise was the official reason given, i.e., that since the US Air Force was technically the client and they did not themselves desire to prosecute the case criminally, civilly, or otherwise, the DoJ itself was going to pass on becoming involved or prosecute.

However expected, this was disheartening all around. The reasoning was also very curious, because even though the Air Force was potentially being bilked to the tune of $1 billion in Northrop contracts, the DoJ's clients were actually the US government and the American taxpayers. They were the victims of the possible fraud, not just the Air Force.

We will never know what the real thinking or motivations were behind the decision not to intervene, but one of the federal agents involved made an observation that will remain with me forever: There were many in the DoD, quite possibly in the Department of Defense, and the Air Force itself who were afraid of Northrop's power and reach. In point of fact, in the aftermath of this decision, there were a number of Congressmen who thought the reasoning absurd. One of them reportedly suggested this was a little like the defense contractor holding up the bank with the US government and the DoJ driving the getaway car. They did, in fact, initiate investigations into the matter, most especially to issues of cost overruns related to the Stealth Bomber. But to no one's surprise, they found themselves out of Congress and out of their jobs in relatively short order, all with controversies exploding about their lives in very public ways.

The one useful consequence of the DoJ's decision was that it finally came out from under seal on August 27, 1992, with Northrop notified on August 31, 1992. We could now finally proceed as an active civil case, complete with the ability to resume new fact finding, depositions, and official action, albeit now on an even colder trail with Northrop having had three more years to bury evidence. The decidedly unwelcome aspect of having it out in the open was that Northrop was now free to take action to stop the complaint in its tracks if possible, and, barring that, draw it out to drain our resources until we were impotent.

To this end, Northrop immediately took two sweeping actions. They filed a challenge motion claiming that the qui tam claim as filed was too broad. At the same time, it slapped me and, I believe, each of my co-relators with an eleven-million-dollar lawsuit claiming defamation of their so-called spotless reputation, as well as accusing us of filing a frivolous lawsuit.

Ron assured me that if we won the case, the eleven-million-dollar lawsuits would disappear because, as he put it, the truth is a 100% defense against a claim of libel, and what Northrop had filed against us was a libel suit. Aside from the general sense that we were facing an almost unde-featable enemy, it is a little difficult for an individual who already finds it difficult to provide for his family to take a lawsuit of that size lightly.

The court did, in fact, dismiss the qui tam claim as filed as too broad. What was encouraging to me was that, in spite of Northrop throwing its legal might at getting the case dismissed altogether, and/or summary judgment[10] in its favor, the court did allow us leave to amend it and re-submit within thirty days. This meant that at the end of the first skirmish, Goliath did not win and we were still very much in the game.

It would be only the first of many times, and we now had the opportunity to refine our case.

Our legal team did refine and re-file within the allotted thirty days, with limited but significant involvement from Rex and me in revisiting and reviewing information we had provided and, in my case, actual documentation that I had collected as an informant. I cannot say for certain if the issues related to the allegations of the other two co-relators were pared down, but for the time being, they remained listed on the case.

This initial process of motions and countermotions, back and forth, with multiple forms of resistance, alleged obstruction, and Northrop's claim of abuse of attorney-client privilege would define the nature and challenges of the next year or so as we proceeded without the formal involvement of the DoJ. Fortunately for us, we had the ears of some assistant US attorneys

---

10 An immediate and final judgment.

whom we needed to keep in the loop as a matter of course. They would prove to be critical allies later on as Northrop made every effort to build our case difficult, if not impossible. Particularly frustrating was getting any useful information via a court order or by accident, then keeping what we acquired. They continually filed motions to recall useful information as protected under attorney-client privilege. Their antics did not go unnoticed nor were they appreciated by those in the DoJ whose responsibility it was to oversee the case as it moved through or got stuck in the courts. Northrop's lawyers' tactics may have prevented or obstructed our ability to make our fraud case against it, but they also provided mounting evidence of their disregard for due process and demonstrated a willingness, as we claimed, to obstruct justice from those whose job it was to assure it.

We would gradually (and on Northrop's part, grudgingly) make progress in compiling important information through painstaking acquisition of records and documents, and even more so through depositions of other Northrop employees and executives. These depositions offered mounting evidence of misrepresentation of bids and billings to the government. We compiled still more evidence from many who knew what was happening and lied to the government in their reports and claims of system accuracy. Then there were those who very diligently and systematically set out to commit what, to our eyes, was unmistakable fraud to cover it all up. Two particularly damning discoveries would soon come up and serve to win favor with the DoJ and other allies.

But as both sides continued doing battle over requested information and continued with depositions of key players, two things were to occur that would change my life in ways none of us expected.

One was Northrop's particularly malevolent focus on me as the source of some of the strongest evidence against it. The second was the unexpected consequences of their doing so. It sometimes seemed an open question as to whether or not I would even survive.

My own depositions were noteworthy at the outset from the Northrop side of things in that I was the last one of the original four relators to be deposed. I was not deposed by just any attorney on the opposing team but by their lead counsel himself, along with a couple of other attorneys and paralegals thrown in for good measure. It went on for days and days with increasing overt frustration, hostility, and outright abuse on their part.

For my part, it was noteworthy because, on the first five-day round of questioning, I was working my newspaper job all night, thus coming in with almost no sleep. In the long run, it was more noteworthy because of the addition of a new attorney to our legal team who would become my legal champion and, in some ways, my emotional savior. My deposition was also one of those events in life that deals a crushing blow you can let destroy you or use to become more whole.

I remember the day we converged at the Chicago offices of Northrop's attorneys to see what seemed a small army on their side, with only Ron and me on ours. This intimidation tactic may have been effective in making me feel as though I was being swallowed up by the experience, but in my sleep-deprived state, it was dulled. What I knew going in was that when you speak the truth you only have one story to remember, and this mantra would be my sword and the key to keeping it simple. They were notions very much supported by the recovery programs I was still an active member of.

These musings brought to mind interesting recollections of my father, one being that the great thing about telling the truth is you do not have to try and remember what it was you said and to whom you said it. The second thought that reverberates throughout this book is when is it ever wrong to do the right thing?

I knew I was doing the right thing. I also knew that Northrop and its minions were not. They were quite committed to doing harm and apparent wrong to me at every turn, piling layer upon layer of wrongdoing, abusing or torturing the truth and whoever offered it up wherever they were. I did not know what to expect. I simply hoped my support team would get me through it somewhat intact and still breathing.

One of the things I did not expect and did not occur until the second day of depositions was the addition of Michael I. Behn, a new attorney to the case. He would soon prove pivotal to the case itself, and to helping me get through the entire ordeal. I could not have anticipated to what extent he would champion me during those days of intensive questioning, to what extent we would bond in that time, and to what extent we would begin setting a foundation for things to come.

My deposition began as anticipated, with endless and repetitious questions, challenges, and attempts to dismiss or minimize any and all of my allegations and/or credibility as their source. The efforts were aimed at tripping me up, getting me to answer questions asked repeatedly or with slight variations in any way that might undermine my consistency. Or, better yet, to create an opportunity for me to contradict myself. Beyond that, much of the questioning was simply aimed at wearing me down and turning me to blithering mush. As all of the questioning was being recorded by court recorders sitting there typing everything in shorthand, their words were chosen carefully so as to create one picture for the record, and another for me, meant to break my spirit. Above and beyond it all, they also tried over and over again to embarrass and denigrate me as being nothing more than a clerk who had neither the credentials, intelligence, or actual perspective to make the allegations I had made at all, let alone credibly.

To this latter end in particular, and to my knowledge then as well as now, I was the only one among the relators in the qui tam claim who had the distinct privilege of being interviewed by their lead counsel himself. He was bent on minimizing me, wearing me down, breaking me. He wanted to catch me in a contradiction or anything that could be construed as a lie or anything he could twist into prosecutable perjury. Unknown to me at the time, I was also in danger of misstating information that could undermine my eligibility to be part of the qui tam case as the "original source" of the fraud allegations.

On the first day, I was asked one dismissive and demeaning question after another, punctuated with reminders that I was just a clerk, culminating in a particularly pointed question: Had I ever actually seen billings submitted to the government by Northrop? Given all I had seen and the amount of documentation that goes into generating them, it was a more complex question than it appeared. I did not want to answer no, but I did not want to lie, either.

Further, he asked the question in a double-negative type of format such as, "Mr. Holzrichter, you never did see any billings actually presented to the government, did you? After all you were nothing but a *clerk*." He emphasized the word "clerk" to insult my intelligence, to try to get a rise out of me.

I thought for a bit, which irritated him in ways that would only grow over the next few days. Finally, he asked in a very insulting tone, "Do you understand the question?"

Having been given very strict instructions by him earlier that I was always to answer the last question asked, I waited a few more moments and answered, "Yes."

As I expected, he assumed I meant "yes" to the question of whether or not I had directly observed actual billings to the government.

What I was not prepared for was what happened next, especially as this was our first day of my being deposed. Ron called a lunch recess and when we were out of hearing of the others, he absolutely laid into me, cursing and unintentionally spitting in my face. In his fury, he swore at me and demanded to know "What the f--k is wrong with you?" and "What the f--k were you thinking?" in answering those question that way. He was yelling at me that I was killing our case and further, demanded to know if I had any idea how my answer to the question would hurt us.

I let his fury somewhat run its course, then explained why I had an-swered the way I did, and reminded him that I was following their lead counsel's own instructions at the beginning of the depositions so as to skirt directly answering his misleading question. There simply was no right way to answer it as it had been asked.

Ron looked at me and said I would need to be careful in doing this in the future because the courts frown on that sort of possible subterfuge. More calmly, he said we could go back and do a couple of housecleaning responses to some of their questions, but did not then and never did apol-ogize for his attack on me. It was a glimpse into the man I had never seen, and it would carry forward with me from that point on. As I was to dis-cover much later, some of his displayed frustration fury was a result of just how badly the depositions had gone with the two fellow relators.

When I arrived for the second day of my deposition after another sleepless night of working my newspaper job, there was no Ron Futter-man to be found. Instead, I was greeted by Michael Behn, who introduced himself and said he had been hired to help with the case, and would be defending me in my depositions that day. As it turned out, he would do so from that day forward. No mention was made of the encounter with Ron the day before or his attitude toward the case at this point.

In retrospect, given the timing of the two problematic relators' removal from the case, negotiations must have begun at once for them to
voluntarily be dismissed with prejudice.[11] It was necessary for Ron's office, Northrop, and the court to agree on this. Their initial involvement
had been based on vague allegations that they knew of wrongdoing, but
they could not communicate more specifically until, with each step forward in the case, Ron's law firm acquired the necessary security clearanc-
es. More and more it seemed that their involvement could possibly be
deemed frivolous by Northrop (threatening the entire case) and their contribution less than nil.

As my own questioning resumed, I listened to all questions very carefully and, to the chagrin of opposing counsel but increasing appreciation of
my own, answered them very slowly and thoughtfully, staying as closely
and clearly as possible to what I knew and believed to be the truth. I an-
noyed opposing counsel to no end by asking repeatedly for clarification of
what exactly they were asking rather than allowing myself to be trapped in
intentionally confusing or misleading questions. The frustration I created
for them was in listening to both the intention and content of their questions
and, to a great extent, getting both of them on the record. This may have
contributed to my initial respect from attorney Michael Behn.

Unfortunately, it also stoked the flames of the frustration and growing
malevolence of opposing counsel and sparked the implementation of the
protocol for dealing with problem and potentially dangerous employees.
Once again, this roughly includes beginning with isolating and discredit-
ing the person or threat and, to whatever extent that fails, do what is necessary to make them seem unstable or outright crazy.

This latter focus would raise its head shortly in devastating ways, but
totally unforeseen at that moment. For now, I was becoming a surprise
thorn in the side of this grand inquisitor. His confidence in his ability to
trip me up or wear me down and break me was beginning to crack. The
degree to which I frustrated him and, perhaps, caused him to show a hint
of his true colors became more apparent when he began to yell at me. He
challenged my audacity in asserting any of what I had and daring to

---

11 "With prejudice" means they could not re-file the claim.

question the integrity of his client in any way. He repeated over and over with increasing fervor, "You are just a CLERK!"

Whether this tactic was his own frustration with being thwarted by someone so common and low, or was meant to get a rise out of me, it hit me as sad and funny. Without my even realizing it, my response to his badgering was to smile to myself and chuckle softly with a weary but profoundly clear appreciation of the absurdity of this charade. It was my first real grasp of just how low they would go to construct a version of reality that could twist, torture, or bury the truth. It did not consciously hit me until the writing of this book that part of what moved me to smile and chuckle was that this presumably overwhelming force could not make what is true untrue or make what is untrue true. There was something slightly pathetic and even comic in seeing this man of power so accustomed to getting his way so desperate and at such a loss.

I may or may not have been a clerk or whatever title one wanted to put on things. I may or may not have had degrees or credentials he and others would find impressive or convincing. I was, however, the person whose perspective and skills had built the tracking system that had led us to this confrontation. This was a foundering inquisition by a man of power, a corporation that, for all its credentials and claims of credibility could manipulate appearances and twist perception of reality to serve their needs.

The one thing they could *not* do was change the truth.

And my consistency in adhering to the truth undermined their determined efforts to dismiss me or make me appear crazy.

When we took what was a slightly longer than usual break, I commented to Michael that it was too bad the transcription would not capture the frustration, volume, or tonal abuse of the questioning, especially in the most recent round of having them yell at me, "You are only a clerk." He agreed and said he wished I would have commented on it to get it in the record.

As our break continued, one of the paralegal assistants on the opposing team was standing next to me at the table where coffee was provided. She leaned in and asked a question that threw me for a moment. "Do you always do that?"

"Do what?" I responded.

"Laugh out loud for no apparent reason," was her flippant reply.

I realized she was referring to my response to the particularly angry questioning earlier, and that she was actually wondering if I was crazy. I have to admit that hurt a little to think I might have given anyone any ammunition in that regard.

But when Michael heard of it, he cornered the assistant and told her in no uncertain terms she was never to speak to me in that way again or speak to me when he was not present, for that matter. I was a profoundly important witness and I was to be treated with all due respect.

When I asked Michael, whom I was already coming to like and respect, if the opposing team actually thought I was crazy, he answered, "No. They don't think you are crazy. They think you are f--king crazy."

Whether they genuinely thought I was crazy or not, whether or not that was due to disbelief I would dare risk opposing them, the questioning and the attitude just got worse over the next few days. The questions being asked over and over again had ceased being anything new, and were nothing other than abuse.

Make that *angry* abuse. [12]

It finally came to pass that Michael, who seemed to grasp and actually care about my exhaustion after five such eight-hour days, with little sleep, stepped up and cut it off. He announced that for now we were done and that this had disintegrated and degenerated into nothing short of abuse and futile questioning. He suggested that if and when they had anything new to ask or address, they could contact us and we would reschedule. This mercifully ended five days of hell and the beginning of a case-long collaboration and lifelong friendship.

I was still decompressing three or four days later when I got a bone-chilling call from Ron. There was something I should know about that was coming in the next round of interrogations. In my fog of exhaustion I thought to myself, *What could possibly be worse than what I have already gone through?* and *What could warrant a warning call with that tone of voice?*

I almost did not want to kick over that anthill, but I did. "What is it I need to know?"

---

12 This would now be considered unmitigated abuse and no longer allowed under civil rules of procedure both at the state and federal levels.

There was a long and disconcerting pause. "They have your hospital records."

"Hospital records?" I asked. "What hospital records?"

Then, at almost the exact instant I knew what he was referring to, he said it out loud. "They have the hospital records for when you were in rehabilitation for alcoholism and drug addiction. They have everything."

Everything, of course, was everything I shared while baring my soul in what had been promised as an inviolate sanctuary. *Everything* included every observation ever made by the team that presumably existed for the purpose of providing a safe haven and place to face and address one's demons. *Everything* was a record of the hell I thought I had faced, owned up to, and left behind.

Fortunately, I was already sitting or I think my legs might have given out at the knowledge of what they had: nothing less than a lifetime of demons and monsters every alcoholic and recovering drug addict used as an excuse to abuse themselves. What kind of devastating harm they could and would do with it—to me and those I loved—was beyond comprehension.

"Who has it?" I asked.

"Their entire legal team and ours," was the answer. "They had to let us see it before we resume your deposition and they bring it into the next round of questioning."

Michael's last words came back to me. *Let us know when you have something new to ask or discuss.* It just so happened to be something that was also very old, and in my efforts to reconstruct my life and make amends to my family, I had hoped it would fade into oblivion. There is no describing how thoroughly violated or physically ill I felt. There was a brief silence while he let me take this in.

"I want to see what you have," I told him. "I want to see what they have."

But I did not want it mailed or sent by messenger to my house. Mary or one of the children could get it and open it before I had a chance to speak with them.

I was still working all night, as I had been now for several years. It was not only abusive in its own right, but I had had almost no sleep at all for those grueling five days with Northrop's council. Recharging my emotional batteries had already been pretty much of a fantasy. Now I knew I had to go back, with complete sleep deprivation, and endure more abuse for who-knew-how-many more days. The next day, I found myself on an early train to Ron's office in Chicago to pick up my medical records, and the documented observations of doctors, psychiatrists, and counselors during my rehabilitation.

When I arrived, I spoke to Virginia, who gave me a three- to four-inch notebook, then added, "Ron is too busy to speak with or see you today and also left the message to not call him, either."

I found this rather odd, considering I had made this special trip to the city, and I now had a lot of questions and concerns about the new round of depositions, not to mention concerns about the medical records now in everyone's possession. These were my innermost thoughts and darkest secrets all laid out in print for everyone to see and use to abuse me. Notes taken while under the care of the hospital. Notes taken in aftercare. Notes taken in what I believed was the most private setting and strictest confidence—privileged and sanctified confidentiality meant to protect the candor and confessions intended to help me leave my past behind and turn my life around. Here they were now, in the hands of those who would use them most cruelly and add to the violations and shame of my past.

It may have been me, but it seemed from that time forward that Ron had started acting differently towards me. I could not bring myself to look at or even open the binder while standing there in the outer vestibule of Ron's office with Virginia seeing the pain on my face. I felt Ron had, no doubt, read at least some of it and that he would never see me the same again. Like those in my past, he found me lacking, as if the so-called shining bright everyman witness had fallen into something disgusting and had acquired a foul stench about him. Then again, standing there and thinking in the moment this was nothing compared to what I thought this information would do to my already suffering family.

With my head lowered, I, ashamed and dejected absently thanked Virginia and asked her to have Ron call me later. He never did.

But Mike Behn did.

Somehow I found my way back to the station and was on the train ride home, the binder with the ghosts of my past in my lap, unopened. I just did not want to see it. I did not want to know what Northrop and its minions had in their hands. What was I about to encounter, being openly exposed to everyone in that room when I found myself there again? I could only imagine what use they would make of it and me after that.

I opened the sealed confidential binder and began looking though its pages. The pain I felt almost immediately in my chest was not just of the body but of the very soul. How could they have done this to me? The doctors and the so-called caregivers who had so assured me of the sanctity of what I was to reveal to them. The empty promises that death threats would not make them reveal what I told them. That they held my revelations as sacrosanct. It now turned to dust and ash in my mouth and ears. The power of the injuries and ghosts that had diminished with distance and time all came rushing back.

It felt worse than physical rape. It stole any faith or trust in anyone or anything other than my family, the family I imagined would be devastated by the indiscriminate release of this information. The weight of the pages sitting in my lap and their possible repercussions bore down on me with a cruelty I could never have imagined. It took something more away from me, now that whatever vestiges of hope I had in Northrop to act honorably were gone. On that very public train, I sat with those pages on my lap, and I cried. Quietly, my shoulders shuddering with my efforts to not attract attention, tears dropping silently onto those damming papers.

When I arrived home, I immediately called Ron's office to find some grounding and get some sense of what to do next. Virginia reminded me that he was not available and could not speak to me, and that Mike would be my contact at the office if I needed to speak with anyone from now on. It appeared the change I had picked up on at his office was on the mark. It was a repeat of the neglect, abandonment, and physical and emotional rape that had defined my childhood and so scarred my teen and early adult years. I again thought of the psychiatrists and other physicians who had promised me they would be a trustworthy safety line in a life that had known none. I again thought to myself, *What have I done?* and *How could they?*

When I did reach Mike, two important things happened as I sat there in shame, with all the irrational guilt that comes with being a victim to those kinds of events.

First, he assured me that there was no way he would allow Northrop or any of their attorneys to introduce the material into the case as evidence, or to use or disclose it to anyone in any fashion. I told him that for the most part, I did not believe that was possible. I was overwhelmed with just how apparently malevolent and downright evil this company, or at least its puppeteers and representatives, would and could be.

Mike then added something on a surprisingly genuine and personal note (considering we had only just met). He added the reminder that while some of what was contained in these records included behaviors and errors in life I was not proud of, most of it was about things that happened to me as a child. I was a victim, not a perpetrator. He reminded me, in marked contrast to what I felt in my chest, that it had not been my fault. I realized, in a life-changing moment, that what this man had discovered about me and my past gave him greater respect and empathy, not less. He was in that dark moment with me, more committed to me, this cause, and the family he knew I wanted to protect.

It is difficult to say whether or not I have ever fully communicated to him what a champion he was for me in that dark moment, but it gave me the grounding and hope for doing what I knew I had to do next: I now had to be the one to tell my family before any of them heard any of it from some other source. What Mike said to me that day gave me the strength to do what I had to do. Nobody else could do it for me. My faith in Mike's capability and intentions in that moment was matched and exceeded only by my mistrust of Northrop's. I knew that however painful and shameful it was, I had to get ahead of this. I had to take the power to affect my life back from these people who would do it and my family harm, and defuse the impact of their threat by putting this information to my family myself.

To that end, I spoke first with Mary.

Afterwards, sitting together with her and holding her hand, we had never been quite so together. With her encouragement, I gathered my children together and shared with them what was likely to come their way from some other source. I let them know I loved them and that I expected the information would bring me down in their eyes. Worse than the expectation was the reality of it—to watch it happen and imagine what cost it had taken from their little hearts and souls as the view of how they saw me changed. Now when they looked at me they saw me for what I was, where I had come from, and those faults a parent never wants their children to know about. In that moment I knew the image of me was a little dimmer in their eyes.

Perhaps only another parent can appreciate this, especially one already feeling the inadequacy and guilt in being unable to take care for their family they want to, but as I spoke to my children and even more in the aftermath, I kept thinking, *What more can Northrop do to me? What more can they take away or kill?*

I cannot say I was happy about the prospect of meeting with opposing counsel in the next round of questioning, but at least now I felt more ready. Unbeknownst to them, they had empowered me, and that as a consequence, they were about to face off with an unquestionably decided foe.

They also gave me almost two months to think about it. The interrogation was held off until it appeared there was some new purpose for meeting again—a period during which they would not allow us access to any of their people for our deposition until they had completed their questioning of me.

When we regrouped for the next and final round of my depositions, Michael began with the announcement that we had some housekeeping to do. He began by announcing that there was no way those records, which had been acquired through questionable means, would ever be used in court or public discourse of any kind. Northrop's attorneys insisted I had opened that door in claiming stress and duress, which gave them standing to challenge the claim and my stability. Michael then conceded we would drop those claims and suggested we all turn the records over for safekeeping to a court-appointed special master pending determination of their relevancy in the case.

Northrop's legal representatives grudgingly agreed, then resumed their prior abuse of me by taking up where we had left off just a few short months earlier. Little, if anything, had changed. I was slightly insulated by a bubble of raw-nerved relief that Mike had been successful in getting my medical records set aside.

I had a newfound strength and distance from these people. Anything like disappointment or guilt over not being able to help them do what was right (even if I still felt the wound where that hope had been) went away. Those feelings had been replaced by a new sort of disbelief and sadness for them. In my eyes, these were simply evil people, willing to do harm to complete innocents and manipulating events around those they could not threaten, harm, or intimidate. Mostly I just watched them go through the motions of asking their questions, looking for some weak or vulnerable point in which to get to me, hoping for some hint of contradiction to put things in a spin. It seemed to me they were just hopelessly, irrecoverably, and morally lost.

As was to become the way of life after my depositions, Northrop's new goal was to make us as logistically and strategically lost as possible. It was an attempt to punish me for having the audacity to accuse it of anything. In our efforts to get our hands on documents and data we knew existed, had existed at some time, and/or came to believe existed, their ploy was to delay, distort, and distract in every way possible. We requested many documents we never got our hands on, most notably their copies of the documents I had taped to my body to sneak out of the facility and give to duly authorized federal agents. These mattered because the contrast could have helped show how they were modifying records. Still other documents were recalled under the claim of attorney-client privilege.

The effort to get information from them (quite separately from being able to get access to deposing key figures) was very much like trying to find a needle in a haystack, only with the needle removed in advance and not one haystack sent sans needle, but several. Aside from the sheer volume of paperwork (when anything was provided at all), it was provided in ways to assure we could not find what we were looking for and we would have to burn up endless hours trying to make sense of it.

Over time, hundreds of boxes of documents were delivered, but out of sequence, with gaps in Bates numbers[13] and no explanation. Not only

---

13 Bates numbering (also known as Bates stamping, Bates branding, Bates coding or Bates labeling) is used in the legal, medical, and business fields to place identifying numbers and/or date/time-marks on images and documents as they are scanned or processed, for example, during the discovery stage of preparations for trial or identifying business receipts. Bates stamping can be used to mark and identify images with copyrights by putting a company name, logo and/or legal copyright on them. This process provides identification, protection, and automatic consecutive numbering of the images. (Source: Wikipedia, http://en.wikipedia.org/wiki/Bates_numbering, accessed 4/25/2013.)

did the documents within individual boxes or groups of boxes jump around in time, the pages of specific documents would be separated and dispersed throughout many boxes, many of which would not be delivered at the same time, often many months apart. Multiply that by the three-million-plus paper documents and the seven million computer entries we reviewed. To make matters still more complicated, Northrop consistently refused to provide a list of box contents that, in theory, would have created a checklist and a paper trail of what we received, but in practice would have been verification that we were not getting what we asked for and would have been a demonstrable lie. Given that the contents of the boxes were so incoherent and scattered, such lists would have been next to im-possible in most cases anyway.

In any legal case, there are ongoing and ultimate milestones to be met and drop-dead dates beyond which all efforts must stop.

They repeatedly claimed they had sent us what we asked for. When we suggested they had not, or asked where an item was, they answered that it was in the boxes provided and told us to look for ourselves, as it was not their place to point us in the right direction. To me, this was an obvi-ous ploy to burn up valuable time and resources, wear us down to the point of collapse, and run out the clock.

Northrop's claims that it had provided us with what we had asked for, and that they were acting in good faith echoed their prior (demonstrably dishonest) communications and interactions with the government. These echoes would cause their undoing in the distant future. Like their past interactions with the government, their efforts to bury us in materials and confuse us with chaos was, in part, to hide what we said:

That none of their continuously changing systems for materials man-agement, accounting, and reconciliation should qualify them to be a gov-ernment contractor, let alone be allowed to submit bills and receive compensation.

As to the practicalities of building a case, we were still digging our way through the morass and trying to focus on actual instances of fraud. All of this was mixed with motions and countermotions aimed at preemp-tively terminating the case if possible, dragging it out if not, and continu-ously burning up massive resources in any case.

One of the ironies unknown to me at the time was that the government of the United States was picking up the tab for Northrop's legal fees.

What many people don't know is that the government itself will underwrite legal fees for contractors such as Northrop to defend themselves against allegations of fraud and/or wrongdoing until such time as the contractor has been found guilty or not guilty, even from allegations made by the government itself. Contractors only have to repay those monies if they lose their cases and only 80%, at that. Not only did Northrop have vast resources and deeper pockets than we did, its hands were in the deepest pockets of all, the United States government.

Had the DoJ intervened and joined our case, the playing field would have been significantly leveled, at least in theory. The working assumption is that the DoJ would have and could have stepped up to the challenge with all its resources, conviction, and might. As it was, we were seriously overmatched, sometimes overwhelmed, and endlessly engaged in what seemed an ever-present, neverending resistance. Getting information from Northrop and wading through all the motions, countermotions, and repeated court orders enjoining Northrop to comply with requests made each and every member of our team—which by this time was really a team—feeling very much like Sisyphus.[14] Our problem was not that it would go on forever (although at times it seemed that it would), but that it could not go on endlessly without results and within governing timelines, regulations, and limited resources.

The only thing in our favor other than the truth (if we could last long enough) was that Northrop's lack of cooperation and noncompliance would help win needed allies and resources, and force us to shift our focus on what documents we wanted. As we progressed, it would also force them to change some of their own tactics and strategies. The last thing they wanted was for us to communicate with, let alone win over, these potential allies who would become dangerous to Northrop. This was especially true as government officials discovered how extensively, systematically, and intentionally they were misinformed for years.

---

14 The king in Greek and Roman mythologies who was punished by the gods by having to roll a huge boulder up a steep hill only to see it roll back down and have to be rolled up once more over and over again for all eternity.

For some time to come, we were still very much on our own and struggling against a giant that threw everything it could at us and for the most part, threw it all at once.

11
CHANGES IN TIDES

Following the completion of my depositions, two key things ensued, one new and one already old and soon to get older.

First, now that they had completed their depositions of me, we were able to proceed with deposing those working with and for Northrop. Second, they escalated their lack of cooperation in providing requested materials in defiance of subpoenas and court orders. Northrop continued to claim attorney-client privilege to recall most of what useful information they did provide, and filed a very long chain of motions, countermotions, and power play requests for summary judgment in their favor.

These were the scattered pieces of what should have been an emerging picture.

What we discovered over time was a snowstorm of intentionally confusing and overwhelming information, with only intermittently useful pieces of the puzzle on the table at any one time. Fortunately, what we also had was an ever-growing picture of the extent to which Northrop and its representatives engaged in ever more blatant obstructions of justice. With two potential smoking guns that made a delayed, but timely, appearance, our mighty opponent could be knocked a little off balance. Better still, we had growing potential for alliance with players Northrop thought were out of the picture who could be offended by its maneuvers and apparent disregard for the courts, government, and taxpayers.

There was also one very obvious change that occurred early in a phase that would last about four years. The two co-relators who had become an apparent threat to the case were suddenly no longer in it. I was told that, given their lack of anything substantive to support the case and devastatingly inappropriate performance at the initial meeting with the DoJ, their depositions were the reason for their dismissal. I had already long wondered how or why they were involved to begin with. I did not know about the whole "We can tell you what we know when you have proper clearance" issue until much later. As time went on, it seemed to me that it was Rex and I who had anything concrete and relevant to bring to our qui tam suit. The documentation I had gathered provided the most sound evidence and served as a compass to even more evidence.

In any case, within weeks of the completion of my depositions, then several months after the completion of theirs, I was informed that our two former colleagues had not only been removed from the case but dismissed with prejudice by their own agreement with Northrop, the court, and Ron's legal team (who had initiated and negotiated it with all parties). Aside from the importance of their no longer being participants in the case, the two key aspects of this to note for future reference are that they *agreed* in their withdrawal at the time *and* that they agreed to being *dismissed with prejudice*, meaning they could not at any time in the immediate or distant future step back into the existing case or re-file another qui tam or pursue related civil litigation on their own—nor could either Rex or I take up any portion whatsoever of their original allegations. Rex and I had no knowledge of any of this until it was announced as a done deal, although we understood that it was a deal that needed to be done. It would not be until years later, after we finally reached an end to the seventeen-year case and thought the ordeal was finally over, that they would show up with an inexplicable notion they deserved part of the settlement.

What I learned during the writing of this book was that the credibility of our case was vulnerable and at risk of dismissal. If Northrop pressed the point that the allegations of the two former co-relators were invalid because they had been dismissed, our case could have been construed as frivolous. Northrop began what would be a steady stream of motions, not the least of which was a challenge of the very laws under which it was being sued. Its first area in seeking summary judgment was against one of the co-relators, challenging that they had anything of substance at all. It was this very issue of filing what could be considered frivolous lawsuits (which is a charge that applies to representing counsel as well) that would come up again after the Northrop case was settled, and the two dismissed relators reappeared seeking a portion of the settlement.

Unfortunately, their removal had an unexpected effect on Rex, who had been friends with the two ex-relators. They also had a work history with the Stealth Bomber. The difference of course was that 1) Rex's allegations had bearing on a qui tam lawsuit; 2) Rex had seen and gathered actual evidence directly related to his allegations; 3) Rex had valid and recognized standing as an original source of that information for the case. For a time, these differences seemed to be lost on Rex who, in spite of thinking he was the most important witness and evidence for the case, believed he was next to be removed, and was the object of a conspiracy by our attorneys and myself.

You need to understand something about Rex. He had always been somewhat of a loose cannon in several ways. First, he had been very vocal about his concerns with Northrop even while working there and especially after being fired for vague reasons that turned into an age discrimination lawsuit. He was also a bit reckless, seriously impatient, constantly wanted to go the press, and throw whatever he could at the enemy, swearing he would never give up until the day he died.[15] He was also prone to seeing conspiracies in everything and everyone, albeit not without some grounds. Unfortunately, he was beginning to see them here with his own team.

I had received a call from Ron not long after our legal team had chosen to dump ballast, so to speak, about Rex having called his office wanting to fire all the attorneys and get new ones, and how this would be good for me. (To me, Ron sounded very pleased and excited). I told him Agent Zott had just spoken to me a little while ago, and when Ron heard that I was going to be meeting with Agent Zott, he told me he would like to be part of that meeting, but did not say why. I guessed in part it had to do

---

[15] Just before the end of the case, Rex died from a cancer one can only get by ingesting certain industrial chemical toxins that he had never come in contact with. He speculated that someone had gotten into his house and poisoned his food, causing him to get the cancer that ultimately killed him. The same cancer also took the life of his son, who had been living with him at the time of the alleged poisoning.

with the fact that all contact with Agent Zott had a touch of adventure by virtue of the work he did and worlds he moved around in. I also suspected that, at this juncture, Ron could use some kind of booster shot of hope and motivation to keep going. He had been through a number of understandably debilitating jolts during this case, and may have needed a little inspiration or encouragement. Otherwise, it would have seemed a bit odd to me that he, and not Mike (whom he had essentially put in charge of the case), wanted to meet with Agent Zott and me, with no Mike in attendance.

Ron and Agent Zott came to see me at my home, arriving within minutes of one another. In all, the meeting took about an hour. After speaking with both of us, Ron asked me to leave so he could have a private conversation with Agent Zott. I went outside to join my family who was already sitting in the yard. Mary asked me what was up. I said I didn't know. Ron wanted to speak with Agent Zott privately so here I was, outside with her. Their meeting took about fifteen more minutes, after which they both came outside, thanked me for my time, and left with no explanation. I found this strange and disconcerting.

Shortly after they left, Rex called, yelling that he had been trying to reach Ron (or anyone else in his office, for that matter) with no success and no one returning his calls. He was frustrated by the slowness of the case, and was suspicious that Northrop would get to our attorneys and get them to sell us out. Considering his friends had been dismissed from the case without consultation with or explanation to us, he feared that he was going to be next. He feared that "they" were already conspiring to oust him as they had ousted our two ex-relators, who had voluntarily agreed to be dismissed with prejudice. It did not help his state of mind when, without thinking, I told him that Ron and Agent Zott were not conspiring to oust anyone and had, in fact, just left my house. In his mind, I was instantly added to the potential list of conspirators out to get him off the case, or rather, get rid of him.

He wanted to know why we were meeting without him and why they would not return his calls. Again, he was always convinced he was the most important relator, perhaps in part because his issues were so closely tied specifically to the Stealth Bomber project, which was pretty sexy. I reminded him that while we were co-relators whose cases had been combined for the overall strength of the case, we were each handled separately, as our issues and evidence stood on its own, as it needed to. I also reminded him that we had been encouraged not to even to talk about the case or our issues amongst ourselves with no attorneys present because that raised issues of vulnerability to discovery. In other words, opposing counsel would call those unprotected conversations into depositions and court testimony along with the corresponding danger of our testimonies becoming tainted or just too similar. My reasoning did not really register or quell Rex's exploding frustrations, fear, and anger. I did not bring up the fact that we had not even touched on the issue of our prior colleagues in the meeting that morning. It was not something the attorneys would have discussed with us nor should we have been expected to have discussed in any case. I suspect it would have mattered little if I had pointed that out.

I was very troubled by this phone call and his state of mind. I wondered what Ron might have wanted when he requested time alone with Agent Zott to discuss some so-called other aspects of the case that did not necessarily have to do with me. I assumed it was to honor of the privacy of the others, so I left them to their conversation without any personal questions or concerns about plots or conspiracies.

I would only discover later that day the extent to which Rex had spun out of control. In fact, Rex showed up on my kitchen doorstep, very distressed, and unknown to me at the time, carrying a gun. As he sat in our kitchen, fuming, it was Mary who first realized he had it.

She asked to have a word with me in the other room where she said, "Jim, I saw a gun sticking out of his belt when his coat slipped open. It is stuffed into the belt in the front of his pants." Upon returning to the kitchen, knowing he was armed and more than a little angry, the notion that he would go off and take us all out became a conceivable and imminent possibility. Mary, me, all of our children . . . All of us gone in a violent flash of uncontrolled rage.

The sudden ringing of the phone made me jump out of my skin.

"Hello?"

The voice on the other end of the line was the last one I wanted to hear at that exact moment. It was Ron. He said he was calling to tell me that he had a vitriolic message on his office answering machine from Rex accusing him of conspiracy and wanting to get me to go along with him to fire Ron and all the existing attorneys and hire a whole new team. I was trying to keep my pounding heart from exploding in my chest as I turned to look at Rex, who was watching me suspiciously. Before I could think of something to say to convey my situation, Ron added that he thought Rex was losing it, and asked my opinion of what we should do. As casually as I could muster, I cleared my throat to make sure I even had a voice and passed along the fact that Rex was sitting in my kitchen at that moment, and suggested that I would call back later after Rex and I had "finished talking."

Assuming, of course, we were all still alive to do so.

Rex got enough of the drift to ask if that had been Ron. He again became just furious, fuming that he could not even get Ron to return his calls and here he called me at home again after already being there earlier. It made him particularly furious that I did not have to call him first to get a call. As I tried to think of the words that might get through Rex's haze of anger, let alone make a difference, all I could picture was taking yet one more wrong step and having him go off, drawing his still unacknowledged gun and taking his rage out on anything or anyone that moved or ran.

Fortunately, he finally calmed down and left, with Mary and me quite shaken and unsure what to make of the event or what to do next. I was still shaking as I called Ron back. I let him know what had transpired, along with repeating that Rex wanted us to fire our legal team. He had accused me personally of conspiring with Ron and Agent Zott to get them to kick him off the case. I waited through what seemed like a minute or so of silence only to hear Ron ask if I thought Rex was going to come after him. He did not ask how we were or how we were coping after Rex's visit.

More specifically, Ron's sole concern was to ask if I thought Rex knew where *he* lived, and if I thought Rex might shoot *him*, or if he might come after him at his office. Where I had hoped for support and perhaps a little informed guidance, I instead found myself reassuring Ron, the person in charge of my case and, to a great extent, the person most in charge of my life that no, I did not think Rex knew where he lived. I did not think Rex would shoot him. I did not think Rex would come after him at his office. In what others would have recognized as a dig, I pointed out it had been my house and my home, after all, that Rex had visited in a blind rage, armed with a gun, conspiracy theories, and irrational tirades.

I may have been shaking somewhat less, but I was disturbed in some ways more when I called Agent Zott. He did not challenge my deepening surprise and disappointment in Ron as a person, and crucially important ally and guide. What he did do, which impacts me even to this day, was simply ask if there was anything I needed or anything he could do. For that moment, beyond caring and asking, there was nothing more. For that moment, it was almost enough.

My wife spoke her mind only briefly about it afterwards, saying she understood I would have to have interactions with Rex by virtue of the ongoing case, but that he was under no circumstances to *ever* set foot in our home again. This was yet one more example of just how remarkable she was and has been through all of this. She understood beyond my comprehension those things I would have to deal with and do, ever protecting our children, our home, and us.

This game and its high stakes also brought home the extent to which the one thing we had to rely on was each other and, fortunately for us, our shared faith. In retrospect, it is interesting to note how much these traumatic things strengthened both of us. We had no idea how many more tests and "opportunities" were still to come.

As I said at the beginning of this chapter, one of the positive consequences of surviving Northrop's extended and brutal deposition, was that my own team was now free to begin deposing all those on Northrop's side that we had not had access to until they finished deposing me. This included the likes of my past immediate supervisor, Tom Clyder, our combined supervisor, Amy Selen, as well as others like Petra Schiller (the informant who recanted her sworn testimony to federal agents) and Dan Quealy, head of internal investigations at Northrop, among others.

This had been part of the strategy meeting at my house, to discuss whom we should depose, when, and what to go after, with Agent Zott providing some of the guidance, and Ron and his team formulating a concrete plan. Our focus was on Schiller, who had been offered up by Northrop as their expert on data management, their so-called expert on "Financial Reconciliation," in response to our 30-B-6 request to have access to such a specific resource.

There was much I did not know about the situation with Schiller and its ironies or implications. Unlike so many similar cases in which relators file a case then go away, or try to survive whatever is left of their lives while the case unfolds (usually with unfavorable results), I was very active in this case all the way through, whenever things were actually happening, and whenever my understanding of some of Northrop's inner workings could be a contribution. As to the latter, I actually chose to sit in on all the above depositions and more, with the exception of Selen, who had left the company and moved to Arizona; she was deposed on camera by Aram Hartunian. I wanted to do this to remind those being deposed of reality, and perhaps to get them a little off balance or prompt them to be a little more honest, knowing there was someone in the room who knew the truth and, by implication, someone who knew when and how they were lying outright or torturing the facts.

The decision to sit in on these depositions was mine, but I later learned it was very much appreciated by my entire team of federal agents and personal attorneys. They grasped the very human element involved in prompting greater truth where possible and increasing discomfort with untruth where necessary. In addition, whatever insights I could provide in discerning fact from fiction at these depositions was also acknowledged and appreciated. I was also included in strategy sessions and planning that others in my situation would not have known of at all, let alone welcomed. I came to appreciate just how my involvement and my team's need to manage information was a delicate balance. In certain ways, they even managed me, what I did and did not know, and when I would come to learn of it as a witness.

This was especially delicate given the expanse of time the case took to unfold. In that time, learning or knowing too much more than I had at the beginning could undermine my continued credibility as the original source of allegations and facts. It was important to make sure my knowledge and testimony were not tainted or corrupted by any new information that I received from others. For Rex, this was maddening. His sometimes volatile unpredictability and constant threats of going to the press or firing everybody caused most of the legal team to keep him at arm's length.

The implications of all this throughout the rest of the story are significant and not only worth noting, but probably necessary. The scale of this increasingly epic tale and much of what it involved often fell outside of my direct observation and knowledge even as it continued to shape my life. Because this is a very personal story, putting faces and a little humanity in what so often felt inhumane, we will not address the minutiae of thousands of legal filings, motions, and challenges, the three million documents reviewed, or the seven million computer data entries. We will continue to look at this journey from ground level and the human experience, highlighting only the most significant events and trends as they touched my life.

In terms of understanding this unfolding story in its broadest phases, we are still very much in what could be considered the first phase of the case itself. That is to say that while we were very much aware of Northrop's intentionally created chaotic inventory and accounting systems, our focus was on demonstrating that they had knowingly defrauded the government.

At this point in the story, neither I nor my legal representatives had more than an incomplete picture of what we would later find, and were still primarily focused on getting the documentation and data that would prove the kinds of fraud we had initially set out to prove: erroneous or nonsensical billings, erroneous and nonsensical contract bidding, false inventory numbers, hidden excess inventory, misrepresented project milestones, and misapplied funding from one project to another. You can see why Northrop spent millions of dollars and used multiple legal teams to prevent us from proving it. Over the course of the next four years, Northrop continued to bury us under documents and data.

Northrop's continued use of these tactics began to win us some important allies Northrop did not want us to have. Though we were alleging fraud, it began to appear that Northrop's attempts to hamper our ability to build the case were strenuous efforts to cover something up.

By doing this, Northrop also gave us new angles to focus on, ones we would be able to prove (e.g., adding the allegations of obstruction of justice on top of our original claims of fraud).

Lastly, Northrop set in motion some of the ways it would get caught in its own web of deceit. Their convolutions and distortions would later lead us to a third point of attack: that nothing they presented could be trusted or considered accurate.

One requirement for any and all government contractors is that they keep accurate, trustworthy records. It would take us some time and much effort, but once Northrop claimed it could not provide even the most basic information,[16] it had painted itself into a corner because we accepted that argument at face value.

It is important to note that if we had been able to prove that Northrop was destroying the data we were requesting, that proof in itself would make the case. Our efforts to document any and all of Northrop's original sins were increasingly tied to their attempts to resist providing anything useful while blitzing us with nonsense and noise. Its battle cry seemed to have become *How do we make it all work in a way that it makes it look good or at least gives the government information it will find acceptable without further scrutiny?* The guiding protocol was that they "could not tell the truth."[17]

Further, we had come into court with affidavits from three witnesses who testified that: 1) Northrop had destroyed and was in fact still massively distorting or destroying data and records; 2) Northrop and its legal representatives were claiming anything and everything that was useful as protected by attorney-client privilege; and 3) Northrop's actions were specifically retaliatory and targeted at me.

To put some of this in perspective, Northrop spent over $10 million just having outside accounting and investigative teams dig their way through literally everything I had ever looked at, reviewed, or reported in my tenure there. As it had done before, these teams were hired through their legal team rather than directly by Northrop for the purpose of being protected by attorney-client privilege. Thus, it was not discoverable by

---

16 Northrop CEO Wallace Solberg, in his deposition, acknowledged this when he said GIGO (Garbage in Garbage Out) when asked about alleged computer system inaccuracies.

17 In fact, entire training programs were put in place to train data people, specifically the program managers, to "violate the system within the system," on how to twist or hide data. One of these included an actual PowerPoint presentation put together by Selen that bluntly stated, "We cannot tell the truth." They had to hide the fact that they were unable to track or report on anything accurately, even when they did want to do so.

and/or usable in court against them. They also sought protective orders to prevent us from sharing anything else with anyone (meaning the government) in the future.

The accidental discovery of this practice became our second semi-smoking gun along with the three witnesses mentioned above. If the reader will remember, I had suggested to Selen perhaps Northrop should bring in its own internal auditors to evaluate and fix the problems I had found. Unbeknownst to me at the time, Northrop had already hired the independent auditing firm Arthur Young to examine their internal systems of material tracking, auditing and reporting.

The surprise twist was that this outside auditing firm had already issued a scathing report to Northrop at the time of my conversation with Selen. The report was critical of exactly what I had found, and the same issues the Attrition Committee wanted to hide, along with millions of dollars of excess inventory.

These two sources of information would give us some needed leverage to get Northrop's attention and give it a real and immediate sense of vulnerability. It demonstrated the chess-game nature of cases like these in which it does not matter what you know or can prove *outside* of court. What matters is what evidence can be gathered and retained throughout the convoluted processes to prove it *inside* of court.[18] Fortunately, what counts in acquiring allies are truth, tenacity, and the occasional gifts of blind chance.

Thus, at the time we launched our own depositions and discovery, these three things emerged to help us win the Department of Justice's assistance in an unprecedented instance of their joining a case they passed on ten years earlier:

1. the discovery of the aforementioned 1988 independent audit Northrop had contracted, which resulted in a devastating evaluation. ;

2. the discovery of three prior employees who claimed their job was to falsely stamp anything and everything of use to us as "attorney-

---

18 Northrop had referenced this commissioned report to the government, but cloaked it in such a way as to present it as a positive one.

client privilege," that Northrop altered and/or destroyed data in an ongoing purge and cover-up, and that Northrop had and continued to engage in retaliation against Rex and me;

3. the shifting status and claims of Schiller, the person who had been responsible for the hands-on data manipulations associated with our allegations pertaining to Financial Reconciliation.

Then came a related bit of a circus by way of a particular magistrate who very nearly decimated our case.

In the earliest stages of commencing depositions and discovery, considerable focus was placed on undercover informant Schiller, the person who had overseen so much of the distortion and destruction of data. She had proved helpful to me in understanding how and where so many of the bodies were buried. She had also helped me to understand that the process of converting to a central computer system (which would replace a great deal of manual data collection and tracking) was revealing previously vague or contradictory information, as well as the dubious practices it reflected. At the point we began moving forward with depositions and discovery, Schiller received immunity and a waiver of prosecution from the AUSA, then, unfortunately, immediately recanted the information she gave to the government.

At this time, Schiller was known only as CH05 in government reports and was still under its protection as a confidential informant. Her recantation, in which she claimed to have previously been in error and/or to have misunderstood the questioning, did not sit well with government investigators. First of all, she had been a potentially valuable witness. What she knew about the original abuses, the efforts to cover them up, and key players in charge of it all was at the heart of what we were trying to prove. The related aspect was her lying to federal agents to begin with or in seeking immunity, a federal offense either way. Agents Zott and Deery wanted to prosecute her for lying to federal agents in their duties of conducting a federal investigation.[19] Further, they felt that as government agents conducting an investigation, they had been had by her and Northrop's attorneys. However, the AUSA who replaced Chris didn't

---

19 Interestingly, this charge was the one Rod Blagojevich was convicted of in his original trial.

want to bother; he said it would only burn up a great deal of time and throw the strategies built on her information into a spin.

I do not know if the attorneys who advised her to request immunity or the attorneys who showed up with her were provided by Northrop or not. In the short term, it served Northrop well. Her position led to the slightly surreal twist that she became an expert witness for Northrop. This tactic may have seemed desirable at the time, but it finally revealed that Northrop threw everything it could at us except the truth. Oddly, when her status as a confidential informant (and being stripped of her secrecy) became an issue, Northrop dismissed her, their own expert witness, as being nothing but a clerk.

Suffice it to say that, in the short term, the loss of her testimony was a serious blow to our case. It was the loss of the closest thing we had to a smoking gun.

Finally, though, we believed we had enough to go into court and ask for a final determination on our original complaints. Then we could enter into the court record the testimony of the three affiants whose sworn statements supported our allegations that Northrop had made it impossible to prove our initial case because of their obstructionist tactics. We then made the more boldly explicit charge that in obstructing our discovery, Northrop had engaged in obstruction of justice, supported by our additional allegations of abuse of privilege.

We were making progress.

But what happened next was both unexpected and, for a time, potentially devastating.

The sitting magistrate stepped up to broker an offer for settlement. Because he had let motions sit so that the case languished for an extended time, his supervising justices wanted the case wrapped up and off his docket. He thus had personal and professional incentive to move the case along. He did, but not in a way that was beneficial to us, the government *or* the taxpayer.

After having our hopes raised one more time, then seeing them dashed, it appeared to be the end of us.

♦

What ultimately made some small sense of it to me was the realization *not* that we had gotten a glimpse into the heart of a monstrous machine, but that it had no heart at all. It was the full and horrifying realization Northrop was, in fact, a giant, unfeeling, and limitless machine, with cold and lifeless fingers, and even longer creeping tentacles that seemed to reach everywhere. In my darkest moment, I could not help but wonder, *How do you fight something like this?*

I would soon get the beginnings of an answer, which would grow like a tree taking root and growing, stretching out to the sun. It was not what I would have ever expected. It would be a wonderful reminder that however much one tries to torture, distort, or bury the truth, one cannot kill it or make it go away.

After having been told over and over by my counsel that, because now too many people knew about me, I had nothing to fear, I was lulled into a false sense of security. Thus, I did not expect that someone might try to kill me in the not too distant future and, after failing, make the exact same attempt on two of my children.

It seems cold machines arrive at the notion that the closest thing to successfully killing the truth is killing the messenger. But that was in the future, with a roller coaster ride in between.

12
A JUDGE INTERRUPTED

The Department of Justice had never been totally disconnected from the case, however disinterested it was in joining the civil case at the outset, or pursuing further criminal investigations and prosecutions. As a matter of course, we had continued to send updates, all the way up to Gordon Jones, who had made the decision to pass. Our legal team had also become more assertive in getting the attention of the assistant US attorneys under Jones. They had begun attending some of the ongoing court hearings and status meetings; their mere presence made Northrop attentive, if not nervous, as would be expected. However, its lawyers did not appear to be nervous in the least, and their behavior was almost mechanical. This was strange and triggered a *What is wrong with this picture?* reaction.

I may have tried to write this off to my utter exhaustion. I was, after all, still working for the *Tribune* twelve to fourteen hours a day, seven days a week, 365 days a year. Delivering papers in bulk was a job that afforded me little sleep and not a single day off in five years. The lawsuit seemed to have already gone on forever, and with my children now no longer quite children (several now in young adulthood), trying to live life after so much of it had been stolen was more than taking its toll. My health was in shambles with diabetes and related problems that arose during this ordeal. My wife had long since lost any hope of a positive outcome to the case. And now, as my legal team had the best case ever, Northrop did not seem to care.

It would be reasonable to assume that the confident, even imperturbable, posture of the legal team representing Northrop was just that, a posture.

Part of the game was to psych out and wear down the opposition; in this case, not just our legal team, but specifically Rex and me. But there was much afoot in 1998 that should have generated at least a flicker of concern or humanity in Northrop's attorneys. There should have been more variance in their moves and counter moves beyond their new tactic of filing mountains of motions to prevent us from sharing information with the government. But even that seemed mechanical. There was just something wrong with this picture that I could not put a finger on or share with my legal team. They were growing more confident as evidence accumulated and the possibility we could once again gain the attention and support of the DoJ.

There were concrete reasons for renewed hope.

Yet I was almost too tired to be able to rally one more time. More than anything, my wife and I wished for it all to be over. The juice it would take to keep going seemed to have drained from us; we wanted the ability to walk away and provide for our family without ongoing retaliation from persons and or entities unknown. Put most simply, we were feeling used up.

Rallying for yet another moment or round of hope, which had been key to our surviving this long, seemed more and more out of our reach. It required more energy than we could muster. That said, as had been the case now for roughly ten years, we had no choice. We had to keep putting one foot in front of the other, much like a person trudging through the desert in search of a drink of water. We had to maintain some kind of hope that it would come to a resolution and set us free. Mary was always wiser than I in regards to needing to get on with life independently of how the case went. By this time, however, the case and all its demands promised to be endless.

What kept hope alive was a little different for each of us, although what ultimately kept us going was each other. My wife, having come from a life in which her expectations were that it would be hard and you did the best you would within that, remained more present and focused than I in her goals and intentions. Mother hen that she is, the protector of the family order and spirit, she was ever vigilant. I was as attentive to and present for the kids and her as I could be, even though I worked endless hours for the newspaper and put in more hours when I could on the case. I managed to trudge through years of sleepless effort to provide for my family and to find a way through the morass of this case. Everything that could have put us at odds made for a degree of balance that kept things going, kept things together, and helped get us through.

I bring this up here because it was this harmony of purpose and combination of efforts that allowed us to get through a situation in which most families come apart. It is also to acknowledge the sacrifice imposed upon my family, all of them, and what they were forced to go through. But I did what I thought was necessary to get through it intact *and* made whole.

If there are any two things I would like to rewrite in history other than the case never having come up at all, is that my family had suffered less, and that I had been more present. The reality is that in my exhausted, overextended, and overspent state, I thought I was more present than I was. They all paid a price for the extent I was not. The fact remains, however, that had I not done what I did, put time and energy where it went, we would not have had the outcome we did and could have been trapped in the brutality and abuse of the situation forever. More likely, we would have come apart as other families do in less trying circumstances. The issue at this point was how to keep hope alive for Mary, my children, and myself when we were continually disappointed.

Though more than anything we wanted the ordeal to be over, I had to stick with any effort that could bring the case to a successful conclusion. Unfortunately for my family (and unbeknownst to me), that also meant they felt as though they did not matter to me, or at least not as much as the case did. A more accurate way of putting it is that in doing the best I knew how, I did not know how to balance it all. I could not separate my family from the case and, as time proved, I was right to see it through. It was the only means to be free of it and become more fully whole and present in life.

In the meantime, my legal team had been compiling more and more formidable, if fragmented, information. They were very excited about a summary judgment motion they were prepared to file they thought showed that over the years, Northrop had been destroying the documentation and that the three affiants could prove it. I was told it would soon be all over for me and my family, and we would be able to get on with our life.

It was within the imperfect context of our family that we gauged what to make of this newfound hope that we found our respective hopes and expectations being rejuvenated.

The magistrate handling the case, Judge Rosemond, took on the role of arbiter and ordered everyone on both sides to appear in court to sign a settlement agreement that could end it all, set us free, and, to some extent, make us financially whole.

Thus, it was in this context we found the energy, the heart, and the way to rally hope one more time. This time, however, we really could have found our end to the ordeal. After all these years, with one judicial order, the case could be settled in a day or two.

In hindsight, the fact that neither my legal team nor Northrop had requested this or (as I know now) was particularly interested, getting our hopes up at all was ill placed and about to set us up to have them dashed like never before. It was also one of those occasions where something that looks really bad causes a shift in circumstances that turns out to be as good as it was unexpected. It was also one of those occasions that brought home the merits of tenacity and determination even when facing a bigger foe.

By this time, now several years after the case had come out from under seal and the wrestling match with Northrop had begun, we were ready to step into court to add the affidavits of our three key witnesses from the Northrop legal department. While not exactly a smoking gun, the affiants' allegations and the potential viability of their source presented an implicit danger to Northrop's defense.

By this time, my legal team had grown to include Steve Miller, a particularly able litigator and strategist who would later play the role of lead counsel in the mock juries we set up to test our case. I found out later that soon after he joined the team, he wanted to push harder to bring the DoJ officially on board. Additional firms had been brought in to share the risk and spread the escalating costs, as well as to help carry the burden of labor. Even though the team had grown somewhat weary of the battle, they still remained invested in spite of the difficulties. Thus, prospects seemed somewhat more hopeful when the presiding magistrate, Judge Rosemond, who had been handling the case for some time, initiated brokering what we hoped could be a final settlement agreement.

Not only Rex and I appeared, as requested, with our entire legal team, but so did the legal representation for Northrop. I remember sitting there in court and having it strike me once again just how emotionless and indifferent the Northrop team seemed in spite of the fact that my team wanted to submit the affidavits from the three former Northrop employees. Further, my team was prepared to request a final determination based on evidence submitted already, along with the new testimony that essentially supported the claim that Northrop, in making it impossible for us to make our case, had made the case for us under what is known as "spoliation of evidence." We were ready to file motions formally accusing Northrop and their representatives of obstruction of justice.

I remember being particularly struck by the incongruence of what was in front of them, their lead counsel's ever-present arrogance, and his less explicable calm. In looking back and forth between them, I wondered how the proceedings would go because the judge was in his chambers leaving us all to wait outside in the main courtroom. And who was this judge about to proffer an agreement to end this dance? Reflecting back on Northrop's attorneys' faces, it was as though they knew something we did not. However, with hopes that this could actually be the end of it all, I did my best to set these qualms aside. I was satisfied, as was my legal team, I believe, that for the moment their intentions were on record, that our leverage and the judge's offer would be taken seriously.

Judge Rosemond called our legal team into chambers. I was told that they conveyed our terms of settlement, including a bottom line for Rex and me, and for legal fees. It totaled $44 million. My team returned to the courtroom and Judge Rosemond then asked the Northrop representatives to join him in chambers.

While we waited for Northrop to come back out, our legal team explained to us that the judge had refused to allow us to file the affidavits or our motions of obstruction. He said it would be moot, because he was going to get us to settle and the case would be over.

What happened next was not only more than a little strange, it supported my sense of why the Northrop team seemed indifferent to the proceedings. They were, perhaps, even a little smug and too well informed of what was unfolding, and especially what was to come next. And it took place during Northrop's time in chambers.

Judge Rosemond should have given our offer to Northrop and then gotten their offer as a beginning point of negotiations. Instead, he simply conveyed Northrop's offer as if it were a done deal. It was a demeaning and dismissive offer of $1 million each for Rex and me, and a mere $1 million to our legal team, which had already invested millions. Worse, it meant the judge, who held our lives in his hands, had shared our attorneys' position with Northrop *ex parte*, and made himself their messenger as to what they would pay.

Unfortunately, he was a messenger with a black robe and a gavel who wanted this old case off his docket. All protocol and any sense of neutrality or fairness had just gone out the window. It was not just an insult. It was not even what one would consider a fair mediation or arbitration. Judge Rosemond presented it to us as a done deal, although not with a take-it-or-leave-it attitude. He seemed to expect that we would simply take it and be eternally grateful.

Since I had never considered this as looking to win the lottery, I had not made any calculations of how much any settlement would be after attorney fees and taxes. Mercifully, I did not yet know that many whistle-blowers who actually won their case could still wind up in a deep hole for taxes they could not pay.[20]

This is to say that the very government for which they risked and lost everything to defend added to their ruination with an unpayable tax debt that the whistleblower would never be able to pay.

Rex and I asked our attorneys what they advised, because we all had to agree on final settlement. As I had reminded Rex when he wanted to dump our team, the consequence would have been owing them the millions they had already invested, due and payable immediately. In this case, they would have taken a hit for millions themselves, but they told us the call was ours. As was his nature, Rex was understandably immediately furious.

Me? I was numb. If I had any feeling at all, it was nausea. The Northrop team had gone back in chambers with the judge, which left us all mercifully alone in the courtroom. The offer was so strange and offensively small after so many years of this ordeal, my befuddled mind could barely take it in.

---

20 Prior to November 2004, federal taxes on awards were calculated before deducting attorney fees.

As I sought some kind of grounding—almost anything that seemed solid and real—it occurred to me to ask, "What about the United States government?"

"What about them?" was the response.

"What do they get out of this so-called settlement deal?"

They were to receive nothing, as the DoJ had opted not to join the case; thus, they were not party to it. I didn't understand how the entity that had been defrauded and, by extension, the taxpayers, whose hard-earned money had been so wantonly stolen or wasted, could *not* get anything. This was incomprehensible to me, and wrong.

No compensation. No justice.

Rex and I asked one more time what our attorneys suggested we do, then I asked them what they would do in my circumstances if they were the ones who had put so much at risk for this outcome. Both Aram Hartunian and Lowell Sachnoff spoke out as one: "Personally, I would walk away." I don't think they meant it quite as literally as we acted on it, but Rex and I looked at each other, shrugged, and nodded. Without speaking, we stood up and walked out of the courtroom, down the empty corridors, into the elevator of what was *supposed* to be a building of justice, out the front door, and into the cold night air.

I am not quite sure what happened inside the courtroom in those next few minutes, but the fallout over the next weeks would be as strange as what had just occurred, and would seem to redefine questionable legal protocols and impartiality.

For the moment, however, Rex and I returned to the train station to make the less-than-happy return trip home. We talked about what had just happened and we each tried to come to terms with it. Rex was angry, as would be expected, and wanted to take some kind of action. At the time, I could not imagine what kind of alternative action would make a difference without making things worse, and I did not hold our legal team any ill will for the unexpected turn of events. I was even empathetic with Rex, who had, by this point, become terminally ill.

Rex's train station was a couple of stops before mine, but after I got off at my stop, I got into my freezing car, hung my head over the steering wheel as the engine warmed up, and rehashed this entire nightmare. I replayed scenes from the first disturbing discovery to the incomprehensible event that had just occurred. As I drove home, knowing that I would have to disappoint Mary and my children yet one more time, anger and resentment began to brew. What came to me over and over was the simple question:

How dare they?

Darker feelings toward this giant unfeeling machine and its minions would come a bit more slowly. But they were definitely coming and beginning to take a cold, hard, and ever more monstrous living form in my heart towards Northrop and those who represented it.

I found myself thinking about the deposition at the hands of the Northrop inquisitors, their callousness in getting my hospital records. I remembered how devastated I was and how violated I felt, that I was required to reveal things to my family I never wanted to reveal.

Until then, I had thought I was dealing with a partial and select group of bad people connected to an organization. I had still harbored some hope someone or something good would come through and do the right thing. Almost home now, I could not imagine what else they could take away or want to take away from us, because we had nothing left. I had had to watch my kids grow up in poverty, suffering embarrassment and shame at different schools because of their ragged clothing and lack of spending money. Northrop had stolen my children's childhoods from them and me. They had forced me to remain cut off from those I loved. This night, so many years later, my hurt and devastation took on a different form:

Anger.

I was tired of other people deciding what was best for me and my family. I was tired of being a victim. I would no longer allow anyone the privilege of taking away what was ours.

When I entered my home that night, where Mary was waiting to hear how my day had gone and thus how all of our lives might finally go, I experienced another one of the worst moments of my life. After over a decade of enduring this saga, with so much of our lives in the hands of others, my own best diligence seemed to have been for naught. I wanted to be encouraging for her. I wanted to be strong. I wanted to feel like less of an impotent failure. I think a part of me really wanted to be able to rally and wrap myself in the insulation of anger. Seeing the look in my wife's eyes and feeling the full weight of my own disappointment settling in, all I could do was accept her strength and support and, in frustration, weep.

I cannot say if she cried as well. She has always been a master at keeping things in and keeping them together. We just sat there, holding each other, and she reminded me we still had what mattered. We had each other. We had our children. Fortunately, we also had our faith.

As was our way, when one of us was down or had fallen more than the other, the one who had fallen less helped hold both of us up. In leaning against and with each other, we did not fall. We stood our ground to face the next challenge. We stood as best we could so we could be there for our children, even as close to adulthood as some of them were. In truth, there was nothing else we could do.

Our legal team returned to court to continue slogging along with the case as before and to complete filing the delayed affidavits, allegations, and motions of obstruction of justice as previously planned. And we had a bigger surprise than the so-called arbitration and settlement meeting. From that moment on, Judge Rosemond demonstrated what a landslide of decisions against our side could look like.

Fortunately, what promised to be the rapid decimation of our case turned out to be the straw that broke the camel's back.

The judge's actions created an emergency shift in tactics and strategy by my legal team—as well as a corresponding rejuvenation of interest by the DoJ.

This series of events, taken together, was the tipping point in the whole journey.

As I said before, there were already AUSAs from the DoJ sitting in on hearings and status meetings from both the criminal and the civil departments. To me, this made Northrop's understandable motions to prevent us from sharing information with the government a bit odd. What I did not know was that my legal team had stepped up their efforts to renew the DoJ's interest in staying on top of the case. Northrop's legal team may have been getting away with much, and seemed to have had their way in the courtroom in ways we did not fully comprehend, but outside the courtroom, my team was actively pursuing other strategies.

Unbeknownst to me, my team, guided by Michael, made contact with the DoJ. They had, in fact, brought representatives of the DoJ and other government agencies together for powerful presentations to bring them fully up to speed. The evidence they had compiled was telling, not only for the original allegations of fraudulent bidding and billing, it also demonstrated the higher-ups knew of the problems and that there were widespread efforts to keep that information from anyone outside the chain of command at Northrop. Our team showed the government that Northrop had lied, then lied more, and continued to lie about lying to us, to them, and to the courts.

Meanwhile, Northrop had stepped up its efforts to cover up the misrepresentations they had made to the government all along. Northrop was not just uncooperative and evasive, they were actively obstructing justice.

Our focus and the DoJ's interest shifted somewhat from the initial allegations of fraud to the obstruction itself, including the abuse of attorney-privilege. As it was to turn out, this was a wiser and more timely strategy than anyone had anticipated, as the magistrate (who was openly furious about our declining Northrop's offer) appeared to be doing everything within his power to turn the case against us and/or destroy it. We would never accuse him of it, then or now, but it was as though Judge Rosemond had turned against us and joined the other side.

Ruling after ruling suddenly went against us and for Northrop. Our efforts to get the court to pressure Northrop to comply with court orders seemed suddenly impotent. Within a matter of weeks, he was very close to annihilating our case.

Chances were we would have rebounded and possibly prevailed in the long run, but the cost of resources and loss of time was incomprehensible. Time was running out, as court deadlines approached rapidly. And time was more personally salient now, as well, because it was clear that my friend Rex was dying.

We needed to get the court schedule back on track and the case back under control. The bottom line was that this apparently rogue judge had to be deterred from ending our case. Instead of getting the footing and momentum we should have had, the ground beneath our feet was shaking and, in some places, opening up and disappearing.

Fortunately, our concern was now shared by some within the DoJ, which could no longer sit idly by and wait. The DoJ now had renewed interest in not only the civil case but possible renewal of criminal investigations. It was at this point that the DoJ made an unprecedented decision: It formally stepped back into the picture. More than that, they stepped in with their full attention on the criminal investigation and possible prosecution of parties as yet unnamed. It filed a motion on March 21, 2000, to stay the civil case.

This had much the same restrictions to everyone as it had when the case was originally filed back in August 1989. In other words, all forward momentum on the civil case was halted and all motions before the court were held until the stay was lifted.

The motion, submitted to District Judge Guzman was unopposed by Northrop, who strangely had a brief win that same day in a minute order issued by Judge Rosemond denying one of our many languishing motions to compel Northrop to provide documents regarding a specific offense. Just as strangely, the next day, in the brief window between the filing of the motion to stay and its formal approval, Judge Rosemond granted Northrop's pending motion for a protective order. The stay order was issued by Judge Guzman on March 23, 2000.

We filed multiple objections in those few days regarding both the denial of our motion for compelling Northrop's cooperation and its being granted the motion for a protective order.

When Judge Guzman granted the DoJ's motion to stay the civil case, he explicitly acknowledged the fact that the alleged abuse of privilege put Northrop's legal team, particularly its lead counsel in the court's cross hairs for violating the law. Judge Guzman, in open court, noted to Northrop's lead counsel that he assumed Northrop grasped that both my legal team and the US government were aiming torpedoes directly at him.

His response was, "Yeah, but they won't hit me." For the moment, the lead counsel was partly right that the torpedoes would not hit him, but only partly right, and very much for the wrong reasons.

The effect of staying the civil case was immediate and significant for both sides. It meant the case was again under seal and nothing of any import could move ahead until the DoJ completed or decided to dismiss criminal proceedings, or the time allowed by the court for the stay expired. This was critical for us because we felt that any further damage by Judge Rosemond was effectively halted. It meant Northrop could not file any motions to protect themselves from our sharing information with the government. It also meant that, for the moment, they were stymied in getting the independent audit report back and out of any open courtroom proceedings, though they would later partially win this motion. On the downside for us, it meant our hands were tied, as well.

This included the ability to get Rex's testimony recorded and on file before he died. He was not likely to survive to see the case's successful completion. It was here in one of our darkest moments that the most remarkable game-changing thing happened.

Make that several.

First, when District Judge Guzman entered his minute order to stay the pending civil case, he also explicitly stayed Northrop's motion for a protective order filed in a narrow window of time. This ruling contained comments regarding the fact that there had been *ex parte* contact between Judge Rosemond and the Northrop legal team that resulted in Judge Rosemond returning documents to them, with his added comments that he had not reviewed them and they had not impacted any of his prior rulings.

The next thing that occurred, although not quite out of the blue, was that Michael went with Assistant US Attorney Linda Wawzenski to the DoJ offices in Washington D.C. to give a four-and-a-half-hour comprehensive PowerPoint presentation regarding the content and state of the case to date. Northrop, who had already put much effort into our not being able to share any information with the government, would have been more than a little chagrined that this meeting happened at all. They would soon be even more surprised by its ultimate outcome, which is where the remarkable comes in.

The DoJ gave the green light for Linda to proceed and intervene on behalf of the DoJ and join the civil case on behalf of the United States of America. This in itself was remarkable and unprecedented. Never before had the DoJ passed over a case then reversed itself and intervened, let alone a ten-year-old case. However, since the civil case was stayed, though the DoJ wanted to intervene on the civil side, they could not file their intent to file their own civil case nor could they proceed with fully allocating resources to pursue and to prosecute it.

Here is where the last and most remarkable thing happened, which Northrop never saw coming: With Judge Rosemond essentially sidelined, my team returned to court, now in front of a much higher-level judge, with the Northrop legal team very much present and at full attention. Both criminal and civil sides of the DoJ appeared with a most unique and, as Northrop would note and argue, precedent-setting request.

The criminal side of the DoJ put in a motion to request the court lift the civil stay long enough for the civil side of the DoJ to file their motion to officially intervene and join the case on behalf of the United States of America. Then, once done, to immediately put the stay back in effect without hearing or taking any other motions. It was the most remarkable fifteen minutes to occur thus far. It changed my life and the course of this case forever.

In that fifteen minutes on June 4, 2001, while the stay was briefly lifted for a matter of minutes, Assistant US Attorney Linda Wawzenski and the civil side of DoJ were able to submit a motion on behalf of the United States of America for leave to intervene and file a new and superseding complaint against Northrop.

The Northrop legal team protested vehemently, claiming this was unprecedented and should not be allowed. They asked if the judge wanted to risk setting new precedents by ruling in such a fashion, particularly with the government having already passed on intervening so long ago. In truth, they were correct; this was both unprecedented and precedent-setting. That said, their arguments were heard and very quickly dismissed without much concern passing over Judge Guzman's face. In that moment the nature of the game changed.

Upon completion of the DoJ filing its motion, the stay was immediately re-imposed, but with two very different circumstances now in place that would prove to be a tipping point in the case, and provide the grounding for all that would follow. One was that we now had the considerable resources of the DoJ and the United States of America in tandem with our efforts. The other was that seemingly rogue judge would very shortly be completely off the case.

All of these were obvious and important changes, and we all secretly hoped they would build to the power of an avalanche.

There was one more thing that had changed, although I do not know if anyone had noticed it yet. I now saw the enemy for what and who it truly was. It was one of the ironies of this saga that, in Northrop's dismissal of me and my family as something that did not matter—a necessary casualty of doing business—it gave me a renewed purpose and dedication. In its willingness to lie, cheat, and rob us, the American people, they made me a more determined foe. The question was, with all the demands on me taking their toll, would I physically last long enough for it to matter?

Up to this point, my legal team had preferred not to have Rex or me in court for motions, hearings, or status meetings for a variety of reasons, some sound and some (for me) not so sound. Remembering what took place during the previous so-called settlement negotiations with Rosemond and the day the DoJ filed to join the case, I insisted on being present for virtually anything and everything I could manage to attend.

My reasons were simple, and came to be embraced by Mike and the rest of my legal team in much the same way that my appearance at all depositions had been. Years before, I had wanted to be in the room so those being deposed knew there was someone sitting there, looking them in the eye, who knew when they were lying and when they were telling the truth. In my new commitment to being present whenever possible, it was to put a human face on the case. It was to remind everyone (including my own legal team) that, even though this case had been filed on behalf of the United States government against a massive corporation, it was also about and for very real people. It was, in my own limited way, my respectful but unwavering effort and intent to hold everyone accountable, and to remind them that at every step of the way, the execution of this case and its outcome depended on and directly impacted real lives. And this real person—me—was tired of being a pawn and a victim to anyone, even if they thought it was for my own good.

For far too long now, my life and the life of my family had been shaped by others' priorities, processes, and decisions that, for good and bad reasons kept me largely in the dark, isolated, and impotent by default and by design. In reality, this could change only a little, especially because this case was about to take on players and a scale no one would have imagined. I would have to trust my team. My wife and I would have to continue to find some way to have faith. But I was going to be right there, with all those people who were making decisions that would shape almost every aspect of my life, and I was going to make sure they did not lose sight of the flesh and blood and tears involved. I may have been one very small player, and, by nature, a very polite and respectful one at that, but from this moment on I would be there to look every judge, every attorney, and every witness or clerk in the eye. Whether it registered or not or even whether they thought it mattered or not, they would have to look me back in mine. This case was about my family, my country, and my life.

13
BUILDING A CASE IN EARNEST

The danger to Northrop of the Department of Justice becoming more officially involved was twofold. First, the scope and level of resources the DoJ could bring to bear were clearly far more vast than what we could manage on our own. Part of this was because of money and resources. Another part was the DoJ's access to all other sectors of the government, allowing them to gather additional information, coordinate, and build support to prosecute the case. While there were certain aspects of the civil stay that restricted both sides, it was the contact between the DoJ and other government agencies that was the more immediate concern for Northrop. This meant that almost everyone Northrop needed to keep in the dark could be brought into the loop and brought up to speed on what had allegedly taken place.

It was because of this that Northrop's attorneys tried *ad infinitum* to challenge the entry of the DoJ into the civil case, and filed motions and protective orders to prevent us from sharing information with them. The reality was that regardless of how the civil case went, Northrop did not want the government scrutinizing its business.

One government individual to whom we now had access was Major General Charles Henry. He would eventually join our roster of powerful allies as our expert witness on military contracts and appropriations. What he said in his deposition is interesting to note: Had he known, when he was working with then-Chairman and acting CEO of Northrop, Kent Kresa, what was going on in Rolling Meadows, he would have formed a group to investigate the practices and procedures and that, knowing what he did now, this would have affected the progress payments, and in all probability the continuation of the contract, He would have led this effort and in the end the contract would be terminated for cause.

These expanding connections allowed the case to get its full footing, would define the case's end, and would redefine how Northrop could play the game. Even though Northrop eventually succeeded in getting the official external audit excluded from evidence *and* negate the credible use of the three affiants, the cat was out of the bag, the game was on, and we were not alone anymore.

Technically, the DoJ was not fully joined in the civil case based on the June 4 fifteen-minute Hail Mary motion for leave to intervene. This would take a brief bit of time and some standard legal hoop-jumping, including allowing Northrop to file its objections by June 21, 2001, with our projected response July 12, 2001. During this time, there would be several changes of magistrates, with the court's executive committee issuing a final order on October 1, 2001, terminating the case referral to Judge Rosemond and referring the case to Judge Michael T. Mason. On October 15, 2001, Judge Guzman granted the DoJ/USA motion to intervene, as well as granting Rex and me each the right to re-file separate complaints to preserve our individual claims. These complaints were filed on October 16 and October 17, 2001, respectively. Northrop, not surprisingly, moved to have both the original and all amended complaints dismissed, but was not successful.

By this time in October 2001, with all tandem complaints now filed, and with Judge Mason having been formally assigned to oversee all discovery proceedings, it had been well over a dozen years since we filed our initial qui tam complaint. Mercifully, none of us knew it would be three more agonizing years before these concurrent cases would be settled. I could not then imagine it would be still another five years before the ordeal was over, requiring me to win a second separate case against the two former co-relators. Though they had dropped out of the original case with prejudice some ten years earlier, they showed up after the final settlement to demand a substantial (although inexplicably calculated) portion of it. This case was beyond anyone's expectations of justice, and a true challenge to sheer human endurance.

One of the most important aspects of the DoJ's intervention and subsequent action, was that it provided a crucially needed respite for us all. It was a moment for us to take a breath and regroup, as the scope of aid in the form of allies, connections, and resources expanded. During this period, however, Northrop had to contend with renewed concerns of criminal investigations and possible prosecutions, up to and including our allegations of obstruction of justice. And we used this period to pursue other aspects of the case. It left us with unusual room to move while Northrop was bound by short-term restrictions. They could do little else than anticipate what we would do next and, perhaps, continue manipulating data.

In July 2000, even with the stay in place, we were allowed to record on camera Rex's testimony and statements. It was not likely he would live long enough to testify if we did go to trial. At that time, it seemed this was as close as he would ever come to seeing an end to the case. By then, this highly trained and skilled engineer, who once worked on not only the Stealth Bomber but all of the Apollo moon launches was living in abject poverty. He was reduced to survival strategies like renting bowling shoes for a dollar and walking out the door wearing them as his means of getting shoes.

One of his final lasting injuries came after he told one of the two former relators that he had terminal cancer. This former colleague and friend sidestepped that information with the announcement that he wanted a million dollars from any settlement or he would sue all of us (including Rex's heirs) for everything we had until all the money was gone and none of us would get anything. Notably, though this person did not bring up the issue of aliens again, he eventually found lawyers who were only too glad to represent him to attempt to do just that.

If the reader will remember, the two ways for a stay to end are for it to be lifted by the court or be allowed to run out. Ours ran out. With the referral of Judge Mason to the case, the wrangling moved back into full gear. He was tasked with handling all aspects of ongoing discovery except for issues extending their cutoff dates. Those determinations remained in the immediate jurisdiction of Judge Moran's supervisor, Judge Guzman, who came under the jurisdiction of the senior and Honorable Judge Moran.

With the addition of the DoJ, we had to battle back and forth over much of the same ground, inch by inch, so that every action could go through the court (the proverbial eye of the needle). In our quest to get clear documentation, our day-to-day battles with Northrop's counsel continued. Northrop challenged the DoJ's intervention at every turn, though at the time, who the real puppeteers had been, how business had been conducted, and how the current battle was being waged from its highest reaches were still somewhat fuzzy and undefined. From the documentation we had gathered thus far, it looked like Northrop's various alleged sins were traceable to the top of the corporation *and* predate my initial discoveries by several years.

With the DoJ joining and bringing its resources, our team grew in size. In what was to be a precedent-setting and striking aspect of our case, Michael Behn not only continued as first chair and orchestrator of all the additional team members, he was also able to juggle the combined cases filed by us and the DoJ. We may not have known who was behind the scenes for Northrop, but Michael was proving to be a master conductor of a golden collection of talent. Win, lose, or draw, I would forever be impressed and grateful for their combined talent, dedication, and effort.

Equally amazing was Northrop's continued fight to stymie our discovery by ignoring subpoenas, court orders, and even dancing on the edges of court sanctions for failure to comply with our requests. They made repeated attempts to have the case dismissed, including claiming the DoJ did not have jurisdiction and challenging the status of qui tam suits as valid or constitutional by law. They filed motions for extensions for the sake of extensions, created delays with motions for permission to submit motions of longer than the standard fifteen-page length. They continued providing useless information we did not ask for without providing much of what we did request. While this slowed things down, it also alienated those who worked with us and made these apparently obstructionist tactics clear.

The issues specifically tied to Petra Schiller illustrate Northrop's kaleidoscopic logic and the lengths to which it would go to twist anything to their favor. In our favor, we still managed to gain damaging internal memoranda that pointed to the chaos of the data system as well as the company's seeming full knowledge. Moreover, these memos and depositions also supported our allegations that identifiable players intentionally misled the government by claiming to have an accurate reporting system and sound billing practices. Most damaging was their demonstration of how they hid their noncompliance from the government, including the appearance of covering it up.

It should be remembered that Schiller, responsible for Financial Reconciliation, was a secret government informant, who, once she was given immunity from prosecution in exchange for her information, recanted and ceased cooperating. She claimed that Agent Zott misrepresented what she had told him (basically calling him a liar) which Northrop used to question his integrity. Further, Northrop then offered her as its 30-B-6 expert witness on all aspects of its data systems and related materials management, billing, and general accounting—only to later dismiss her and her testimony as coming from "nothing more than a clerk" who didn't know anything about anything.

Most significant, however, was the wrangling over her status as a confidential informant, which had not been revoked when she recanted during the Grand Jury investigation. While she had escaped federal prosecution for lying to federal agents, she had not been revealed to the world as an informant. She still had her protected status as CH05. When AUSA Wawzenski decided to reveal her name as an informant, Northrop went to great lengths to keep that information secret and out of court.

What I find strange in this was how hard they fought to keep this from happening. Usually it is the government that fights to protect the status of an informant, but not in this case. The court finally decided that Northrop could not have it both ways. Schiller was revealed, in open court, that she was the CH05 informant.

The questionable soundness of her various testimonies could now be seen as dishonest legal contortions by Northrop in order to keep that information out of the public record.

The Northrop legal team was more successful in eliminating the information provided by the three affiants from the Northrop legal department, who had said that Northrop was destroying or distorting data, had engaged in retaliatory actions against me, and were routinely committing abuse of privilege by knowingly and intentionally stamping everything they did not want us to see as protected by attorney-client privilege. Ultimately, the affiants' depositions proved devastating in terms of how a jury might have viewed their testimony, no matter how accurate and true it might have been.

To me, it is still a galling irony that Northrop made a very big issue out of the fact that one of the affiants had a prior felony conviction. This raised the whole issue of why he had been working in that capacity after Northrop itself had recently pled guilty to and paid fines for thirty-seven admitted violations of federal law on the MX missile program. It struck me as more than a little hypocritical. The upshot, in any case, was that while the previous testimony of the three affiants had put the return of the DoJ back in motion, the use of these three witnesses and their specific testimony was removed from the game plan. In the overall scheme of things, this made getting complete copies of the Arthur Young report on the record much more important.

We originally came upon portions of this report when assessing Northrop's compliance with the necessary requirements to get any government contracts at all. For several years, we had tried to get our hands on the full report without success, because, if the reader will remember, Northrop had commissioned the report through its legal department and thus could be claimed as attorney-client privilege. Northrop was doing that now, even while under stay. It was not that they denied the evaluation ever occurred; it was that they referred to it as proof of their compliance with governing standards for data management and government reporting. Eventually, though, once the stay on the civil case ran out, they did win the battle over control of the final report, and we were required to return all copies of it. They might have won the battle in keeping the information off the record, but we had won the war with that information.

With the reassignment of all the concurrent civil cases (the government's, Rex's, and mine) to Judge Mason, battle resumed. Motions were accepted and ruled on, and some had to go up a judicial level to Judge Guzman, the more senior US District Judge. Many of these motions pertained to gaining the full Arthur Young report. We claimed that though the report had been ruled protected under attorney-client privilege, that same protection did not apply to the research and data it was based on. Thus, we were allowed to interview the auditors themselves and get access to much more extensive raw data and their personal notes.

Now we had devastating information that truly supported our claims of how Northrop had misrepresented the accuracy of its bidding and billing practices, and documented the chaos of their information management systems as a whole. This documentation proved Northrop knew of their offenses at very high levels, and exposed the layers upon layers of attempted cover-ups. And while the wrangling went on as to what could and could not be admitted into court or revealed in any public record, the facts had been seen by many in the government. Another benefit of having the DoJ involved (besides their enormous resources), was that they could communicate with anyone they wanted and pass this information to other parts of the government.

The effect of the unprecedented cooperation between various offices and branches of government became apparent in relation to our recurring requests for massive amounts of data that Northrop alternately said no longer existed or had been misplaced or was still classified. They doggedly fought our efforts to have some materials evaluated by the court under protective seal. A great deal of data should have become declassified automatically by law over time, but in those cases, Northrop made the excuse that it could not provide the information in any format we requested and that they could not afford to go through it all to convert it and/or determine which parts should have already become automatically declassified, after having presumed we could not afford to take on the expense.

They were no doubt surprised when the Air Force (which had declined to prosecute them at the beginning of our claim) offered to pick up the tab. Though they were essentially busted, they back-peddled and still managed to side-step or ignore some of the requests related to classified material. Eventually they were compelled to provide substantial quantities of computerized data in whatever form it existed, with our taking on the responsibility and expense for converting it to anything useful. The fact that we were now dealing with technology computers in a way that had not existed when the case began helped immeasurably. It was one of the few benefits of the case having dragged on so long.

It was in this context that the truly remarkable involvement of Major General Charles Henry came into play. Our ability to share information with him and get his input was not hampered by many of Northrop's maneuvers to keep information from him or his ilk (even if some of it would be recalled by the court or deemed inadmissible). Nor could Northrop prevent us from getting input or information from him, as they would have preferred. All that considered, it was most specifically with him that they made their most blatant and, frankly, boneheaded move.

In a moment that will live in all of our memories forever as something beyond comprehension, the attorney deposing Major General Henry on behalf of Northrop, as if trying to impugn him as nothing but a clerk, asked him if he had ever overseen the handling of substantial amounts of military equipment and materials. After a pause during which, I must assume, he was trying to decide if the question was serious or just unbelievably insulting, he answered with a yes, if things like battleships, tanks, aircraft, and aircraft carriers counted.

The reinforcement of his position during the time I was at Northrop, and having on the record that he would have led an investigation which might have led to the possible cancellation of all contracts was a significant blow to Northrop, not only because he was positioned to be able to do what he said, but because of Northrop's ignorance of who he was. This, after all, was the man who was responsible for all the logistics of Operation Desert Storm in Iraq. The notion that they could intimidate or attempt to humiliate anyone of his accomplishments and stature was nothing short of incompetent and, in my eyes, obscene. It was also very foolish. Courtesy and respect aside, you probably should not be that ill-informed of or insulting to someone who has that much power over you.

At the end of Northrop's deposition of Major General Henry, we had those representing Northrop and those in the know at Northrop as much on their guard as we had probably ever mustered. His testimony was not just devastating in its own right, it came from someone who, though retired, was still connected to those who could cause Northrop insurmountable grief with a stroke of a pen. It reflected Northrop's arrogance that even after this, they kept stepping up their game to outdo us, with an ace-in-the-hole attitude, an attitude of being "too big to fail."

So in the aftermath of that, what made my life and continuing role in all of this so important that someone would make an attempt on my life?

Who tried to kill me remains unknown to this day, but when that failed, attempts were made on several of my children. The mechanism was simple: loosen all the lug bolts on the right front tire. At some point, the wheel would come off, which would make the hub hit the ground, dig in, spin, then flip the car. Had I been driving the same route and speed I normally would have been, instead of the route and much lower speed I was driving that night, I have no doubt I would have joined my now-deceased co-relator Rex, a life cut unnecessarily short, or at the very least been seriously injured.

It was never considered an accident or fluke, which raised the issue of witness protection for me and my family yet again.

The morning it occurred, I had almost taken the other family car, which could have been even more disastrous if my wife had then used mine, and been injured or killed. That prospect must have been clear to whoever arranged the accident because they removed all the oil from the car I mostly used for work. It could not be driven. In fact, when I tried to start it, lights went off immediately and it made some unsavory sounds. I took the family car and called the tow truck to pick up my work car later that morning. After the work car was picked up, I drove to work and, with whatever bit of grace was in motion, did not take my normal route nor did I drive at the high speed I usually would have. When the entire wheel came off, I lost control of the car.

I was rattled by the accident itself, of course. I also had to admit I was unnerved, but in a bit of denial about it whether it was intentional or not because I wanted to believe it was some freak accident. But Agent Zott was immediately on alert after hearing what happened. This was (as he told me later) a well-known technique for sending a message or taking someone out while making it look like an accident.

Whatever residual hope I had of believing all the lugs on one wheel happened to shear off at the same time, it was dashed when I got a call from the mechanic evaluating the other car, who asked me who had drained all the oil out of the engine. I asked him what he was talking about. He said the engine did not have a drop of oil in it, and that he could tell it had recently had the drain plug removed and put back in.

Even after many years of living in some degree of fear for my life, it is difficult to describe that not only had you had come very near death, but that someone had carefully planned it. I suddenly had visions, later con-firmed by Agent Zott, that, no doubt as we slept, someone had crawled un-der one of our cars parked in our driveway and carefully drained all the oil from the vehicle they did not want me to use, leaving no trace of ever having been there. We found additional evidence when we returned to the scene of the accident. As I walked along the road with the DCIS agent investigating the incident, we found all five sheared-off lug bolts with their respective lug nuts loosened to the exact point at the end of all the bolts, which is exactly how this kind of hit, made to look like an accident, is done.

Then the same type of accident occurred twice in a matter of weeks with my children, first my oldest daughter (who had her younger sister with her at the time) and two weeks later with my oldest son. The tire that had been tampered with was the same right front one, with bolts we found at the ends of the stems.

Yet for all the talk of witness protection, there were at least two prob-lems with it.

When I asked the federal agents if they would be able to relocate us and make sure I had gainful employment to support my suffering family, the answer came back no. With no real identity or work record to market, I would be as bad off as before, if not worse. At least with the newspaper, as punishing as the hours and demands were when matched with the de-mands of this case, I could care for my family. If we relocated, I could not even consider trying to promote any of my best skills working with elec-tronics (let alone related systems analysis) as that could be used to hunt us down. It would have been something of an occupational fingerprint. Not knowing if I could support my family, and putting them on the run to spend their own lives hiding was not an option.

What was truly difficult for me to accept was the fact that witness protection would even be raised, let alone encouraged. This was supposed to be the United States of America, not Russia. We were not going up against the mob and I wasn't a criminal and I had not done anything wrong. We were simply challenging a corporation whose purpose was to protect American citizens.

It was as it had ever been. There clearly was no way out of this night-mare other than continuing to push forward and come out the other end, whatever that was, win or lose, for good or ill. The question resurfaced and grew: Would I and could I physically and emotionally continue?

While it is impossible to say who made the attempts on our lives, it was pretty clear to me and my legal team that a truly substantial case against this giant contractor had been put together. After conducting a mock trial with not one, but three, separate mock juries, we would soon discover just how compelling a case we had to take to twelve everyday citizens of the United States of America, who would listen and pass judgment on behalf of their country, their own tax dollars, and all their fellow citizens in this remarkable country of ours.

We had to assume that at least some at Northrop shared this view because the legal team that had been such a relentlessly condescending foe was replaced by another firm, and, though still representing Northrop, were pushed back to second chair and handling the grunt work of the case. The torpedoes we had aimed at them may not have sunk them (or Northrop) altogether, but we had definitely winged them. I have to admit it gave me more than a little satisfaction to know not only the strength of our position, but that the leader, who had dismissed others as being little more than clerks, was now, by and large, little more than a clerk.

Unfortunately, as we were soon to discover, the new law firm and its lead counsel were arrogant and smug beyond all apparent reason. They considered themselves unbeatable and, we must assume, quite happy to collect the fees they were being paid courtesy of the taxpayers of the United States of America. They would also prove to be a ridiculously insurmountable wall before my own deteriorating health gave out altogether, leaving my legal team without a live client and my family without a husband and father.

Fortunately, there were some key moments that helped put things in perspective and helped lift my spirits, like the day Northrop deposed General Henry. That day, while we were alone in the elevator on our way to join others for lunch, he looked me in the eye and said, "Thank God for people like you."

This great man, whom I have come to respect even more and have the privilege to speak with still today, saying that at that moment was like a fresh cool breeze on a hot summer day. I still felt the weight of the world on my shoulders, but now I felt a desire to stand a little bit taller, and it was a reminder I was not standing alone. It was also a reminder of sorts, even if only in the back of my mind, that if it had not been for the support and endurance of my family through all this, I would not have been standing at all.

14
WHEN WORLDS COLLIDE

It is now 2004. A court date has been set for a jury trial. We are getting ready for what we all believe will be the final and hopefully brief leg of the journey. My once unpredictable but now missed co-relator Rex Robinson is gone. Northrop now has a new law firm guiding their defense strategy.

I think everyone was beginning to wonder how much longer I could physically and emotionally last, given my full-blown diabetes, perpetual fatigue, and intermittently waning optimism. For fifteen years, since the case formally began in 1989, my entire family has been robbed of much of what it deserved. It has now been seventeen years since I initially discovered my employer's alleged wrongdoing. I am hoping for the best. My chronic exhaustion is beyond description and my health is failing.

We only needed to fine tune our case and its presentation, and gird our loins for the push to see it through. What we were not prepared for were delays introduced by the enemy's new legal representation. They even expressed a willingness to let the case drag out indefinitely (presumably while they collected fees for it) and we wore down, died, or caved. But we knew something they didn't: We were not about to cave. We were approaching the most crucial tipping point in the case, and for almost everyone involved, it was now more than just a case. It had become for each and every one of us something personal.

There were aspects of this case that were always personal for some of the key players and my most important allies. This is not to say that they were ever anything less than professional in ways that met all standards and often raised the bar. They saw in this case wrongs they could not ignore and felt a need to address them just because it was the right thing to do. What I only learned well after the case had ended was how much they appreciated me in providing a cornerstone for the endeavor. My presence gave them the chance to right some massive wrongs. What I did not comprehend at the time (especially as we prepared for trial) was the extent to which they balanced their goals of seeing the case through a jury trial and winning against me, and my family's ability to endure any more punishment.

To some extent, I think my insistence on being present for the building of the case had its intended effect of putting a much-needed human face on the proceedings. And since some of my allies had spent time with my family, they had a much wider sense of the human impact in my little sphere. But the real kudos goes to them for allowing their own humanity to enter into the picture.

They allowed themselves to care.

They allowed themselves to care about their jobs in spite of endless compromises. They allowed themselves to care about what this case meant to them. Most of all, they allowed themselves to care about me, my family, and the entire citizenry of the United States. Their caring helped keep them going, because what they were doing *mattered* and they could not think of giving in to a corporate megalomaniac.

What was most moving to me was that they could not bear the thought of failing me or my family after everything we had suffered. They could not bear the thought of abandoning the battle and thus abandon us. Rather, they could not bear the thought of our feeling and being abandoned, so they often found strength when needed so as to not allow that to happen.

What I did not know—and even now gives me moments of contemplative pause—was that in their eyes, I was their hero. I "suited up and showed up," as they put it, so they could do the same and have a real shot at success. I kept putting one exhausted foot in front of the other, guided only by the belief that I had to respect and honor what was true. My unusual perspective, knowledge, and ways of thinking helped them understand much of what they were digging their way through.

With all their credentials, high position, and incredible ability and diligence, they were all my revered knights in shining armor, and I, without my having the faintest clue, was theirs.

At that time, then, considering my declining health, the only positive way to proceed was to have such a strong case that we could get a summary judgment in our favor or win a (hopefully) short enough trial for me to survive. Those options failing, we could also settle out of court for a less than optimum impact on Northrop.

As Northrop's new law firm stepped in, it appeared to us that they arrogantly believed they could withstand anything we had to throw at them so much that running the case on for many more years was just fine with them. It struck us as very strange that they could be so cavalier, given the case we had. Then again, it was also true that Northrop was writing some very big checks, and the American citizenry was still picking up the tab for now.

Our next step was putting together a mock trial with three mock juries to hone not only our case but the presentation of it. Court cases are not totally won or lost on truth alone, but on what can and cannot be admitted and how the jury perceives and cares about what is presented. As it turned out, how it was presented in our mock trials and how it was perceived by our mock juries was important in unexpected ways. What I found to be most important was to have faith that the power of the truth and the wisdom of good citizens would prevail even in the face of obfuscations.

With our goals in mind, our legal team and the DoJ agreed to hire an independent research firm to set up a one-day presentation of the trial with twenty-eight jurors recruited from a random pool of people. One of our attorneys, Steve Miller, argued the most salient features of our side of the case as he would do in reality if it went to trial. Another of our attorneys, David Bowen, took the part of Northrop's lead litigator with disconcerting prowess. I appeared as myself. The questions and dynamics of all three juries played out in our favor in similar stages and fashion.

Initially, they wanted to know if I was the real me or someone playing my part. We intentionally declined to answer that question.

The next question arose as to whether or not I (or the real me) was the good-guy everyday citizen I appeared to be or if I had actually been a wrongdoer myself and was cooperating for personal benefit or to escape criminal prosecution.

The third thing that came up in all three juries was an observation about my appearance. In regard to the issue of damages, evidently I did not look as though I had suffered that much. I was well dressed and did not show any adequately observable lasting damage. I had no visible signs of distress, no broken bones or bruises and black eyes. To the naked eye, I looked all right.

It was a fourth and separate issue that most impressed us and gave us the most hope: The jurors could follow the very complex information.

After both sides of the case were presented to the entire group, they were broken off into three distinct juries and isolated for deliberation. My team broke up as well to sit behind one-way glass and listen in on the juries' discussions.

The most notable idea amongst these deliberations was the opinion that if the government of the United States was stupid and inept enough to award contracts and pay money to this kind of corporate giant to begin with, and so inept at monitoring them that they got ripped off, well then too bad for them. They deserved whatever they got.

This was, in one way, reassuring, because, based on what we presented, they really did see the massive and appalling wrongdoing on Northrop's part to the tune of hundreds of millions of dollars. True, this would have done us little good if they decided the government deserved to be ripped off and punished, as if they could agree on the sins of the giant but still decide some aspects of the case against us.

But soon, their shared question proved to be both insightful as well as impactful.

Sometime during the brief deliberations, several people would point out that while the crimes committed did not reflect well on the government and those charged with protecting the citizenry's interests, they asked the question, "Isn't that our money that had been and possibly still is being stolen and wasted, not the government's money and it is not all right with us for them [the government] to decide for us without our knowledge if we should or should not seek to get it back?"

This simple and inescapable fact resonated with and shaped the final deliberations of all three juries. In every case and in all ways we won, hands down. Some of us suspected that if Northrop was conducting its own version of this test and doing it realistically, they were probably getting much the same results as well. The key point here, aside from our winning, is that this very issue was playing out in our national political and economic arenas while these pages were being written.

By the time the mock trials were finished and we were filing our pre-trial brief, we had built a very strong case against Northrop that now included several key elements. While some of the specific issues in the originally filed qui tam complaint had been dropped or lessened in emphasis, several concrete examples remained. The case was ready to go forward and had accrued more clarity by the time spent doing battle with Northrop over the years. Too, we had incorporated some of Northrop's transgressive legal tactics in our final allegations.

Looking back with the advantage of time and distance, our focus had shifted from documenting specific secretive practices intentionally designed to systematically gouge the US government, to taking them at their word. While we did still believe their claims to be the truth in many instances, *accepting* Northrop's own claims about not being able to provide us with the massive amounts of information we had asked them for became our tactic.

You can think of this shift in focus as being a little like looking at one of those pictures in which you either see two faces looking at each other or the outlines of a vase. In this case, we argued (and they denied) that they had committed fraud by being unable to operate cleanly and accurately. This chaos, we said, provided cover for people who clearly knew that there were major discrepancies in their tracking and billing systems to commit fraud. More to the point, we claimed the fraud manifested in: 1) lying about the accuracy of the data when bidding and billing; 2) proactively setting out to hide the chaos of the system itself; and 3) the ongoing false reporting to the government that its materials management and accounting systems did meet the government regulations and contract standards.

In short, the shift in our focus helped document the existing *systemic* flaws. Thus, we had solid ground on which to demonstrate that they had committed fraud just by covering up their systemic flaws.

Now we were ready for trial with the large number of alleged transgressions soundly documented. Between the False Claims Act, the qui tam provisions, over seven million computer data entries, and three million paper documents, Northrop was staring down the barrel of over $1.2 billion in fines.

This was soon to play itself out in ways that were as unexpected as they were dramatic. The paradox that stands out for me is the contrast between what Northrop project managers and resident government monitors knew and did not see versus how much internal communication moved about for years and how overtly. This internal correspondence reached to top division management, along with actual training programs to effect emergency cleanup.

Still, though, it remained unclear as to just who knew what and who was ultimately pulling the strings. Those at high levels remained hidden.

And even though Northrop had dragged out due process and crossed the line well into what many felt was obstructing justice, it never seemed to go quite the way they expected it to go. We wondered if anyone on their side was getting a true take on what they were really facing, and the ways in which their tactics cumulatively weighed against them. Their guiding presumption that they could just outlast us and wear us down was wrong, but almost held true in terms of my own endurance.

I remember that the first thing we heard upon the arrival of the new legal firm was their assurance to the court that the transition in representation would not cause any delays in the progress of the case. The second thing we heard, after the transition was granted, was that their new lead counsel was going on a two-week vacation and needed to ask for some extensions.

What I only recently discovered was that Northrop executives had finally discovered the prior legal firm had misinformed them for years with repeated assurances that they should not worry because we had no case. They also found out (thanks to a few articles that trickled out through the *Chicago Tribune*) that they could be looking at massive fines that could multiply depending on how detailed the government wanted to get in defining any one offense down to single data keystrokes. Northrop's top-tier board members and executives were now getting a real clue as to what had really been going on in a case they had been advised was well under control.

Once they had had the chance to settle the case for a mere $21 million as the lowest figure my legal team was willing to offer, to which they had made their counter offer of $1 million each. Now they had concern that the cash cost could be in the billions, not to mention the loss of all contracts for the defense division for two years.

To have been a fly on the wall when they discussed what had been happening in this case over the years and how could they be now facing a $1.2 billion loss with sanctions (*What happened?*) would have been sweet . . .

In certain ways, the arrival of a new legal team was a case of good news, bad news for us. In retrospect, while it appeared Northrop's new legal firm realized we had a case and did not continue dragging out the case, it meant they really had to focus and come up with a strategy. The prior firm's arrogance and negligence left the new team with a case they could very well lose as, at this point, it would be almost impossible to fix. The tactics allowing time to run out and motions to expire came back to bite them in that their failure to address our motions had been decided in our favor by default.[21] Where we thought we had another law firm that thought itself unbeatable and able to ride this out forever, they knew they had to have time to come up to speed.

But this time also weighed on my shoulders in terms of my declining endurance. My team's concern for my health and my family's well-being had become quite personal. Thankfully, I did not have the burden of knowing the extent to which my ability to continue would determine how to go forward and how long to assume the next push could be sustained. Fortunately, I also did not know that they had concerns for my physical safety because the stakes were astronomically high, and my having put a face on it weighed heavily in the motivations of my allies, right up to such

---

21 There were many instances in which we filed motions that went unchallenged and thus were deemed decided in our favor.

magnificent people as Major General Henry and our much admired colleague, Linda Wawzenski of the DoJ.

At the time, however, we had no reason to presume that Northrop was particularly better informed than they were before as to the merits of the case and team lined up against it. Because of my precarious health, the challenge was how to light a fire and move things forward more rapidly while turning up the heat to leverage a resolution that would also make sure my family and I were compensated for our long punishment and, to whatever extent possible, be made whole.

To that end, it was decided the pen may be mightier than the sword, and opening a window to let in some fresh air and sunshine would be crucial to this conflict that had been waged in darkness.

Mike came up with the idea of taking our story to the *Wall Street Journal* hoping for some coverage and, after clearing it with others in key positions, that was exactly what we did. Not only did the *Wall Street Journal* pick up our story, it put it on the front page with several of the documents used to argue previous motions before the court. The results were remarkable and rapid.

We had Northrop's attention now.

They came forth and agreed to hear us and allowed us to present our case to their CEO and CFO. But since the case was already scheduled for jury trial to be heard in June 2005, it was decided to present the evidence to an independent mediator in California. The individual to whom we presented the case was a retired appellate judge and, much to our pleasure (and, I am certain, Northrop's chagrin), he suggested that we did, in fact, have a strong case and that Northrop probably would lose the trial. Northrop balked at the suggested $400-million-plus settlement and decided go directly to the DoD, where it traditionally had been able to flex its muscles and pull endless strings. With the stakes now higher than we had ever imagined, Northrop played what they presumably thought was their trump card.

A meeting was scheduled with Major General Henry's successor at the Pentagon. Northrop complained that the DoJ was not being reasonable and was putting in jeopardy some of the toys the DoD wanted. What happened next was unprecedented. Someone at the DoD legal department, who knew of and understood the issues of the case, caught wind of Northrop's complaint and, after the general who had agreed to a meeting was brought up to speed, he instructed the DoD to inform Northrop there would be no meeting on this issue. Not now. Not ever. Northrop's seemingly endless string of contacts within the Pentagon had broken down.

By now, the effort to shut the case down had run the course of almost twenty years. We received a call from Northrop shortly after this thwarted meeting. Another meeting was quickly set up between Michael Behn, Linda Wawzenski, with selected others, and Northrop's CFO, accompanied by a handful of top brass from Northrop. Northrop's stance was as chilling to me as the response from my side was gratifying and caring.

As it has been reported to me, the CFO of Northrop acknowledged that if the case went to a jury trial, we would, in all likelihood, win and Northrop would lose. But, he pointed out, they would still resist and outspend us until there were no longer any living relators or clients to benefit from the outcome. He told Mike, "Both of your clients will be dead." They also insisted that the payout fall under $100 million for the claim itself because, as we understood it, to pay more changed the status of the case and their relationship with the government and ongoing contracting. To comply with this demand to end the case before I left my family without a husband or father, the DoJ allowed some of the monies to be allocated to Rex's heirs and myself for undisclosed damages. For legal reasons, I will not divulge the conditions nor the amount of that settlement.[22]

As is standard in this kind of case, the payment of a settlement meant that they were admitting to no wrongdoing, and that the conditions of the issues and case's outcome were to remain secret. While an additional $40 million would have to be paid back to the United States government in reimbursement of legal fees incurred over the almost-eighteen-year course, this did not affect the desire to stay under the $100 million dollar settlement. That was to be divided between the United States government, my legal team, me, and Rex's heirs, as they were separate purses. What is

---

22 The particulars of that settlement can be found in the court records of the suit filed against me by the two parties who had dropped out of the qui tam case. The case was filed in McHenry County Illinois and the case number was 05 LA 137. Northrop itself released the details of the settlement in open court, not Rex's heirs or I.

significant here is that $40 million was only 80% of the total fronted to them over the years.

Had I been able to think about it with any distance or perspective, I would have been somewhat disappointed at how insignificant this amount was to Northrop. The Northrop Corporation that we alleged had bilked the taxpayers of billions of dollars, had gotten off with what for them was little more than a rounding error. More to the point, they got off without having to admit wrongdoing, and for all I knew then or know now, they may have continued with business as usual and changing nothing.

But it was over.

Or so I thought.

We celebrated the fact that we had at least shown the giant they were not as untouchable or omnipotent as they liked to believe, even if they rolled along largely unchanged after the fact.

As for me, my wife, and our family, we shared a sigh of relief and more than a few tears, unaware of what was to come next. It became worse than anything Northrop had ever put us through, and we didn't even have a hint.

In the best of circumstances, no one comes through that many years of tragedy and trauma unmarked, no matter how much money people may think they may have afterward. As we soon realized, this case had not ended when the original case did and the settlement was paid out. Of course, once any settlement is parceled out, what is left over is much smaller than it sounds, even before getting hit with taxes. The award given in these cases is not tax exempt and there is no income averaging, so it is considered income for a single year—instead of a seventeen-year-long battle. The tax burden, after the attorneys take their 40%, is another 40%.

For example, say there are two relators and the award is $10 million after seventeen-and-a-half years of not working. The attorneys take 40% off the top leaving you with $6 million. At that level, the IRS takes 40% (no deductions), so that is another $2.4 million. This leaves $3.6 million to be split in half, or $1.8 million per person. Divide that by 17.5 years and it comes to about $100,000 a year to have your life ruined and your dreams and those of your children stolen—only to have defense attorneys for such corporations claim we do it for the money. They claim that it is a big lottery win for us and that we are mercenaries.

In reality, the only winners are the corporations who never claim responsibility, and the attorneys who represent them.

It is now April 2005. As you can imagine, the initial period following our "win" was one of almost disorienting relief mixed with a host of other jumbled emotions for everyone involved, most especially for my family and myself. It was the first time in years my wife and I could even begin to entertain the notion of a life that is not consumed and/or defined by the battle with Northrop. It was the first time in my children's lives that they didn't have to think about it. We did not know what it all meant or what we were to make of it, but the whole question would become short lived. What we did know, each in our own way, was that it was a time to take a breath, perhaps take stock, and most of all begin regrouping as individuals, and as a family to begin the slow process of healing.

There is nothing I would like more than to tell you now that at this point the struggles, fears, and conflicts were over for my family and me. There was nothing we would have liked more than a complete and decisive end to all the litigation and stress that had so defined our lives for so many years.

Unfortunately, this was not to be the case. Almost before the ink was dry on the final settlement agreements, the two claimants who had been dismissed with prejudice from the original qui tam suit decided they still had some claim on the settlement or "winnings," as they saw it. Their claim was based on a document we had all signed when the case started (one that I had actually declined to sign for over a year) to assure payment to the attorneys upon settlement of the case. It became moot, or so I was told, when they dropped out. For me, it was a horrifying time of renewed personal threats and obscene legal wrangling at a time I was trying to move on. I was also trying to do some good with groups to help whistleblowers, and those brought with them its own stress.

It would take another five years of legal wrangling, hundreds of thousands of dollars out of pocket, and still greater duress on my family and me before it would be done and the bulk of the settlement finally released, hopefully without the conflict of any further legal battles.

It was for me very much like the odyssey of Ulysses who, having endured the unimaginable and survived to find his way home, discovered on his return that creeps and parasites had infested his home, and that he still had one great battle to reclaim his life. In my case, and thus that of my family, the reappearance of these two treasure hunters was an unexpected echo of the odyssey we had all just survived. This saga would continue for another five years in ways that complicated our needs to cut free of the past and be able to move forward unfettered from this seemingly endless nightmare.

While we had received a portion of the settlement and thus had some ability to regroup financially and otherwise, we not only had to fight once again for what was now ours, but to endure threats and abuses that were more up close and personal than any Northrop had conjured.

The most graphic and telling of these was when my youngest son found animal entrails piled neatly on our doorstep the day we were served with their lawsuit. It was as if someone had taken a picture of entrails in an anatomy book and recreated it at our back door. I still have the pictures to this day. Suffice it to say we were, as no doubt intended, terrified.

The ensuing years brought with them many ups and downs as well as fears. After I informed Agent Zott of the animal entrails, a federal agent and two uniformed sheriff's deputies paid them a visit to remind them I was a government witness, and that any intimidation of a federal witness is a federal offense and would be dealt with swiftly. A couple of years later, their hired gunslinger would make this a particular sticking point during my deposition, when he accused me of abuse by having them visited in this fashion.

The case came to its conclusion five years and two trips to the Illinois Supreme Court. During that time, I had earned a degree in law and paralegal studies and now acted as my own paralegal. When the case finished, the lawyer who held our escrow finally agreed to release it to us if we spent more in more legal fees.

Mary and I were in Door County, Wisconsin, taking a break when we got the news. This was on a Friday, late in the day. Mary and I cried and laughed at the same time. It was over. It was *finally* over. We were so happy.

That ended two days later when I lost my younger sister tragically and suddenly from causes and circumstances I will not mention here.

15
A LITTLE MATTER OF MEANING

When I first went to work for the Northrop Corporation in 1984, all I wanted was a steady job to provide for my wife and family. They had already been through too much and had too little in life, due to our nearly constant moving to find erratic and often barely viable work. Sadly, it escaped me that they were still paying a price for the rapidly escalating late phases of my addictions to alcohol and other drugs. To our very great surprise, however, the rapid succession of promotions and the stability that came with my continuing sobriety gave us unprecedented hope for a quality of life we had never had and almost stopped believing in.

I saw a succession of opportunities to do work I was well trained for and eager to do, despite the lack of advanced degrees these opportunities normally required. For the first time as a young married couple and family, it appeared I had a real chance to provide for my family in the way they deserved and that I had not known as a child. It appeared we had a real shot at the American Dream. While it turned out to be something of a mirage, the challenges to survive and triumph served us well to keep us going, to take one impossible step after another, doing whatever it took to keep family and soul together, and honoring what was true, right, and good.

I would love to be able to say that all was financially and legally well, complete and whole, at the conclusion of the nearly two-decade-long battles with Northrop. I would love even more to be able to say all was well in my life story and the newfound liberation and healing of my family. If nothing else, the writing of this book has helped me to better understand how the two are interconnected. These hopes of healing, completion, and becoming whole were to remain elusive and, to some extent, still are. They continued to elude us for more than five years after the Northrop case was settled. There would continue to be reverberations from my childhood and surprise unfinished business with the Northrop case. Things are ever so much better now, but for a time, there were multiple challenges in the new and uncharted course of personal, professional, and family life post-Northrop.

I will spare the reader the minute details of this period that are still playing out even as I write these final words. What I will say is that the insanity and costs of inescapable litigation arose anew when the two participants in the original qui tam suit who had dropped out decided they still had some inexplicable claim against the final settlement for a case they had long since ceased to be any part of.[23] As a result, much of the hard-won settlement, which had already been massively diminished by legal fees and taxes, was placed into a holding trust as the litigation progressed. They filed one unfounded variation of their claims after another until their own attorneys were in jeopardy for wasting the court's time with frivolous lawsuits. And once again, my former fellow workers and friends made repeated personal threats, including the pile of animal entrails on our doorstep.

Worse, my new attorneys bled what limited monies had been released through inept service and unscrupulous billing. In fighting this case, huge additional costs piled up and my trust was gone. It was this continued litigation that kept my family and me in cruel and intentional turmoil for over five more years following the settlement of the original case and well into the writing of this book.

I was not able to return to my family in full as I had planned because, in addition to this new litigation, I was applying what I had learned to helping others. In retrospect, this was not so much because my efforts were misguided, but because they were misused by people I trusted as

---

23 Some aspects of the prior case had been handled in ways that allowed and possibly prompted this new litigation to happen.

fellow survivors and dedicated servants of other whistleblowers. All I will say here is that in stepping up to work with others who purported to advocate for legislation on behalf of fellow and future whistleblowers and to develop related support services, I discovered as much self-serving and sometimes despicable deception (among some) as I had ever encountered with my nemeses in the qui tam lawsuit. Agendas were often not what they appeared to be at all or were often conflicted between the parties involved. Some sought to capitalize on my own successes, reputation, and bank account for their own ends.

Part of the problem in "winning" any kind of settlement is that almost everyone in your personal and work life see the award as winning the lottery, as if you didn't work for it, as if it is found money. The fact seems to escape them that it took twenty-five years of punishing legal battles, horrible poverty, homelessness, and delayed access to the actual funds to arrive at the point all these conflicts are settled and we are free to move on. It breeds strange resentments among many who, for one reason or another, feel they have some claim on the "spoils."

When I began writing this book, with the last reverberations of litigation still playing out, I thought I was beyond looking back to find some kind of overriding purpose and meaning. It would have been perfectly natural to seek order that said life is and can be better than the worst that we endured. It would have been natural to seek meaning that would allow us to nurture what was best for our lives. What my mind and my heart *accepted* was faith in the goodness and purposefulness of things. Not only did I believe that there was some grand and valuable reason for all we went through but that, in the end, what we went through actually mattered and in some way stood to make a difference. For me, it was what it was. The only questions that mattered were not how to explain or justify what had happened, but to figure out how to find our way forward.

It is this last point that had the most to do with beginning the journey of writing this book, which was my need to convey to my family that what they survived mattered. In some ways, this is simply because I care and want them to feel that what they endured was worthwhile. After years of being isolated from my own family, I want them to know me (in contrast to all the ways I did not know my own father) and I want to better connect with and know them. Most of all, what I want for us now (what I did not so explicitly realize at the beginning of writing this book) is to know how to let go of the past, move forward both as individuals and as a family, and make the most of our lives. This involves healing, allowing ourselves time to grieve and feel the pain we want to leave behind. It means ceasing to be defined by those events that bore down on us and boxed us in. For me, it includes finally being free of residual, if irrational, guilt.

This latter point cannot be overestimated nor should it be misunderstood, even outside of the context of this story. It is part of what plagues and paralyzes all those who have been through a similar experience. What must be understood here is that guilt is part of the worst evil whistleblowers suffer. Though the whistleblower makes the choice and takes the action, the individual does not face the consequences alone. All those the whistleblower cares about will be impacted as a matter of course, and, all too often, devastated by well-planned, punishingly coercive intention. In my own very blessed case, my family survived and is finding its own while still finding ways to heal. In most such circumstances, this is not the case. Relentless manipulation using guilt as a weapon is one of the most effective tools to discourage initial action and the most concrete block against moving on.

The insidiousness of guilt made itself known in my case which, unlike the vast majority of such cases, ended with what most would consider a positive outcome. By many measures, we won—"we" being everyone involved from my immediate family to my extended family made up of agents, attorneys, officials, and colleagues I had collected along the way. Still, it is difficult to let go of the injuries and losses we would like to erase or change. The challenge, even in those rare cases in which there is a positive outcome, lies in the fact that though the family has paid endless tolls and suffered many losses, they will not experience any recognition for enduring it or bask in the glory of success. It is the strange nature of whistleblowing that everything for and about the family comes to be defined by the attacks made against the whistleblower. It makes everything seem to be caused by and/or about them—even when one tries to protect the family from the effects of attacks. The unfairness and isolation is prolonged, in that recognition and praise never include the family with the whistleblower.

From the first, this book was meant in part to acknowledge my family's sacrifice and to share the many accolades that have come and continue to come my way. On a more selfish note, it was also meant to validate that the effort we all went through as a result of my choice to engage in this battle was worth it, that there was something worthwhile and even admirable in it and in my role in it. One of the most unbearable costs in this kind of journey is the relentless ways in which one is made to look and feel culpable and incompetent to the world at large, made to feel like a failure and a loser in the eyes of those they love most, and made the struggle to support and protect those loved ones from the impacts of the situation.

The primary problem in *sharing* recognition, of course, is that these public manifestations of appreciation and praise *are* about my role in sustaining and, to some extent, winning the case (and thus about me), and not about what the family went through just to stay together and survive. There needs to be a form of recognition more appropriately attuned to their sacrifices and scars, along with acknowledgment of the specific costs they paid along the way—because they were never given any choice in the matter. This is something my family and I are still finding our way through.

The second and, in some ways, most strategically challenging problem is that they may not want any acknowledgement of anything except to be done with it and move on, even when many of their needs and behaviors are still defined by the experience and its aftermath.

As I stated at the beginning of this book, it is the story of my family that mattered and still matters most to me. It challenges us each and every day of our lives in ways much smaller and more subtle. This need has as much to do with deciding how to go forward as it does with making sense of what happened. Where the two overlap, it has to do with the faith, meaning, and the purpose we choose to ascribe to the experience.

Whenever I share our epic story—me, my family, and all those who rallied to our cause—I am asked two or three fairly consistent questions from others trying to make sense of this story and events in their own lives, as well as from those who seek to assist and serve them.

First, what have I learned or been able to take away from all of this?

Second, what advice or insight do I have to offer to others who may be facing similar circumstances, or who are just trying to get their lives in order to do right in a world and (at the moment) country that seems so accepting of such wrong?

Third, what would I still like to do or create with the time I have left in this world, for me, my family, and others trying to find their way in a complicated world?

While my answers are still evolving, I will try to share what is currently relevant to me, my family, my country, and you, the reader.

First and foremost, I learned over and over again just how precious my family is to me, as is my beloved motley crew of wonderful individuals. I learned how much my love for them and my desire to shine for them can keep you going when you could not go on for your own sake. Another takeaway I can offer is how devastated and lost I would be without each and every one of them, and most especially my wife, Mary, who made everything work when nothing did.

Second, as for what may have relevance to others' situations, I learned only while writing this book just how easy it is for the head of the family (if you are the primary target), to think you are doing and showing more than you are. Conversely, I learned (with more than a little pain) that how well everyone seems to be doing, and however much you believe they know they matter to you, it may very well be a form of nearsighted wishful thinking.

The only way forward and out of this kind of long-term trauma is to face and feel the pain, to see things as they were and are now, and accept both your strengths and limitations, not out of critical judgment but in proactive and realistic assessment of your resources. Perhaps the biggest lesson I learned is the extent to which you must be willing to let go of your take on things both past and present, no matter how neutral or charged they may be. What I learned is the extent to which you need to see things honestly to get through them, and may be exactly what you need to let go, get real, and move beyond.

As a parent in the present, I learned the need to act out of responsibility instead of out of guilt or a need to undo the past. I learned to allow people to show up differently than you may expect. I was reminded that it is better to allow people to live up to your expectations rather than down to them. I learned how much my family kept their suffering to themselves, which served to magnify my appreciation and celebration of them. I learned how far love and humor will go in keeping you together and allowing you to heal.

Perhaps most of all, I discovered that in allowing yourself to be imperfect in front of those you most want to impress, that in accepting all your frailties and shortcomings, doing so allows you to do your best to show up and be a real hero. In fairness to Mary, who has been telling me this for years, I also fully got what she meant when she said over and over that this is not just all about me—either in my preoccupations with the case when it was going on or in my need to make a difference and save the world when it was over.

But before I go on to a list of other issues, I need to also acknowledge the need for proper help.

In our case, much help came in the form of a consultant, whose eclectic experience and knowledge of the myriad dimensions of what we were going to undertake in the writing of this book made a substantial difference at every turn. He understands the worlds of corporations and whistleblowers, and I met him when he was providing support for some national groups I was involved with. He came up with strategies, organizational development, and media plans to make it all work well for them.

In walking me through and drawing out the facts of the case as I knew or thought I knew them, he saw patterns and connections between things I had might never have seen. He made seeing these things in whole new ways both comfortable and rewarding. Most of all (and I cannot overstate this to those who want to provide or receive help in these matters), he always seemed to know what would happen next and made that seem normal when we otherwise could have thought we were crazy. We never felt lost even when we were not sure of our way. In fact, he was our best and most enthusiastic cheerleader. With humor that fit right in with our family's, and a reassuring smile, he answered my wife's oft-repeated question of how he could be so patient with us, that it was because we were doing so well. Moreover, he was patient, waiting for facts and insights that would not all come out at once, but would show up in waves and successive stages of clarity. He knew when our observations and opinions did not make sense, and would suggest there was something wrong with what we had presented. From that, he was able to get at the heart of a story, then put it together.

I share this here in appreciation of his friendship and guidance in the journey to and writing of these pages for my family and me. More importantly, I (with his permission) share this to highlight some of the things individuals and their families need to survive this kind of ordeal and thrive. Those who seek to support and guide whistleblowers must bring a considerable fund of knowledge and skills to the table, and to do so sensitively and successfully. As I highlight the range of diverse support needed in these circumstances, I am struck to the core by how wonderful and important family is and how enduring it can be. Equally, I have come to appreciate how fragile it is, subject to damage from things we can and cannot control. I am awed and grateful at the endurance and tenacity of my own.

A greater lesson I learned from this long saga is that the running of our country cannot be left to powerful corporate interests or to any government that is beholden to them. The greater lesson is what can be accomplished when we, as employees and citizens, rally in ways that match who we claim to be and/or hope to become, when we allow other honorable people to do their jobs.

It is all too easy and convenient to indiscriminately disparage all those who seek to serve, and dismiss the government itself as the enemy, even as we give away our own power and responsibility for shaping it. There is no such thing as a viable and free market without accountability. There is no such thing as sound representative government without the rational, informed, and diligent participation of those represented. It is here once again that I salute and thank all those who rallied around this case for its own merits, and most particularly all those who came to see it as more than just an abstract case or chance to do their job. They are one and all true heroes.

This all brings me to the grand lesson I hope is embraced by those who can and do care, whether they live in this country or not. We must not only support whistleblowers (although that is a part of it), but confront the crossroads we, as a people, are at.

Aside from the unusually high-security and high-risk setting from which my saga arose, and the fact that it involved the official designation of "whistleblower," this story is really about any working person who must deal with small things, such as inefficiencies that can be improved, to serious wrongs and dangers to the public. We as a people need to not only take our conscience back, but to assume the responsibility of choosing our representatives wisely and holding them accountable. Just as I never set out to be labeled a whistleblower or have my life and that of my family dominated for decades by litigation, I am not a political person.

That said, what I do know is that if there is any real and lasting solution to such wrongdoing, it has to come from all of us. We should be protecting those who come forward, and all of those who do so in the future. Most of all, we need to stop living in fear and resume ownership and stewardship of our values. As we do so, we must never lose sight that on the ground, this is always about people and families who risk much and sometimes all, only to be discarded or disregarded by those they seek to help and protect. We need to remember that it is up to us as individuals to prove our values and hold accountable all those who would undermine or destroy them.

It is worth remembering where the term whistleblower comes from: the whistles used by British bobbies to call out a warning or to alert others to possible danger or harm and interrupt wrongdoing.

This brings us to the conclusion of these pages and my journey in writing them, and back to the questions as to what advice I might have for others and what I would like to do next. Since these are interconnected, I will handle them together.

Above all is the well-being of my family and the lives we now carve out for ourselves as individuals finding our way forward. We have been much more fortunate than most simply in staying together as a family. We learned much in this process I would like to pass along to those individuals and families who find themselves in similar circumstances, and to those who would support or, by necessity, rely on them. To the former, my advice is on how to get help and guidance that can make all the difference. To the latter, it is a reminder that you are dealing with people faced with overwhelming challenges who need understanding and guidance.

My first advice for those who find themselves in work or community situations that could be more efficient or that have real problems is to get help and guidance on how to handle that while issues and potential conflicts are small. There is far more information available these days on communication and problem resolution than existed when my situation arose.

In those cases that are serious enough to involve any kind of personal risk, get a handle on the likely risks, know your rights, and get advice on how to best handle the situation. The aim here is to approach each situation as a problem-solving opportunity rather than a conflict doomed to escalate into enmity. It may sound obvious, but in my own experience and subsequent work with others I have discovered we tend to avoid or ignore problems that could have been handled while small and only engage them when they have grown to become confrontational and explosive. In those cases, it is all the more crucial that you get supportive guidance on how to effectively handle the conflict. In those extreme cases in which any kind of secret reporting absolutely must occur, it is most important to get knowledgeable guidance.

The challenge, of course, is in knowing how to tell if your available resources are appropriately knowledgeable about the range of issues and related skills and strategies you are called upon to deal with. Fortunately, there is now a wealth of information and organizations available online that can get you headed in the right direction. The problem with most of them, in my estimation, is that most are oriented to those already formally designated as a whistleblower. Those types of resources are geared for escalating and formalizing the conflict rather than resolving or scaling it down. The other problem with many existing groups and resources is that they are politically oriented to impacting whistleblowing legislation and issues, and can also lose sight of the people involved.

There is an inverse set of implications here for: 1) all those who would provide guidance and support for these individuals and their families; 2) all those attorneys and government agents who may become involved in more extreme cases; and 3) all those organizations and companies themselves who can proactively equip themselves for problem resolution that makes whistleblowing at any level unneeded.

Just as those individuals who are in work-related conflicts and their families need a wide range of skills and expertise available to them, those who work with or rely on them need to know what those needs are. This ranges from work-related organizational problem-solving and communication skills, to personal and family emotional support, to legal advice and alliance-building where necessary. From a proactive/preventative standpoint, organizations need to be sensitive and responsive to the kinds of problem-solving most resist.

For my own part, there are several areas in which I will continue to serve. Perhaps the most obvious is my work with Taxpayers Against Fraud (TAF.org), an organization with which I have been involved for some time to create support services for whistleblowers, their attorneys, and the government entities that work with them. Without going into detail here, its prototype program and exportable training services are similar to the kind of employee assistance program I actually designed and helped put in place at Northrop following my life-changing stint in rehab.

Aside from continuing to support TAF's mission to support whistleblowers and the professionals who work with them, I would hope the resource development training and support services continue evolving for other agencies, professionals, and organizations. Similarly, I anticipate the continuation of the well-received and highly requested presentations and training I have already had the privilege of doing with Michael Behn and Agent Zott for the DoJ, the DoD, and diverse related academic programs. Beyond these and because I must resume making a living, I anticipate consulting for organizations that want to optimize their internal communications and problem-solving abilities to prevent the need for whistleblowing. At the same time, I anticipate assisting law firms and government agencies to decipher their cases and turn their data into concise and coherent presentations for the court or clients.

On a grander scale, we need to recognize that those who take risks on behalf of the public good and in the name of human decency need and deserve optimum protections under the law. If anything, such recognition and protection need to be expanded beyond those who fall into official whistleblower status. In this way, problem identification (short of violations of the law) can be handled in less black-and-white terms with an eye to scaling back the formalization of conflict rather than escalating it wherever possible.

We need to respect integrity and transparency. We need to demand accountability. We need to accept that we do not live in the simple agrarian society of the founding fathers, who never anticipated such globalization as we have today, and the level of governmental power and control. All the way back in the 1950s, President Dwight D. Eisenhower warned of the Military Industrial Complex, which so successfully resists being held accountable and prevents the government from doing its primary job of protecting the rights and freedoms of the American citizen. We cannot hand our interests and well-being over to those who will abuse them. We must become empowered by what we are for rather than being limited by what we are against.

As to the full circle that is my personal life, beginning with my childhood and family of origin, I find myself returning to the acceptance portion of the serenity prayer of AA, which played such an important role in my early program of recovery. As much as I would like to, I cannot rewrite history for myself or my remaining siblings. Letting go of my need to rewrite history and accepting that everyone did the best they were able allowed me to forgive and move on. By doing this, I make it all matter.

I inherited not only my father's alcoholism but, due to my circumstances, I also manifested a similar mental and emotional absence from my wife and children. While I intended that my relationship with them would be different, it was not because of my need to keep secrets and try to protect them from the stress I was going through. If there were one thing I would change in this odyssey, I would have found the strength and sensitivity to be more present with my family. At the time, I thought I was more present than I was, and it was only well after the fact I discovered how often they felt cut off and of less importance to me. Most ironically, when the praise and accolades started to come my way, it made them feel they were of secondary importance to me, when I thought they would be proud of me and know that I appreciated them.

I also repeated some of my mother's behaviors, most especially my attraction to performing and my love of the limelight and party life. It was in the midst of the nightmare, which brought with it surprise blessings, that I learned to step into adulthood and learn the skills to take care of business, family, and self that, as a child, I had never seen modeled. Perhaps, in accepting myself for having done no better than they did, that I find the ability to forgive and embrace them for who they were, while letting go of what they were not.

The three and a half years I have spent writing this book, while the story was still unfolding, has involved much grieving, letting go, and looking forward. As it turns out, it is here that I was confronted with some of my greatest sense of loss and sadness that I still need to move through. After a lifetime of abandonment and conflict, aggravated by envy or resentment from the Northrop settlement, life seems to have cheated me from being able to turn any of that around.

As I noted earlier, my sister passed away during the writing of this book, during a shifting moment when a chance at reconciliation seemed a possibility. This was shattering in itself, but more so because her manner of death was not necessary. My next older brother passed away on June 29, 2012, from lung cancer.

It is perhaps in relation to my similarly ill oldest brother that I feel the most powerful sense of impending loss. I owe him an unpayable debt because he was there for me in my youth, especially on that morning he found my other brother and me naked and hanging by our wrists in the orphanage. In my teens, he was a model for me, after having left the chaos of our family for the order of the Coast Guard—which would later give me my own first taste of order and accomplishment. It was at his home I stayed as a teenager when I met my wife. Most recently, even as ill as he was himself, he was there for me every day by phone as I inched my way through the devastation of our sister's untimely and unnecessary death. It is with great sadness and the humility that comes with being reminded we are just human that I fear he will never fully know what is in my heart, the love and respect I will always have for him, and the sense of loss that we will not have more time to explore or share that.

With these words on these pages, I am comforted in knowing there is still opportunity for joy within my own family and that the journey itself has taught us much about love, laughter, and celebrating connection. I feel blessed to have finally moved through so much of this arduous adventure, made stronger and a little wiser. I embrace and celebrate the opportunity my family and I have to imbue it with great and wonderful meaning.

Now I thank you, the reader, for taking this little journey with me. I wish you well in your life and hope you can take a lesson from this book: That in the darkest and seemingly most hopeless times of life, there is so much that can lay waiting for us. Hope is one of them.

I leave you with the question my father asked that served as my compass and that so speaks to our times now:

When is it ever wrong to do the right thing?

To that, I add, *When is it ever right not to?*

Bless you and thank you again for sharing a bit of this journey. May you be well and travel well on your own.